ELEMENTS OF QUANTUM MECHANICS

ELEMENTS OF QUANTUM MECHANICS

For B.Sc. Physics

KAMAL SINGH
M.Sc., Ph.D.
Vice Chancellor
Amravati University, Amravati
Former Professor and Head
Department of Physics
Nagpur University, Nagpur

S.P. SINGH
M.Sc.
Former Head
Department of Physics
Hislop College, Nagpur

S. CHAND
PUBLISHING
S Chand And Company Limited
(ISO 9001 Certified Company)

S Chand And Company Limited

(ISO 9001 Certified Company)

Head Office: Block B-1, House No. D-1, Ground Floor, Mohan Co-operative Industrial Estate, New Delhi – 110 044 | Phone: 011-66672000

Registered Office: A-27, 2nd Floor, Mohan Co-operative Industrial Estate, New Delhi – 110 044 Phone: 011-49731800

www.**schandpublishing.com**; e-mail: **info@schandpublishing.com**

Branches

Chennai : Ph: 23632120; chennai@schandpublishing.com
Guwahati : Ph: 2738811, 2735640; guwahati@schandpublishing.com
Hyderabad : Ph: 40186018; hyderabad@schandpublishing.com
Jalandhar : Ph: 4645630; jalandhar@schandpublishing.com
Kolkata : Ph: 23357458, 23353914; kolkata@schandpublishing.com
Lucknow : Ph: 4003633; lucknow@schandpublishing.com
Mumbai : Ph: 25000297; mumbai@schandpublishing.com
Patna : Ph: 2260011; patna@schandpublishing.com

First Edition 2005
Reprints 2006, 3008, 2010, 2011, 2016 (Twice), 2018 (Twice), 2020, 2021 (Twice)

Reprint 2022 (Twice)

ISBN: 978-81-219-2539-6 **Product Code:** H6QMC68PHYS10ENAB0XO

PRINTED IN INDIA

By Vikas Publishing House Private Limited, Plot 20/4, Site-IV, Industrial Area Sahibabad, Ghaziabad – 201 010 and Published by S Chand And Company Limited, A-27, 2nd Floor, Mohan Co-operative Industrial Estate, New Delhi – 110 044.

PREFACE TO THE SECOND EDITION

In this edition of the book, Appendix 3 covering the topic 'Probability Current Density' has been added. This topic is necessary for obtaining the expressions for reflection and transmission coefficients discussed in Sections 5.4 and 5.5. To enhance usefulness of the book, the subject index has been given at the end.

We hope that in this form the book will be more useful to the students and teachers in different universities.

Suggestions for further improvement of the book will be thankfully accepted.

Authors

PREFACE

Curriculum Development Centres in various Science Subjects for preparation of a model national curriculum for the undergraduate and postgraduate levels in Indian Universities were established in 1988 by the University Grants Commission. The Syllabi for Physics for the undergraduate and postgraduate levels were finalized in 1991 by the committees constituted for the purpose. Most of the Universities adopted the U.G.C. Syllabi of various subjects in their original or modified forms from the academic year 2002–2003.

For B.Sc. Part III the new syllabi have come into effect from the academic year 2004-2005. This book on Quantum Mechanics which is one of the subjects for B.Sc. (General) Physics, has been written *in accordance with the U.G.C. syllabus covering all the topics of Quantum Mechanics*. A large number of questions and numerical problems are given at the end of each chapter.

We hope that the book in the present form will be useful to the students and teachers in different universities.

We express our sincere thanks to Shri R.K. Gupta (Chairman & M.D), Shri Navin Joshi, General Manager and Shri Bhagirath Kaushik Zonal Manager of S. Chand & Company Ltd. for taking initiative and giving constant encouragement in the preparation of the manuscript for the book.

Any correction of errors and suggestions for improvement will be thankfully accepted.

Authors

CONTENTS

CHAPTER 1

ORIGIN OF THE QUANTUM THEORY

Phenomena such as motions of mechanical objects involving distances larger than about 10^{-6} m can be explained satisfactorily by laws of classical theoretical physics which is based on the following basic laws:

(*i*) Newton's laws of motion,

(*ii*) The inverse square law of gravitational attraction between two bodies.

(*iii*) Coulomb's inverse square law of attraction or repulsion between two electrically charged bodies,

(*iv*) The law of force on a moving charge in a magnetic field, *i.e.*, the Lorentz force.

However, certain phenomena such as spectral distribution of energy in black body radiation, photoelectric effect etc, and phenomena involving distances of the order of 10^{-10} m could not be explained by classical physics. The failure of classical physics to explain distribution of energy in the spectrum of a black body led Max Planck to propose the *quantum hypothesis* in 1900, and this was the origin of the quantum theory.

1.1 BLACK BODY RADIATION

A body having a surface which can absorb all the radiation (*i.e.* radiation of all the wavelengths) incident on it, is called a *perfectly black body*. Its coefficient of absorption, *i.e.*, absorptivity is 1, and its coefficient of emission, *i.e.*, emissivity is also 1.

A perfectly black body is an ideal conception. There is no known surface which can be regarded as perfectly black. Lamp black or platinum black is nearest approach to a perfectly black body . Lamp black can absorb about 96% of the radiation incident on it, and platinum black absorbs about 98%.

For experimental purposes, a perfectly black body consists of a hollow sphere with a small hole in its surface. The inner surface is coated with lamp black. Any radiation entering the sphere through the hole suffers multiple reflections at the inner surface and so it is nearly completely absorbed.

The small hole thus acts as a perfect absorber of radiation, i.e., a perfectly black body.

The radiation within a uniform temperature enclosure in equilibrium with its surroundings is called black body radiation at the temperature of the enclosure. Therefore the radiation coming out from such an enclosure, through an opening in it at any temperature of its walls, is the black body radiation at that temperature.

Distribution of the energy in the spectrum of a black body :

To study the distribution of the radiant energy over different wavelengths, at constant temperature, the sphere is heated to and maintained at that temperature. By means of an infrared spectrometer, and a bolometer (an instrument for measurement of the intensity of radiation) the intensities of the radiation of different wavelengths are measured.

The experimental results as obtained by Lummer and Pringsheim (1899) are shown in Fig. 1.1. The curves are for temperatures of the black body, ranging from 998K to 1646 K. The ordinates represent the emissive powers E_λ and the abscissa wavelengths.

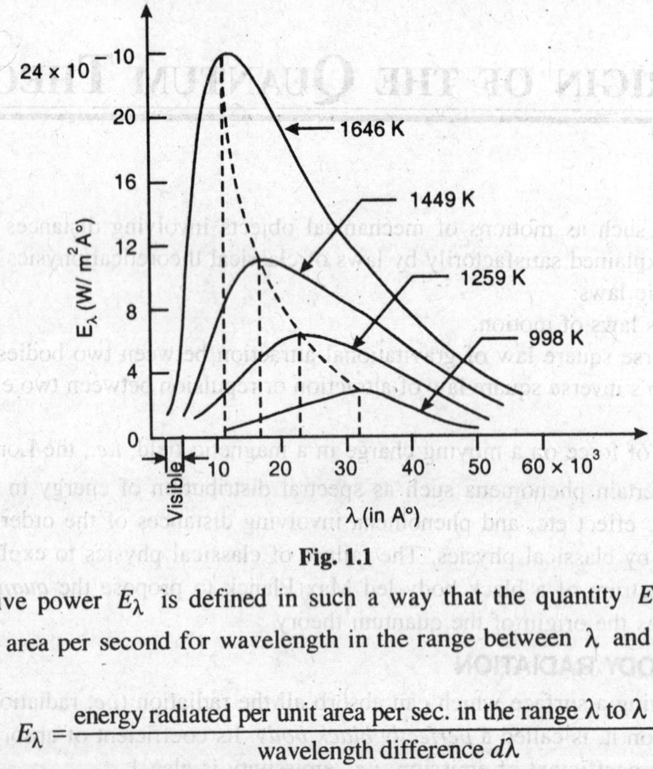

Fig. 1.1

The emissive power E_λ is defined in such a way that the quantity $E_\lambda d\lambda$ is the energy radiated per unit area per second for wavelength in the range between λ and $\lambda + d\lambda$.

Thus

$$E_\lambda = \frac{\text{energy radiated per unit area per sec. in the range } \lambda \text{ to } \lambda + d\lambda}{\text{wavelength difference } d\lambda}$$

Unit of E_λ is 1 watt per square metre per Angstrom unit, and the SI unit is 1 watt per square metre per nanometre (10^{-9} m).

From these curves the following conclusions are drawn:

(1) As the temperature increases, E_λ for every wavelength increases.

(2) At constant temperature as λ increases, E_λ increases till its value becomes maximum E_m at a certain wavelength λ_m and then with further increase of λ, E_λ decreases. At a higher temperature the wavelength λ_m at which E_λ is maximum, shifts towards a shorter wavelength.

(3) The area enclosed between the curve at any absolute temperature T and the axis of wavelength λ, that is $\int_0^\infty E_\lambda \, d\lambda$ increases rapidly with increase of temperature. This area represents the total radiation emitted per square metre per second by a perfectly black body at the absolute temperature T over all wavelengths..

The total radiation emitted per unit area per second by a perfectly black body at temperature T is called the *total emissive power E* of the body at that temperature for all wavelengths.

Therefore, it follows that *the total emissive power E of a block body at a temperature T depends only on the temperature.*

1.2 FAILURE OF CLASSICAL PHYSICS TO EXPLAIN ENERGY DISTRIBUTION IN THE SPECTRUM OF A BLACK BODY

Late in the nineteenth century a number of attempts were made to explain distribution of energy among wavelengths in the spectrum of a black body by using laws of classical Physics. But the attempts were not very successfull. Two well-known classical laws with their limitations are as follows :

(1) Wien's Radiation Formula

In 1896 Wien derived the following formula for radiation from a black-body:

$$E_\lambda d\lambda = \frac{C_1}{\lambda^5} e^{-C_2/\lambda T} d\lambda \qquad ...(1)$$

where C_1 and C_2 are constants.

For obtaining the formula, the following arbitrary assumptions were made:

(1) The radiation inside a hollow enclosure is produced by resonators of molecular dimensions.

(2) The frequency of the radiation emitted is proportional to the kinetic energy of the resonator.

(3) The intensity of radiation of any particular wavelength is proportional to the number of resonators having required amount of energy.

Limitations of the formula :

The formula explains the experimental results fairly well for low values of λT, but for higher values it gives values of E_λ lower than the experimental values.

(2) Rayleigh-Jeans Law

In 1900 Lord Rayleigh applied the principle of equipartition of energy to the electromagnetic vibrations. Then with a contribution from J.H. Jeans this attempt led to the deduction of a formula for energy per unit volume inside an enclosure with perfectly reflecting walls. This formula is called the Rayleigh-Jeans law. According to this law the energy density, $U_\nu d\nu$, *i.e.*, the amount of energy per unit volume of the enclosure in the frequency range from ν to $\nu + d\nu$ is given by

$$U_\nu d\nu = \frac{8\pi\nu^2 kT}{c^3} d\nu \qquad ...(2)$$

where U_ν is the energy per unit volume per unit frequency range at frequency ν, k is Botzmann constant and c is the speed of light in free space.

The Rayleigh-Jeans formula can be transformed in terms of the wavelength λ by using the relation:

$$\nu = \frac{c}{\lambda}$$

and

$$d\nu = -\frac{c}{\lambda^2} d\lambda$$

The energy $U_\nu d\nu$ contained in a frequency interval between ν and $\nu + d\nu$ is equal to that contained in a corresponding wavelength interval between v and $v + d\lambda$, and an increase in frequency corresponds to a decrease in wavelength.

$$\therefore \quad U_\lambda d\lambda = -U_\nu d\nu$$

$$= -\frac{8\pi}{c^3}\left(\frac{c}{\lambda}\right)^2 kT\left(-\frac{c}{\lambda^2}\right)d\lambda$$

$$= \frac{8\pi kT}{\lambda^4}d\lambda \qquad \ldots (3)$$

This equation is another form of the Rayleigh-Jeans law,

Limitations of the law :

The law explains the experimental facts for very long wavelengths, but not for shorter wavelengths. According to the law as λ decreases, the energy density U_λ will continuously increase, and as λ tends to zero, U_λ approaches infinity (Fig. 1.2). This is contrary to the experimental results.

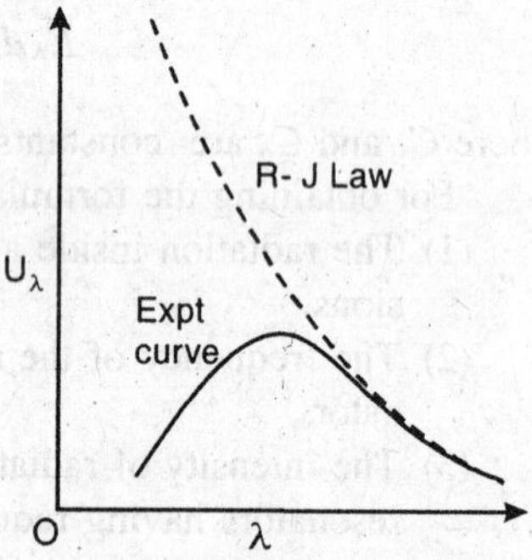

Fig. 1.2

The law leads to an absurd result which is as follows. The total energy of radiation per unit volume of the enclosure for all wavelengths from zero to infinity is given by :

$$U = \int_0^\infty U_\lambda d\lambda = \int_0^\infty \frac{8\pi kT}{\lambda^4} d\lambda$$

$$= 8\pi kT\left[-\frac{1}{3\lambda^3}\right]_0^\infty = \infty$$

This result shows that for a given quantity of radiant energy all the energy will finally be confined in vibrations of very small wavelengths. Thus, if the classical treatment is correct, on opening a shutter in the black body cavity, we would be bombarded with radiation of extremely short wavelengths. But, experimental results show that $U_\lambda d\lambda \rightarrow 0$ as $\lambda \rightarrow 0$. This discrepancy between the theoretical conclusion and the experimental result is called "ultraviolet catastrophe." This absurd result is because of the assumption that energy can be absorbed or emitted by the atomic oscillators continuously in any amount.

Thus, in the foregoing discussion on the distribution of energy in the spectrum of a black body classical theoretical physics failed to provide satisfactory explanation of the phenomenon. This led Max Planck to propose the quantum hypothesis.

1.3 PLANCK'S QUANTUM THEORY

In order to explain the distribution of energy in the spectrum of a black body, Max Planck in 1900, put forward the quantum theory of radiation. He assumed that the atoms in the walls of a black body behave like simple harmonic oscillators, and each has a characteristic frequency of oscillation. In his theory he made the following two radical assumptions about the atomic oscillators:

(1) A simple harmonic oscillator cannot have any arbitrary values of energy but only those values of the total energy E that are given by the relation:

$$E = nh\nu \qquad ...(1)$$

where $n = 0, 1, 2, 3, ...$; n is called the quantum number, ν is the frequency of oscillation, and h is a universal constant called Planck's constant ($h = 6.626 \times 10^{-34}$ Js). In this relation $h\nu$ is the basic unit of energy and it is called a *quantum of energy*. Thus the relation shows that the total energy of an oscillator is *quantized*.

(2) As long as the oscillator has energy equal to one of the allowed values given by the relation $E = nh\nu$, it cannot emit or absorb energy. Therefore, the oscillator is said to be in a stationary state or a quantum state of energy. *The emission or absorption of energy occurs only when the oscillator jumps from one energy state to another*. If the oscillator jumps down from a higher energy state of quantum number n_2 to a lower energy state of quantum number n_1, the energy emitted is given by :

$$E_2 - E_1 = (n_2 - n_1)\, h\nu$$

if $\quad n_2 - n_1 =$ one unit, then

$$E_2 - E_1 = h\nu$$

Similarly, an oscillator absorbs a quantum $h\nu$ of energy when it jumps up to its next higher energy state.

According to Planck the quantum theory is applicable only to the process of emission and absorption of radiant energy.

In 1905 Einstein extended Planck's quantum theory by assuming that a monochromatic radiation of frequency ν consists of a stream of photons each of energy $h\nu$ and the photons travel through space with the speed of light.

Planck's Radiation Law

On the basis of the quantum theory, Planck obtained the formula for an average energy of an oscillator:

$$E = \frac{h\nu}{e^{h\nu/kT} - 1} \qquad ...(2)$$

It can be shown that the number of oscillations or degrees of freedom per unit volume in the frequency range ν and $\nu + d\nu$ is given by :

$$N(\nu)d\nu = \frac{8\pi\nu^2}{c^3} d\nu \qquad ...(3)$$

where c is the speed of light in vacuum.

Then assuming that the average value of the energies of the various modes of oscillation in black body radiation is given by Eq. (2), Planck obtained the equation.

$$U_\nu d\nu = \frac{8\pi h\nu^3}{c^3} \frac{1}{e^{h\nu/kT} - 1} d\nu \qquad ...(4)$$

where $U_\nu d\nu$ is the energy per unit volume in the frequency range ν and $\nu + d\nu$ and U_ν is the energy per unit volume per unit frequency range at frequency ν. In terms of the wavelength of the radiation this equation is:

$$U_\lambda d\lambda = \frac{8\pi hc}{\lambda^5} \cdot \frac{1}{e^{hc/\lambda kT} - 1} d\lambda \qquad ...(5)$$

Eqs. (4) and (5) are two forms of Planck's radiation law.

When the values of U_λ as obtained from Eq. (5) for different values of λ are plotted against the corresponding values of λ we get curves as shown in Fig. 1.3. These curves agree very well with the experimental results over the whole range of wavelengths.

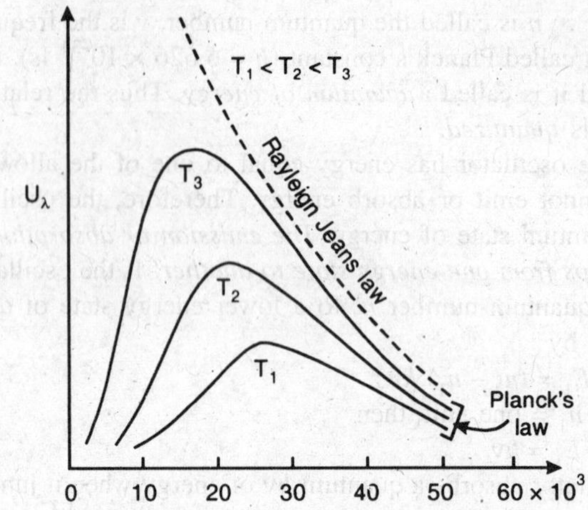

Fig. 1.3

Consequences of Planck's law

From Planck's law in the form of Eq. (5) the Rayleigh -Jeans law, Wien's law and the Stefan-Boltzmann formula are obtained as mathematical consequences:

(1) **Rayleigh-Jeans law**: For small values of $hc/\lambda kT$, *i.e.* in the region of long wavelengths, the exponential term in Eq. (5) can be expanded and retaining only the first term, we get

$$U_\lambda d\lambda = \frac{8\pi hc}{\lambda^5} \cdot \frac{1}{hc/\lambda kT} d\lambda = \frac{8\pi kT}{\lambda^4} d\lambda \qquad \text{... (6)}$$

This is the Rayleigh-Jeans law.

(2) **Wien's Radiation Formula:** In the region of low wavelengths $hc/\lambda kT$ becomes large. Hence 1 in the denominator on the right hand side of Eq. (5) can be neglected in comparison with the exponential term. Therefore, we get

$$U_\lambda d\lambda = \frac{8\pi hc}{\lambda^5} \cdot \frac{1}{e^{hc/\lambda kT}} d\lambda$$

$$= \frac{8\pi hc}{\lambda^5} e^{-hc/\lambda kT} d\lambda$$

It can be shown that for any black body, E_λ is related to U_λ at the same temperature by the equation :

$$E_\lambda = \frac{cU_\lambda}{4}, \quad \text{or} \quad U_\lambda = \frac{4E_\lambda}{c}$$

Now substituting for U_λ in the above equation, we get :

$$E_\lambda d\lambda = \frac{2\pi hc^2}{\lambda^5} e^{-hc/\lambda kT} d\lambda$$

$$= \frac{C_1}{\lambda^5} e^{-C_2/\lambda T} d\lambda \qquad \text{...(7)}$$

where $C_1 = 2\pi hc^2$ and $C_2 = hc/k$

Eq. (7) is Wien's radiation formula

(3) Wien's displacement law : From Planck's radiation law, we have :

$$U_\lambda = \frac{8\pi hc}{\lambda^5} \cdot \frac{1}{e^{hc/\lambda kT} - 1} \qquad ...(8)$$

At constant temperature T of a black body, the wavelength λ_m at which the energy density is maximum is given by :

$$\left[\frac{dU_\lambda}{d\lambda}\right]_{\lambda_m} = 0$$

Taking logarithm of both the sides of Eq. (8), we have :

$$\log_e U_\lambda = \log_e(8\pi hc) - 5\log_e \lambda - \log_e\left(e^{hc/\lambda kT} - 1\right)$$

Differentiating this equation with respect to λ

$$\frac{1}{U_\lambda} \cdot \frac{dU_\lambda}{d\lambda} = 0 - \frac{5}{\lambda} - \left[\frac{1}{e^{hc/\lambda kT} - 1}\right]\left(e^{hc/\lambda kT}\right)\left(-\frac{hc}{\lambda^2 kT}\right)$$

$$= \frac{1}{\lambda}\left[-5 + \frac{hc}{\lambda kT}\left\{\frac{e^{hc/\lambda kT}}{e^{hc/\lambda kT} - 1}\right\}\right]$$

At $\lambda = \lambda_m$, $\frac{dU_\lambda}{d\lambda} = 0$

$$\therefore \quad -5 + \frac{hc}{\lambda_m kT}\left\{\frac{e^{hc/\lambda_m kT}}{e^{hc/\lambda_m kT} - 1}\right\} = 0$$

Let $\frac{hc}{\lambda_m kT} = x,$

then $-5 + \frac{xe^x}{e^x - 1} = 0$

or $\frac{xe^x}{e^x - 1} = 5$

On solving this equation by trial and error method, we will get

$$x = 4.9651$$

i.e., $\frac{hc}{\lambda_m kT} = 4.9651$

$$\therefore \quad \lambda_m T = \frac{hc}{4.9651 \times k}$$

$$= \frac{6.62 \times 10^{-34} \times 3 \times 10^8}{4.9651 \times 1.38 \times 10^{-23}} = \frac{6.62 \times 3 \times 10^{-3}}{4.9651 \times 1.38}$$

$$= \mathbf{2.898 \times 10^{-3}\ m\ K}$$

This relation is Wien's displacement law. The law can be used to determine the temperature of a black body by determining the wavelength λ_m at which the intensity of the radiation is maximum.

(4) Stefan-Boltzmann Law. On the basis of the experimental data of Tyndol and of Dulong and Pelit, J. Stefan in 1879 deduced empirically that the total radiant energy of all wavelengths emitted per unit area per second by a heated body is proportional to the fourth power of its absolute temperature. In 1884 Boltzmann derived the fourth power law by considering the black-body radiation as the working substance for the ideal Carnot Cycle. He showed that the law is strictly applicable to the radiation from a black body. The law is, therefore, generally called the Stefan-Boltzmann Law. The law can be obtained directly from Planck's radiation formula. The derivation is as follows:

The energy density of the total radiation of all wavelengths in a black body enclosure at temperature T is given by :

$$U = \int_0^\infty U_\lambda d\lambda = \int_0^\infty \frac{8\pi hc}{\lambda^5} \cdot \frac{1}{e^{hc/\lambda kT} - 1} d\lambda$$

Let $$x = \frac{hc}{\lambda kT}$$

∴ $$\lambda = \frac{hc}{kTx}$$

and $$d\lambda = -\frac{hc}{kTx^2} dx$$

when $\lambda = 0,\ x = \infty$ and when $\lambda = \infty,\ x = 0$

Hence,

$$U = \int_\infty^0 \frac{8\pi hc}{1}\left(\frac{kTx}{hc}\right)^5 \frac{1}{e^x - 1}\left(-\frac{hc}{kTx^2} dx\right)$$

$$= -\int_\infty^0 \left(\frac{8\pi k^4 T^4}{h^3 c^3}\right) \frac{x^3}{e^x - 1} dx$$

$$= \frac{8\pi k^4 T^4}{h^3 c^3} \int_0^\infty \frac{x^3}{e^x - 1} dx$$

The value of the integral is $\frac{\pi^4}{15}$

∴ $$U = \frac{8\pi k^4 T^4}{h^3 c^3} \cdot \frac{\pi^4}{15} = \frac{4}{c}\left(\frac{2}{15}\frac{\pi^5 k^4}{h^3 c^2}\right) T^4 \qquad ...(8)$$

It can be shown that for any black body the total radiation of all wavelengths emitted per unit area per second at a given temperature, *i.e.* the total emissive power E is related to U at the same temperature by the equation:

$$E = \frac{cU}{4}, \quad \text{or} \quad U = \frac{4E}{c} \qquad ...(9)$$

Substituting for U in Eq. (8), we get

$$E = \left(\frac{2\pi^5 k^4}{15 h^3 c^2}\right) T^4 \qquad ...(10)$$

or $$E = \sigma T^4 \qquad \text{... (11)}$$

where $$\sigma = \frac{2\pi^5 k^4}{15h^3 c^2} \qquad \text{... (12)}$$

Eq. (11) is the Stefan-Boltzmann law of radiation. The constant σ is called Stefan's constant. The experimental value of this constant is

$$\sigma = 5.67 \times 10^{-8}\, \text{W/m}^2\text{K}^4$$

When the value $\sigma = 5.79 \times 10^{-8}\, \text{W/m}^2\text{K}^4$ (this was the value known at that time), $k = 1.38 \times 10^{-23}$ J/K, $c = 3 \times 10^8$ m/s are substituted in Eq. (12), the value of h is found to be 6.57×10^{-34} Js. This was the first calculated value of h. The recent recommended value of h which is now widely used is :

$$6.626 \times 10^{-34}\, \text{Js}$$

this value of h is substituted in Eq. (5) for obtaining the values of U_λ, it is found that the theoretical distribution curves agree excellently with the experimental curves over the whole range of wavelengths.

The success of Planck's hypothesis in explaining the distribution of energy in the spectrum of black body was the beginning of quantum mechanics, We now describe some more important phenomena which are explained by this hypothesis.

1.4 PHOTOELECTRIC EFFECT

When an electromagnetic radiation of sufficiently high frequency , such as ultraviolet light and X-rays is incident on a clean metal surface electrons are emitted from it. This phenomenon is known as the photoelectric effect, and the emitted electrons are called photoelectrons. The whole range of electromagnetic radiation from γ-rays and X-rays to the ultraviolet, the visible and the infrared rays produce this effect. Most metals give this effect when exposed to ultraviolet rays or X-rays. Sodium gives this effect when exposed to all radiations of wavelengths smaller than 5455 Å. Caesium produces this effect when exposed to all radiations of wavelengths smaller than 6438 Å.

The photoelectric effect was discovered by Heinrich Hertz in 1887. Further experimental study was undertaken by Hallwachs in 1888. Then in 1899 Lenard showed that the carriers of electricity emitted from a metal surface, under the action of ultraviolet light, were electrons.

Experimental Study of the Photo-electric Effect

The type of the apparatus that was used for the experimental study of the photoelectric effect is shown in Fig. 1.4 . A photo-sensitive metal plate *A* is mounted opposite to a metal plate *B* in a highly evacuated glass tube *C*. The plates *A* and *B* form two electrodes to which a variable potential difference (p.d.) can be applied. The glass tube is fitted with a quartz window *D*. Ultra-violet light from the source *S* is transmitted by *D* and falls on the surface *A*.

When the applied *P.D.* between *A* and *B* is such that *A* is at negative potential with respect to *B*, the photo-electrons emitted from *A* are accelerated towards *B*. The resulting photoelectric current *I* flowing in the circuit is measured by the micro-ammeter μA and the accelerating *P.D.* is measured by the vacuum tube voltmeter *V*

If the *P.D.* is reversed so that now *B* is at negative potential with respect to *A*, the photoelectrons are repelled towards *A* by the retarding *P.D.* Consequently the photoelectric current is reduced. The photoelectric current is found to depend on the following factors:

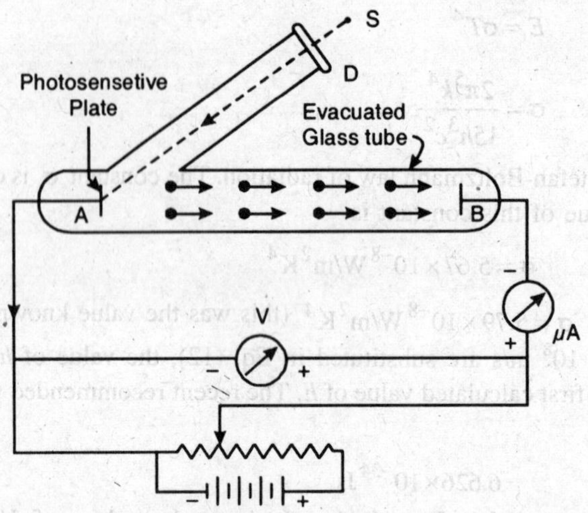

Fig. 1.4

(1) the frequency of the incident radiation,

(2) the intensity of the incident radiation,

(3) the potential difference between the electrodes,

(4) the nature of the emitting surface.

From the experimental study of the photoelectric effect we get the following results:

(1) Effect of frequency of the incident radiation on emission of photoelectrons:

For a given photo-sensitive surface there is a certain minimum frequency, called the threshold frequency ν_0 of the incident radiation, such that if the frequency of incident radiation is less than ν_0, no photoelectrons are emitted . The value of ν_0 depends on the material and the nature of the emitting surface.

(2) Effect of the intensity of the incident radiation on the photoelectric current:

For a given frequency $\nu(\nu > \nu_0)$ the number of the photoelectrons emitted per second from a given metal surface, under a constant accelerating potential difference is directly proportional to the intensity of the incident radiation.

(3) Effect of retarding potential difference on the photoelectric current:

When radiation of a given frequency $\nu(\nu > \nu_0)$ is incident on a given surface, photoelectrons with kinetic energies ranging from zero to a certain maximum value are emitted from the surface. The retarding potential difference V_0 which reduces the photoelectric current to zero is called the *stopping potential for* the photoelectrons. The variation of the photoelectric current with the potential difference for three different intensities X_1, X_2 and X_3 of the incident radiation is shown in Fig. 1.5. The curves show that for a given surface the stopping potential is independent of the intensity of the incident radiation of fixed frequency.

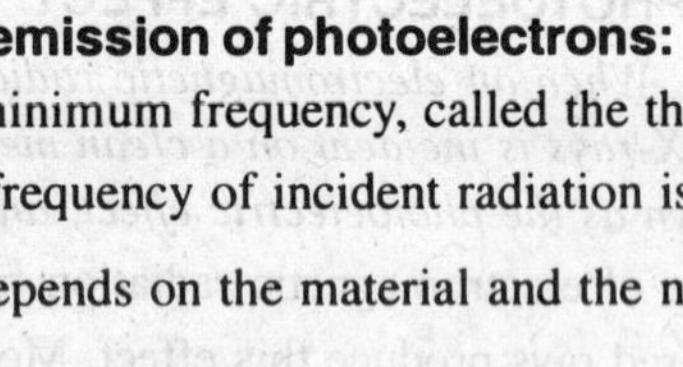

Fig. 1.5

The stopping potential V_0 just stops the photoelectrons having the maximum kinetic energy from reaching the collecting electrode B.

$$\therefore \qquad \frac{1}{2}mv^2_{\max} = eV_0 \qquad \text{... (1)}$$

where m is the mass of the electron, e the electronic charge and $v_{\max}$ is the maximum velocity of emission. Those electrons which are emitted with kinetic energies less than the maximum value are stopped by smaller values of the retarding potential.

(4) Effect of frequency on the stopping potential :

The stopping potential V_0 for the photoelectrons emitted from a given surface increases linearly with the frequency of the incident radiation. The straight line for the given surface meets the frequency axis at the threshold frequency ν_0 for the surface. Fig. 1.6 shows the graph of V_0 against the frequency ν for three different metals I, II, and III. The slope of the three straight lines is the same *i.e.* equal to h/e, but their intercepts ν_{01}, ν_{02} and ν_{03} on the frequency-axis are different. These intercepts are the respective threshold frequencies of the metals.

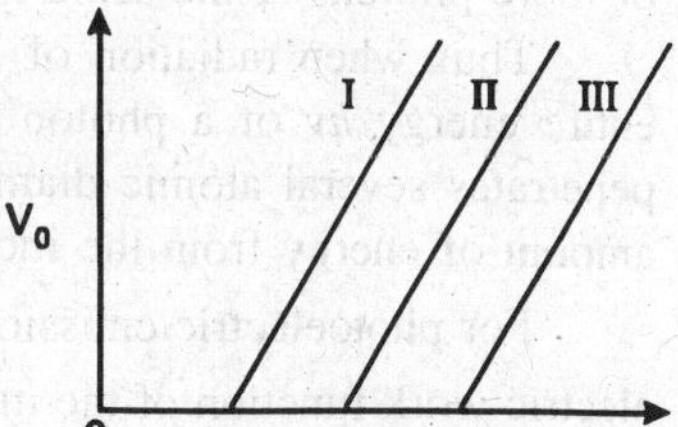

Fig. 1.6

(5) The emission of photo-electrons is an instantaneous process:

As soon as radiation of frequency greater than the threshold frequency is incident on a given photo-sensitive surface, there is emission of photo-electrons.

Failure of classical physics to explain the photoelectric effect :

The following experimental results cannot be explained on the basis of classical physics:

(1) The existence of the threshold frequency:

According to the wave theory of light the emission of the photoelectrons should occur for any frequency of the incident radiation provided the intensity of the radiation is sufficient to supply enough energy to the electrons. But this does not happen.

(2) The non-dependence of the maximum kinetic energy $\left(\frac{1}{2}mv^2_{\max} = eV_0\right)$ of the photoelectrons on the intensity of the incident radiation :

According to electromagnetic theory oscillating electric vector of the incident radiation should cause an electron in the metal to oscillate. If the amplitude of its oscillation is sufficient, the electron is emitted from the metal surface. If the amplitude of oscillation of the incident wave is increased, the electron should be emitted with greater energy. However, this does not happen. The incident radiations of the same frequency greater than the threshold frequency but of different intensities give rise to emission of the photoelectrons with exactly the same maximum kinetic energy.

(3) Absence of time-lag between the irradiation of a surface and the start of the emission:

According to the wave theory, the energy of the incident light is spread over the wave front and since the energy incident on any one electron would be very small, some time will be required by an electron to absorb enough energy to escape from the surface.

1.5 EINSTEIN'S EXPLANATION OF THE PHOTOELECTRIC EFFECT

Einstein's Photoelectric Equation

To derive the photo-electric equation, Einstein in 1905 applied Planck's quantum theory and made the following two assumptions :

(1) A radiation of frequency ν consists of a stream of discrete quanta each of energy $h\nu$ where h is Planck's constant. These quanta are called photons. The photons move through space with the speed of light.

(2) When a photon of energy $h\nu$ is incident on a metal surface, the entire energy of the photon is absorbed by a single electron without any time lag. The probability of its absorbing two or more photons at the same time is negligible.

Thus when radiation of frequency ν is incident on the surface of a metal in vacuum the entire energy $h\nu$ of a photon is absorbed by an electron of the metal. The incident radiation penetrates several atomic diameters into the metal and electrons at different depths absorb this amount of energy from the incident photon.

For photoelectric emission of an electron from the metal $h\nu \geq W_0$, where W_0 is the photo-electric work function of the metal . When an electron at the metal surface absorbs the energy $h\nu$, a certain *minimum* part of this energy is used up by the electron to do work equal to W_0 to overcome the attractive forces of the positive ions of the metal. The remaining *maximum* energy $(h\nu - W_0)$ is in the form of maximum kinetic energy $(1/2)mv^2_{max}$ of the electron emitted from the surface.

$$\therefore \quad \frac{1}{2} mv^2_{max} = h\nu - W_0 \qquad ...(1)$$

where m is the mass of the electron and v_{max} is the maximum speed of the emitted electron. An electron emitted from below the surface will lose some part of the energy $h\nu$ in internal collisions with other electrons. Consequently, it will be emitted with a smaller energy. Eq. (1) is known as *Einstein's photoelectric equation.*

According to this theory, the threshold frequency ν_0 for a metal surface is the frequency of a photon which has just sufficient energy to liberate an electron from the surface with zero kinetic energy. From Eq. (1) this frequency is given by:

$$O = h\nu_0 - W_0$$

$$\therefore \quad h\nu_0 = W_0 \qquad ...(2)$$

Substituting for W_0 in Eq. (1), we get

$$\frac{1}{2} mv^2_{max} = h(\nu - \nu_0) \qquad ...(3)$$

This is another form of Einstein's photoelectric equation.

The three main characteristics of the photoelectric effect which cannot be explained by the wave theory, are in perfect agreement with Einstein's photon theory. Their explanations are as follows:

(1) *The existence of the threshold frequency:* This has been explained by Eq. (2)

(2) *The non-dependence of the maximum kinetic energy of the photoelectrons on the intensity of the incident radiation:*

According to this theory, the intensity of a beam of radiation of frequency ν is proportional to the number of photons each of energy $h\nu$ passing normally through unit area of cross-section of the beam per second, and the energy of a photon is *independent* of the intensity. Therefore, if the intensity of the radiation is increased, the number of photons in the beam will increase in proportion to the intensity. Hence the number of photoelectrons emitted per unit area per second will increase in proportion to the intensity . But the maximum kinetic energy will be the same as before. Thus the maximum kinetic energy of the emitted photoelectrons is *independent* of the intensity, but the photoelectric current is proportional to the intensity.

(3) *The absence of time-lag between the irradiation and the start of the emission of the photoelectrons:*

The energy of a photon is not distributed over an area, as in the wave theory. It is in the form of a concentrated bundle. So when a photon is incident on an electron, all its energy is absorbed by the electron without any time lag.

We have seen that the photoelectric effect is explained by Einstein's photon theory according to which an electromagnetic radiation of frequency ν consists of photons each of energy $h\nu$, and a photon gives up all its energy to an electron in a metal when the radiation is incident on the metal surface. Thus this effect shows that electromagnetic radiation also has particle properties.

1.6. THE RITZ COMBINATION PRINCIPLE IN SPECTRA

J.J Balmer in 1885 showed that the wave numbers $\bar{\nu}\left(i.e., \frac{1}{\lambda}\right)$ of the spectral lines in the visible region of the emission spectrum of hydrogen could be represented by the *empirical formula* $\frac{1}{\lambda} = \bar{\nu} = R\left(\frac{1}{2^2} - \frac{1}{n^2}\right)$, where n = 3, 4, 5 .... . The constant R is the Rydberg constant ; its empirical value is 1.097×10^7 / m. The formula consists of two terms : the first term is a constant and is called the *series term*, the second term is variable and is called the *current term* or *the running term.*

In 1908 W. Ritz introduced his combination principle which is a generalization of the Balmer formula. The *combination principle* may be stated as follows:

The wave number $\bar{\nu}$*(i.e.* $1/\lambda$*) of any spectral line in the emission spectrum of an element may be represented as the combination of two terms : one of which is constant and the other is the variable or the running term throughout each spectral series.*

Application of the principle to spectral series of lines in the spectrum of hydrogen:

According to this principle : the wave numbers of the spectral lines in different series of the hydrogen spectrum may be represented by the general formula :

$$\bar{\nu} = R\left(\frac{1}{n_1^2} - \frac{1}{n_2^2}\right) \quad ...(1)$$

where R is the Rydberg constant, and n_1 and n_2 are integers. The integer n_1 is constant and n_2 variable for a series of the spectral lines. Therefore, for each value assigned to n_1, a different series of the spectral lines was predicted. It has been seen that for the *Balmer series in the visible region,* n_1 = 2. For n_1 = 1 3, 4 and 5 the following series were predicted before they were discovered :

Lyman series : discovered in 1916 in the ultraviolet region:

$$\bar{\nu} = R\left(\frac{1}{1^2} - \frac{1}{n_2^2}\right), \text{ where } n_2 = 2, 3, 4, ...$$

Paschen series : discovered in 1908 in the infrared region :

$$\bar{\nu} = R\left(\frac{1}{3^2} - \frac{1}{n_2^2}\right), \text{ where } n_2 = 4, 5, 6, ...$$

Brackett series : discovered in 1922 in the infrared region:

$$\bar{\nu} = R\left(\frac{1}{4^2} - \frac{1}{n_2^2}\right), \text{ where } n_2 = 5, 6, 7, \ldots\ldots$$

Pfund series : discovered in 1924 in far infrared region:

$$\bar{\nu} = R\left(\frac{1}{5^2} - \frac{1}{n_2^2}\right), \text{ where } n_2 = 6, 7, 8, \ldots$$

A theoretical basis for the Ritz combination principle is provided by the Bohr theory of the hydrogen atom, which is discussed in Sec. 1:8.

1.7. STABILITY OF AN ATOM

Rutherford model of an atom: In this model an atom consists of a very small sphere of radius about 10^{-14} m , in which its positive charge and nearly all its mass are concentrated. This sphere is called the nucleus of the atom. The electrons revolve round this nucleus in circular orbits of radius about 10^{-10}m. The positive charge of the nucleus is equal to the total negative charge of the electrons. The centripetal force for circular motion of the electrons is provided by the electrostatic force of attraction between the negative charge of the electrons and the positive charge of the nucleus.

Failure of classical physics to explain stability of an atom:

According to the electromagnetic theory an accelerated charged particle must radiate energy in the form of electromagnetic radiation continuously . An electron moving round the nucleus in a circular orbit is subjected to a continuous acceleration of constant magnitude directed towards the nucleus. Therefore, it should emit radiation continuously. Due to the loss of energy by radiation, it would move along a spiral path of *decreasing* radius and finally it would fall into the nucleus. In this process of the spiral motion it would emit radiation of continuously increasing frequency and hence would given rise to a continuous spectrum. Calculations show that the collapse of the electron into the nucleus should occur in about 10^{-8} second. But atoms are stable and they show no tendency to collapse. Moreover, atoms of any element emit radiation of discrete wavelengths which form the line spectrum of the element.

Thus Rutherford's model could not explain the stability of atoms.

1.8. BOHR'S QUANTIZATION OF ANGULAR MOMENTUM AND ITS APPLICATION TO THE HYDROGEN ATOM

In order to explain in detail the observed spectrum of the hydrogen atom, Neils Bohr in 1913 used the Rutherford model of the atom. To overcome the difficulty about electron's orbits, Bohr postulated that an electron in an atom can revolve round the nucleus only in certain stable (or stationary) circular orbits without emitting electromagnetic radiation. To determine the radii of the allowed orbits, Bohr postulated that *only those orbits are stable for which the magnitude L of the electron's orbital angular momentum is quantized : being equal to an integral multiple of $h/2\pi$, where h is Planck's constant.* In symbols this condition is expressed as :

$$L = mvr = n\frac{h}{2\pi}$$

where $n = 1, 2, 3, \ldots\ldots$

Bohr's theory of the hydrogen atom:

The theory of the hydrogen atom is based on the three basic postulates (assumptions) which are stated as follows:

1. *The electron in the hydrogen atom revolves in a stable circular orbit round the nucleus under the action of Coulomb's force of attraction between the positively charged nucleus and the negatively charged electron* (Fig. 1.7). The centripetal force which keeps the electron moving in the circular orbit is provided by the electrostatic force of *attraction* exerted on it by the nucleus.

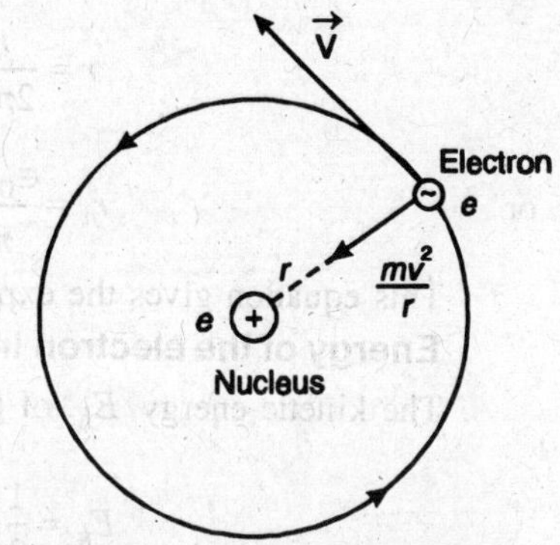

Fig. 1.7. Circular orbit of an electron.

$$\therefore \quad \frac{mv^2}{r} = \frac{e \times e}{4\pi\varepsilon_0 r^2} = \frac{e^2}{4\pi\varepsilon_0 r^2} \quad \text{... (1a)}$$

From this equation, we have

$$mv^2 r = \frac{e^2}{4\pi\varepsilon_0} \quad \text{...(1b)}$$

where r = radius of the allowed circular orbit,
v = liner speed of the electron,
m = mass of the electron,
e = electronic charge , and
ϵ_0 = permittivity of free space.

2. *In an allowed stable orbit the magnitude L of the orbital angular momentum of the electron is an integral multiple of $h/2\pi$, where h is Planck's constant. That is :*

$$L = \frac{nh}{2\pi}$$

or

$$mvr = \frac{nh}{2\pi} \quad \text{...(2)}$$

where n = 1, 2, 3, ...

The parameter n is called the principal quantum number.

3. *Transitions of the electron can occur from one of the stationary orbits to another. When the electron makes a transition from an outer stationary orbit of quantum number n_2 to an inner stationary orbit of quantum number n_1, a photon of energy $h\nu$ is emitted as an electromagnetic radiation of frequency ν. The energy of the photon is the difference of the energies of the electron in the outer and inner orbits.*

Thus,

$$h\nu = E_{n2} - E_{n1} \quad \text{...(3)}$$

where E_{n1} and E_{n2} are the energies in the inner and outer orbits respectively.

Linear speed, Radius, and Energy

Linear speed v of the electron in a Bohr orbit:

Dividing Eq. (1 *b*) by Eq. (2), we get

$$v = \left(\frac{e^2}{4\pi\epsilon_0}\right)\left(\frac{2\pi}{nh}\right) = \frac{e^2}{2\epsilon_0\, hn} \quad \text{...(4)}$$

This is the expression for v of the electron in a Bohr orbit of quantum number n.

Radius *r* of a Bohr orbit:

Using Eqs. (2) and (4), we obtain:

$$r = \frac{nh}{2\pi mv} = \left(\frac{nh}{2\pi m}\right)\left(\frac{2\epsilon_0 hn}{e^2}\right)$$

or
$$r_n = \frac{\epsilon_0 h^2 n^2}{\pi m e^2} = \left(\frac{\epsilon_0 h^2}{\pi m e^2}\right) n^2 \qquad ...(5)$$

This equation gives the expression for r_n of a Bohr orbit of quantum number n.

Energy of the electron in a Bohr orbit:

The kinetic energy E_K of the electron is given by

$$E_k = \frac{1}{2} mv^2 = \frac{1}{2} m \left(\frac{e^2}{2\epsilon_0 hn}\right)^2$$

$$= \frac{me^4}{8\epsilon_0^2 h^2 n^2} \qquad ...(6)$$

The potential energy E_p of the electron is equal to the *product* of the potential at distance r_n from the nucleus due to its positive charge $+e$ and the electronic charge $-e$

Thus,

$$E_p = \frac{e}{4\pi\epsilon_0 r_n}(-e) = -\frac{e^2}{4\pi\epsilon_0 r_n}$$

Substituting the value of r_n in this equation, we get

$$E_p = -\left(\frac{e^2}{4\pi\epsilon_0}\right)\left(\frac{\pi m e^2}{\epsilon_0 h^2 n^2}\right) = -\frac{me^4}{4\epsilon_0^2 h^2 n^2} \qquad ...(7)$$

Now the total energy E_n of the electron in the orbit is given by

$$E_n = E_k + E_p = \frac{me^4}{8\epsilon_0^2 h^2 n^2} - \frac{me^4}{4\epsilon_0^2 h^2 n^2}$$

$$= -\frac{me^4}{8\epsilon_0^2 h^2 n^2} = -\left(\frac{me^4}{8\epsilon_0^2 h^2}\right)\frac{1}{n^2} \qquad ...(8)$$

This equation shows that the total energy of the electron in the orbit of principal quantum number n is inversely proportional to the square of the principal quantum number. If E_1 is the total energy of the electron in the first Bohr orbit, then

$$E_1 = -\frac{me^4}{8\epsilon_0^2 h^2} \qquad ...(9)$$

$$\therefore \quad E_n = \frac{E_1}{n^2} \qquad ...(10)$$

The calculated value of E_1 in electron volt = – 13.6 eV

$$\therefore \quad E_n = -\frac{13.6}{n^2} \qquad ...(11)$$

The values of the total energy of the electron in different orbits are called the energy levels of the hydrogen atom. The total energy is negative because the potential energy is taken to be zero when the electron is at an infinite distance from the nucleus, and when the electron moves towards the nucleus work is done on it by the electrostatic force of attraction. So, it loses potential energy.

The lowest energy level $E_1 = -13.6$ eV is called the ground state energy of the atom. The higher energy levels $E_2 = -13.6/2^2$, $E_3 = -13.6/3^2$, ... eV are called the energies in the excited states.

Origin of the spectral Lines

From Eq. 8 the total energy E_{n2} of the electron in the outer orbit of quantum number n_2 and its energy E_{n1} in an inner orbit of quantum number n_1 are given by

$$E_{n2} = -\left(\frac{me^4}{8\epsilon_0^2 h^2}\right)\frac{1}{n_2^2}$$

$$E_{n1} = -\left(\frac{me^4}{8\epsilon_0^2 h^2}\right)\frac{1}{n_1^2}$$

According to the third postulate, when the electron makes a transition from the n_2^{th} orbit to the n_1^{th} orbit, the frequency v of the radiation emitted is given by

$$hv = E_{n2} - E_{n1}$$

$$= -\left(\frac{me^4}{8\epsilon_0^2 h^2}\right)\frac{1}{n_2^2} + \left(\frac{me^4}{8\epsilon_0^2 h^2}\right)\frac{1}{n_1^2}$$

$$= \frac{me^4}{8\epsilon_0^2 h^2}\left(\frac{1}{n_1^2} - \frac{1}{n_2^2}\right)$$

$$\therefore \quad v = \frac{me^4}{8\epsilon_0^2 h^3}\left(\frac{1}{n_1^2} - \frac{1}{n_2^2}\right) \quad ...(12)$$

Let λ be the wavelength of the radiation. Then

$$v = \frac{c}{\lambda}$$

where c is the speed of light in vacuum, or air

$$\therefore \quad \frac{c}{\lambda} = \frac{me^4}{8\epsilon_0^2 h^3}\left(\frac{1}{n_1^2} - \frac{1}{n_2^2}\right)$$

or

$$\frac{1}{\lambda} = \frac{me^4}{8\epsilon_0^2 ch^3}\left(\frac{1}{n_1^2} - \frac{1}{n_2^2}\right)$$

$$= R\left(\frac{1}{n_1^2} - \frac{1}{n_2^2}\right) \quad ...(13)$$

where $R = \frac{me^4}{8\epsilon_0^2 ch^3}$ is the Rydberg constant.

Using the values of m, e, h, ϵ_0 and c, the calculated value of the Raydberg constant is $R = 1.097 \times 10^7$/m. This value is nearly the same as the experimental value for the hydrogen atom. Eq. (13) is called Bohr's equation. From this equation the emission of all the spectral series of lines in the hydrogen spectrum are explained as follows:

(1) **Lyman Series** (in ultra-violet region, invisible). This series of lines is emitted by transitions of the electron from outer orbits of quantum numbers, $n_2 = 2, 3, 4$, ... to the first orbit of quantum number $n_1 = 1$. The wavelengths of this series of lines are given by :

$$\frac{1}{\lambda} = R\left(\frac{1}{1^2} - \frac{1}{n_2^2}\right), \text{ where } n_2 = 2, 3, 4, ...$$

(2) **Balmer Series** (visible). This series of lines is emitted by transitions of the electron from outer orbits of quantum numbers n_2 = 3, 4, 5 ....to the second orbit of quantum number n_1 = 2. Thus, the wavelength of the $H_\alpha, H_\beta, H_\gamma$ and H_δ and lines are given by

$$\frac{1}{\lambda_\alpha} = R\left(\frac{1}{2^2} - \frac{1}{3^2}\right), \qquad \frac{1}{\lambda_\beta} = R\left(\frac{1}{2^2} - \frac{1}{4^2}\right)$$

$$\frac{1}{\lambda_\gamma} = R\left(\frac{1}{2^2} - \frac{1}{5^2}\right), \qquad \frac{1}{\lambda_\delta} = R\left(\frac{1}{2^2} - \frac{1}{6^2}\right)$$

(3) **Paschen Series** (in infra-red region, invisible) : For this series n_1 = 3, and n_2 = 4, 5, 6, ...

(4) **Bracket Series** (in infra-red region, invisible): For this series n_1 = 4, and n_2 = 5, 6, 7, ...

(5) **Pfund Series** (in far infra-red region, invisible): For this series n_1 = 5, and n_2 = 6, 7, 8, ...

Energy Level Diagram for Hydrogen Atom

In this diagram the energy of the electron E_1 = – 13.6 eV in the ground state, and the values

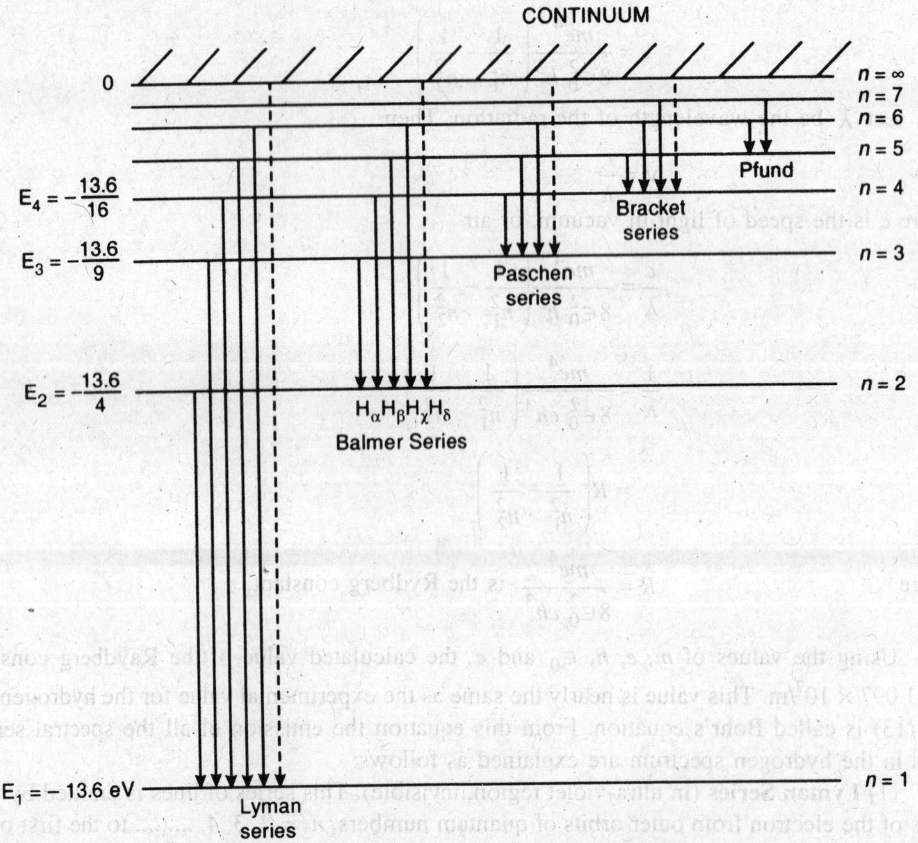

Fig. 1.8. Energy levels and spectra of hydrogen

of energy $E_n = -\frac{13.6}{n^2}$ in the excited states for different values of n are plotted on a vertical scale, These energy-levels are represented by horizontal lines as shown in Fig. 1.8. As n becomes larger, the energy-levels become progressively closer. For $n = \infty$, $E_\infty = 0$. The energy in electron-volt required to remove the electron from the ground state to infinity, *i.e.*, to the zero energy level is called ionisation potential or the ionisation energy for the hydrogen atom. Its value for the hydrogen atom is 13.6 eV

The transitions of the electron, which give rise to the Lyman, Balmer, Paschen, Bracket and Pfund series of lines are shown by vertical arrowed lines in the figure. As n increases the energy difference between successive energy-levels decreases, Therefore, the separation between the spectral lines of higher frequencies or smaller wavelengths in any series decreases.

In a discharge tube at a given instant of time a very large number of hydrogen atoms are excited to different higher energy states. Hence electrons in these atoms will be making all possible types of quantum jumps from outer orbits to inner orbits, so that all possible spectral lines are emitted continuously. The intensity of any line depends on the number of electrons making transitions between the particular orbits in a group of atoms. If the outer orbit has a high quantum number, the intensity of the line emitted will be low, because the probability of an atom getting excited to the energy state of high quantum number is low.

Limitations of Bohr's Theory

Bohr's theory explains quite successfully the spectrum of hydrogen and hydrogen-like ions such as singly ionized helium and doubly ionized lithium. But the theory has a number of limitations. A few of them are as follows:

(1) It cannot explain the experimental observation that many spectral lines extend over a finite wavelength-range, consisting of a small number of lines close together.

(2) The theory cannot explain the difference in the intensities of certain spectral lines in the spectrum of an element. That is, the theory cannot explain the difference in the probabilities of occurrence of certain transitions of electrons between energy levels.

(3) The spectra of complex atoms having two or more electrons each cannot be explained on the basis of the theory.

(4) In the theory the nucleus is considered stationary with the electron revolving around it. But both, the nucleus and the orbital electron revolve around a common centre of mass.

(5) The theory does not provide any clue about the forces of interaction between atoms which form a stable substance.

SOLVED EXAMPLES

Example 1.1. *Find the average number of photons per cubic metre in a monochromatic beam of radiation of frequency* 10 kHz *and of intensity* 10^4 W/m^2.

Solution:

The intensity of a beam of radiation is the total energy of the number of photons passing normally through unit area of the cross-section of beam per second.

Let n be the number of photons per unit volume each having energy $h\nu$. Let us consider a length l of the beam having cross-section area A.

In the volume Al the total photon-energy = $nAlh\nu$. The time taken by this energy to pass through the length l is given by

$$t = \frac{l}{c}$$

where c is the speed of light in free space.

$\therefore$ the intensity I of the beam is given by

$$I = \frac{nAlh\nu}{At} = \frac{nlh\nu}{l/c} = nh\nu c$$

Hence $$n = \frac{I}{h\nu c}$$

Substituting the numerical values

$$n = \frac{10^4}{6.63\times10^{-34}\times10^4\times3\times10^8}$$

$$= \frac{10^{26}}{19.89} = \mathbf{5.03\times10^{24}}\ \text{photons/m}^3$$

Example 1.2. *Prove that in the photo-electric effect from a metal surface, the maximum velocity of the photo-electrons is related to the stopping potential by the equation*

$$V_{max} = 5.927\times10^5\sqrt{V_0}$$

where V_{max} *is in* m/sec. *and* V_0 *is in volts.*

Solution.

We have $m = 9.11\times10^{-31}$ kg, $e = 1.6\times10^{-18}$ C

The maximum kinetic energy is related to the stopping potential by the equation

$$\frac{1}{2}mV_{max}^2 = eV_0$$

$$\therefore\ V_{max} = \sqrt{\frac{2eV_0}{m}} = \sqrt{\frac{2\times1.6\times10^{-19}}{9.11\times10^{-31}}}\times\sqrt{V_0}$$

$$= 10^5\sqrt{\frac{20\times16}{9.11}}\times\sqrt{V_0}$$

$$= 10^5\times5.927\sqrt{V_0}$$

$$= 5.927\times10^5\sqrt{V_0}\ \text{m/sec.}$$

Example 1.3. *The photo-electric threshold wavelength of silver is 2762 Å. Calculate (a) the maximum kinetic energy of the ejected electrons, (b) the maximum velocity of the electrons, and (c) the stopping potential in volts for the electrons when the silver surface is illuminated with ultraviolet light of wavelength 2000 Å.*

Solution:

We have $\lambda = 2000\times10^{-10}\ \text{m} = 2\times10^{-7}\ \text{m}$

and $\lambda_0 = 2762\times10^{-10}\ \text{m} = 2.762\times10^{-7}\ \text{m}$

(a) $E_{max} = h(\nu - \nu_0)$

$$= hc\left(\frac{1}{\lambda} - \frac{1}{\lambda_0}\right)$$

$$= 6.63\times10^{-34}\times3\times10^{8}\left(\frac{10^7}{2}-\frac{10^7}{2.762}\right)$$

$$= 6.63\times3\times10^{-19}\left(\frac{1}{2}-\frac{1}{2.762}\right)$$

$$= 6.63\times3\times10^{-19}\times0.138$$

$$= \mathbf{2.745\times10^{-19}\ J}$$

(*b*) The maximum velocity is given by :

$$\frac{1}{2}mV_{max}^2 = E_{max}$$

$$\therefore \quad V_{max} = \left(\frac{2\times E_{max}}{m}\right)^{\frac{1}{2}}$$

$$= \left(\frac{2\times2.745\times10^{-19}}{9.11\times10^{-31}}\right) = 10^5\left(\frac{2\times274.5}{9.11}\right)^{1/2} = 7.76\times10^5\ \text{m/sec}$$

(c) $$eV_0 = E_{max}$$

$$\therefore \quad V_0 = \frac{E_{max}}{e} = \frac{2.745\times10^{-19}}{1.6\times10^{-19}}$$

$$= \mathbf{1.715\ Volts.}$$

Example 1.4 *A metallic surface, when illuminated with light of wavelength λ_1, emits electrons with energies upto a maximum value E_1, and when illuminated with light of wavelength λ_2, where $\lambda_2 < \lambda_1$, it emits electrons with energies upto a maximum value E_2. Prove that Planck's constant h and the work-function W_0 of the metal are given by*

$$h = \frac{(E_2-E_1)\lambda_1\lambda_2}{c(\lambda_1-\lambda_2)}$$

$$W_0 = \frac{E_2\lambda_2 - E_1\lambda_1}{\lambda_1-\lambda_2}$$

Solution:

The maximum kinetic energy E_1 is given by

$$E_1 = h\nu_1 - W_0$$

or $$E_1 = \frac{hc}{\lambda_1} - W_0 \quad ...(1)$$

Similarly the maximum kinetic energy E_2 is given by

$$E_2 = \frac{hc}{\lambda_2} - W_0 \quad ...(2)$$

Subtracting Eq. (1) from Eq. (2), we get,

$$E_2 - E_1 = hc\left(\frac{1}{\lambda_2}-\frac{1}{\lambda_1}\right) = hc\left(\frac{\lambda_1-\lambda_2}{\lambda_1\lambda_2}\right)$$

$$h = \frac{(E_2 - E_1)\lambda_1\lambda_2}{c(\lambda_1 - \lambda_2)} \qquad ...(3)$$

Now to obtain the expression for W_0, from Eq. (1) and (2) we have,

$$E_1\lambda_1 = hc - W_0\lambda_1 \qquad ...(4)$$

$$E_2\lambda_2 = hc - W_0\lambda_2 \qquad ...(5)$$

Subtracting Eq. (4) from Eq. (5), we get.

$$E_2\lambda_2 - E_1\lambda_1 = W_0(\lambda_1 - \lambda_2)$$

$$\therefore \qquad W_0 = \frac{E_2\lambda_2 - E_1\lambda_1}{\lambda_1 - \lambda_2} \qquad ...(6)$$

Example 1.5. *A metallic surface, when illuminated with light of wavelength 3333* Å, *emits electrons with energies upto 0.6* eV, *and when illuminated with light of wavelength 2400* Å, *it emits electrons with energies upto 2.04* eV. *Calculate Planck's constant and the work-function of the metal.*

Solution:

We have $\lambda_1 = 3333\times10^{-10}\,\text{m} = 3.000\times10^{-7}\,\text{m}$

$\lambda_2 = 2400\times10^{-10}\,\text{m} = 2.4\times10^{-7}\,\text{m}$

Max. energy $E_1 = 0.6\times1.6\times10^{-19}\,\text{J}$

Max. energy $E_2 = 2.04\times1.6\times10^{-19}\,\text{J}$

(*i*) *Planck's constant:* Proceed as in Ex. 1.4 and obtain

$$h = \frac{(E_2 - E_1)\lambda_1\lambda_2}{c(\lambda_1 - \lambda_2)}$$

$$\therefore \qquad h = \frac{(2.04-0.6)\times1.6\times10^{-19}\times3.333\times10^{-7}\times2.4\times10^{-7}}{3\times10^{8}(3.333-2.4)\times10^{-7}}$$

$$= \frac{1.44\times1.6\times3.333\times2.4\times10^{-34}}{3\times0.933}$$

$$= \mathbf{6.58\times10^{-34}\ Js}$$

(*ii*) *Work function*: Proceed as in Ex. 1.4 and obtain

$$W_0 = \frac{E_2\lambda_2 - E_1\lambda_1}{\lambda_1 - \lambda_2}$$

$$\therefore \qquad W_0 = \frac{(2.04\times2.4-0.6\times3.333)\times10^{-7}}{(3.333-2.4)\times10^{-7}}\ \text{eV}$$

$$= \frac{4.896-1.9998}{0.933}$$

$$= \frac{2.896}{0.933} = \mathbf{3.1\ eV}$$

Example 1.6. Show *that the frequency of transition from level n to level n – 1 in Bohr model for large value of n approaches the classical frequency of revolution of the electron in the nth orbit.*

Proof:

In a hydrogen atom the electron's linear speed in a stable orbit of quantum number *n*, and the radius of the orbit are given by (See Sec. 1.8)

$$v_n = \frac{e^2}{2\epsilon_0 hn} \quad \text{...(1)}$$

$$r_n = \frac{\epsilon_0 h^2 n^2}{\pi m e^2} \quad \text{... (2)}$$

Hence the frequency of revolution *f* of the electron is

$$f = \frac{1}{T} = \frac{v_n}{2\pi r} = \frac{1}{2\pi}\left(\frac{e^2}{2\epsilon_0 hn}\right)\left(\frac{\pi m e^2}{\epsilon_0 h^2 n^2}\right)$$

$$= \frac{me^4}{4\epsilon_0^2 h^3 n^3} = \frac{me^4}{8\epsilon_0^2 h^3}\left(\frac{2}{n^3}\right) \quad \text{...(3)}$$

In the transition from an outer orbit of quantum number n_2 to an inner orbit of quantum number n_1 the frequency ν of the photon is given by :

$$\nu = \frac{me^4}{8\epsilon_0^2 h^3}\left(\frac{1}{n_1^2} - \frac{1}{n_2^2}\right) \quad \text{...(4)}$$

Substituting $n_1 = n - 1$

and $n_2 = n$, **the term in the bracket is**

$$\frac{1}{n_1^2} - \frac{1}{n_2^2} = \frac{1}{(n-1)^2} - \frac{1}{n^2} = \frac{n^2 - (n-1)^2}{n^2 (n-1)^2}$$

$$= \frac{2n - 1}{n^2 \cdot n^2\left(1 - \frac{1}{n}\right)^2} = \frac{2n\left(1 - \frac{1}{2n}\right)}{n^4\left(1 - \frac{1}{n}\right)^2}$$

For a large value of *n*, the terms 1/2*n* in the numerator and 1/*n* in the denominator are negligible in comparison with 1

∴ for large value of *n*

$$\frac{1}{n_1^2} - \frac{1}{n_2^2} = \frac{2}{n^3}$$

Hence from Eq. (4), we get

$$\nu = \frac{me^4}{8\epsilon_0^2 h^3}\left(\frac{2}{n^3}\right) \quad \text{...(5)}$$

Thus Eqs. (3) and (5) show that the frequency ν of transition from level *n* to level *n* – 1 for large value of *n* is equal to the frequency *f* of rotation of the orbital electron.

QUESTIONS AND PROBLEMS

1. Find the average number of photons per cubic metre in a monochromatic beam of γ-rays of wavelength 0.003 Å and of intensity 10^4 W/m^2. (**Ans.** 5.03×10^{17} /m^3)

2. What was Planck's hypothesis to explain the spectral distribution of the intensity of radiation from a black body? Derive Planck's radiation law, (Garhwal, 2005)

3. (*a*) Explain the photo-electric effect.
(*b*) Outline the basic facts of the photo-electric effect.
(*c*) Discuss the inadequacy of the wave theory of light to explain the effect.
(*d*) Establish Einstein's equation for the photo-electric effect.

4. (*a*) Define the terms: (*i*) threshold frequency, (*ii*) photo-electric work function, (*iii*) stopping potential. (Allahabad, 2006)
(*b*) Deduce Einstein's photo-electric equation.

5. (*a*) In what way does the wave theory fail to explain the photo-electric effect.
(*b*) Show that Einstein's equation gives adequate explanation of all the facts about the photo-electric effect.

6. (*a*) Explain the photo-electric effect. (Kurukshetra, 2005)
(*b*) In the photo-electric effect, why does the existence of a cut-off frequency speak in favour of photon theory and against wave theory?
(*c*) A photon of energy 12 eV falls on molybdenum whose work-function is 4.15 eV. Find the stopping potential. (**Ans.** 7.85 V)

7. Find the maximum energy of the photo-electrons in electron-volts when light of frequency 1.5×10^9 MHz. falls on a metal surface for which the threshold frequency is 1.2×10^9 MHz. (**Ans.** 1.24 eV)

8. A photon of energy 10 eV falls on molybdenum whose work-function is 4.15 eV. Find the stopping potential. (**Ans.** 5.85 Volts)

9. The threshold wave-length for a metal is 3800×10^{-10} m. Calculate the maximum kinetic energy of the photo-electrons ejected when ultra-violet light of wavelength 2500×10^{-10} m. falls on it. (**Ans.** 2.725×10^{-19} J *i.e* 1.7. eV)

10. A certain photo-tube requires 1 volt to serve as the stopping potential for light of wave-length 5000 Å. If the light has the wavelength of 3750 Å, the stopping potential is 1.82 volts. Calculate h/e from this data.

$$\left[\textbf{Hint: } eV_1 = \frac{hc}{\lambda_1} - W_0 \text{ and } eV_2 = \frac{hc}{\lambda_2} - W_0\right]$$

Eliminate W_0 between these equations and obtain

$$e(V_2 - V_1) = \frac{hc(\lambda_1 - \lambda_2)}{\lambda_1\lambda_2}$$

$$\frac{h}{e} = \frac{[V_2 - V_1]\,\lambda_1\lambda_2}{c[\lambda_1 - \lambda_2]}$$ (**Ans.** 4.1×10^{-15} Volt. sec)

11. The photo-electric threshold wavelength of tungsten is 2300 Å. The tungsten surface is illuminated with ultraviolet light of wavelength 1800 Å. Calculate (*a*) the maximum kinetic energy of the ejected electrons, (*b*) the maximum velocity of the ejected electrons and (*c*) the stopping potential, in volts, for the electrons.
(**Ans.** (*a*) 2.387×10^{-19} J, *i.e.*, 1.49 eV (*b*) 7.239×10^5 m/sec. (*c*) 1.49 V)

12. Potassium has a work-function of 2eV and is illuminated by mono-chromatic light of wavelength 3600 Å. Find
(*a*) the maximum kinetic energy of the ejected electrons,

(*b*) the maximum velocity of the ejected electrons, and
(*c*) the stopping potential in volts for the electrons.

(Ans. (*a*) 2.325×10^{-19} J. (*b*) 7.14×10^{5} m/sec. (*c*) 1.45 Volts)

13. Explain in brief Planck's quantum theory. (Sambalpur, 2005)

14. State the postulates of Bohr's theory of the hydrogen atom. (Purvanchal, 2005)

15. Obtain an expression for the radius of a Bohr orbit of the electron in the hydrogen atom.

16. Show that the radius of a Bohr orbit of the electron in the hydrogen atom is directly proportional to the square of the principal quantum number.

17. Obtain an expression for the energy of the electron in a stationary orbit in the hydrogen atom. (Bhopal, 2006)

18. Show that he energy of the electron in a stationary orbit in the hydrogen atom is inversely proportional to the radius of the orbit.

19. Show that the energy of the electron in a stationary Bohr orbit of the hydrogen atom is inversely proportional to the square of the principal quantum number.

20. Assuming the postulates of Bohr's theory of the hydrogen atom, derive expressions for (*i*) radius of a Bohr orbit (*ii*) energy of the electron in the *n*th orbit.

21. Draw the energy level diagram of complete hydrogen spectrum according to Bohr's theory. (Agra, 2005)

22. Draw the energy level diagram of the hydrogen atom and hence explain the emission of the Lyman and Balmer series of lines.

23. Draw the energy level diagram of the hydrogen atom and hence explain the emission of the Paschen series of lines. (Madras, 2004)

24. Calculate the radius of the first Bohr orbit of the electron in the hydrogen atom, given that

$$h = 6.63\times10^{-34}\ \text{Js}, \qquad m = 9.11\times10^{-31}\ \text{kg}.$$

$$e = 1.6\times10^{-19}\ \text{C}, \qquad \epsilon_0 = 8.85\times10^{-12}\ C^2/\text{N m}^2$$ **(Ans.** 5.31×10^{11} m)

25. Calculate the total energy of the electron in the second Bohr orbit in electron-volt.

(Ans. – 3.4 eV) (Ravishankar, 2005)

26. Given that the total energy of the electron in the first Bohr orbit is – 13.6 eV, calculate the energy of the electron in the second, third and fourth orbits.

(Ans. – 3.4 eV, – 1.5 eV, – 0.85 eV) (Kerala, 2005)

27. Calculate the wavelength and frequency of the first line of the Lyman series of the hydrogen spectrum. Given $R_H = 1.097 \times 10^{7}$ *m* and $c = 3 \times 10^{18}$ m/s.

(Ans.1.215×10^{-7}m, 2.469×10^{15} Hz).

28. Calculate the wavelength and frequency of H_α line of the Balmer series of the hydrogen spectrum. Given $R_H = 1.097 \times 10^{7}$/m and $c = 3 \times 10^{8}$ m/s.

(Ans. 6.563×10^{-7}m, 4.57×10^{14} Hz).

29. The wavelength of the H_β line of the Balmer series of the hydrogen spectrum is 4.86×10^{-7} m . Calculate the wavelength of the H_α line. **(Ans.** 6.561×10^{-7} m)

30. Prove that the orbital speed and the orbital frequency of the electron in the *n*th Bohr orbit in the hydrogen atom are given by

$$v = \left(\frac{e^2}{2\,\epsilon_0\,h}\right)\frac{1}{n}, \quad f = \left(\frac{me^4}{4\,\epsilon_0^2\,h^3}\right)\frac{1}{n^3}$$

31. Using the standard values of the physical constants, calculate the frequency of revolution of the orbital electron in the first Bohr orbit **(Ans.** 6.545×10^{15} Hz)

32. State Ritz combination principle. Show, on the basis of the principle, how could new series be predicted by taking example of H_α and H_β lines of the Balmer series. (N.U., 2006)

33. State the limitations of Bohr's theory. (N.U., 2006)

CHAPTER 2

WAVE PROPERTIES OF MATTER

2.1 WAVE - PARTICLE DUALITY

We know that interference and diffraction of light are produced by the superposition of beams of light. Thus, these phenomena are the result of *interaction of light with light*. From experimental observations on interference, diffraction and some other phenomena such as reflection, refraction and polarisation and their interpretations, it is concluded that light is a transverse wave motion. Therefore, these phenomena are completely explained by the wave theory and the electromagnetic theory of radiation.

However, there is another class of phenomena : black body radiation, the photo-electric effect and the Compton effect which are produced by *interaction of radiation with matter*, and these cannot be explained by the wave theory or the electromagnetic theory of radiation. We have seen that in order to explain these phenomena, radiant energy is considered as a stream of small packets of energy. These packets of energy are known as light quanta or *photons*. The amount of energy assigned to each photon is given by :

$$E = h\nu$$

In interaction of radiant energy with matter, any one of the photons can transfer all its energy to an electron of the matter :

The frequency ν is determined from the measurement of the wavelength λ of radiation, using the equation :

$$\nu = \frac{c}{\lambda}$$

The frequency or wavelength is a concept relevant to a wave, and quantum having the isolated energy $h\nu$ is the concept of a particle. Therefore, *we conclude that radiation possesses dual character, and it never exhibits both characteristics in any one experiment*. Matter evidently has particle properties. Therefore, by analogy with radiation, matter should also have wave properties under suitable conditions. This was first predicted by the French theoretical physicist Prince Louis de Broglie in 1924, and was verified experimentally by C. J. Davisson and L. H. Germer in 1927, and also by G. P. Thomson in the same year. Wave properties of matter can be reconciled with particle properties by combining waves of different wavelengths to form group of waves (wave packets). Since the effect of a particle in motion at any instant of time is confined to a small region in space, a wave packet can be used to represent a particle in motion.

2.2 DE BROGLIE'S HYPOTHESIS FOR MATTER WAVES

The relationship between the energy E of a photon and the frequency ν of the associated electromagnetic wave is given by the Planck-Einstein equation

$$E = h\nu \qquad \text{... (1)}$$

According to the theory of relativity, the relation between the total relativistic energy E and the relativistic momentum p of a particle of rest mass m_0 is given by :

$$E^2 = p^2c^2 + m_0^2c^4 \qquad \text{... (2)}$$

Since photons have zero rest mass, the momentum of a photon is obtained by putting $m_0 = 0$ in this equation.

Thus,

$$E^2 = p^2c^2$$

$$\therefore \quad p = \frac{E}{c} \qquad \text{... (3)}$$

Substituting Eq (1) and $c = \nu\lambda$ in Eq. (3), we :

$$p = \frac{h\nu}{\nu\lambda} = \frac{h}{\lambda}$$

$$\therefore \quad \lambda = \frac{h}{p} \qquad \text{... (4)}$$

This equation represents the wave-particle relation for photons. In this equation λ is the wavelength of the wave associated with photons of momentum p.

In 1924, Louis de Broglie extended the wave-particle relationship for photons to all particles in motion (*i.e.*, electrons, protons, neutrons, atoms, molecules etc.) and put forth the following hypothesis :

All particles in motion have properties characteristic of waves. The wave-length λ and the frequency ν of the wave associated with a particle in motion, are given by :

$$\lambda = \frac{h}{p} = \frac{h}{mv} \qquad \text{... (5)}$$

$$\nu = \frac{E}{h} \qquad \text{... (6)}$$

where, h is Planck's constant = 6.6256×10^{-34} Js

v is the particle velocity,

E is the kinetic energy, and m is the relativistic mass given by the relation :

$$m = \frac{m_0}{\sqrt{1 - v^2/c^2}}$$

Eq. (5) is the de Broglie expression for the wavelength associated with a particle moving with velocity v.

We rewrite Eq. (5) and (6) in the following convenient forms :

$$p = \frac{h}{\lambda} = \frac{h}{2\pi} \cdot \frac{2\pi}{\lambda} = \hbar k \qquad \text{... (7)}$$

where $\quad \hbar = h/2\pi$, and $k = 2\pi/\lambda$.

$$E = h\nu = \frac{h}{2\pi} \cdot 2\pi\nu = \hbar\omega \qquad \text{... (8)}$$

2.3 CONCEPT OF WAVE VELOCITY

A plane simple harmonic wave travelling in the positive x-direction is represented by the well known equation :

$$y = A \sin \omega \left(t - \frac{x}{v} \right) \quad \text{... (1)}$$

where A is the amplitude, v the velocity of propagation of the wave in the positive x-direction, and ω *the angular frequency which is related to the frequency* ν *of the wave by the formula*

$$\omega = 2\pi v$$

The wave velocity is also called the *phase velocity*. The reason for this is as follows. In Eq. (1) the phase ϕ of the wave at position x and at time t is :

$$\phi(x, t) = \omega \left(t - \frac{x}{v} \right)$$

Differentiating this equation with respect to t, we get :

$$\frac{\partial \phi}{\partial t} = \omega \left(1 - \frac{1}{v} \frac{dx}{dt} \right)$$

For a point of constant phase, $\frac{\partial \phi}{\partial t} = 0$

$$\therefore \quad 1 - \frac{1}{v} \left(\frac{\partial x}{\partial t} \right)_\phi = 0$$

or

$$\left(\frac{\partial x}{\partial t} \right)_\phi = v$$

$\left(\frac{\partial x}{\partial t} \right)_\phi$ is the velocity with which a displacement of a given phase moves forward. Therefore, this quantity is called the phase velocity, and it is usually denoted by v_p or v_ϕ.

Thus the wave velocity or the phase velocity of a wave is defined as the velocity with which a displacement having a given phase moves forward.

It is sometimes more convenient to work with the wave equation (1) in the following form :

$$y = A \sin \omega \left(t - \frac{x}{v_p} \right) = A \sin \left(\omega t - \frac{\omega}{v_p} x \right)$$

$$= A \sin (\omega t - kx) \quad \text{... (2)}$$

where $k = \frac{\omega}{v_p}$

The quantity k is called the propagation constant, or the phase constant, or the propagation number of the wave. It can be expressed in terms of the wavelength λ :

$$k = \frac{\omega}{v_p} = \frac{2\pi v}{v \lambda} = \frac{2\pi}{\lambda} \quad \text{... (3)}$$

In terms of ω and k, the phase velocity is given by

$$v_p = \frac{\omega}{k}$$

If the wave travels in an arbitrary direction, the displacement $\psi(x, y, z, t)$ at distance r from the origin of the coordinate-axes is given by the wave equation.

$$\psi(x, y, z, t) = A \sin(\omega t - k_x x - k_y y - k_z z)$$

$$= A \sin(\omega t - \vec{k} \cdot \vec{r}) \quad \text{... (4)}$$

where $\vec{k}$ is the propagation vector, and $\vec{r}$ the position vector of the point from the origin.

2.4 CONCEPT OF GROUP VELOCITY

Analytical Expression for a Group of Waves

An analytical expression for a group of waves was first obtained by Stokes. He assumed that a group of waves is formed by the superposition of two infinite trains of waves of the same amplitude but of slightly different wavelengths, which travel simultaneously in the same direction along the same straight line. On the basis of this assumption, Lord Rayleigh treated the problem in the following way and he first pointed out the importance of a group of waves in the interpretation of optical phenomena and experiments.

Let two plane simple harmonic waves of the same amplitude but of slightly different wavelengths (Fig. 2.1 (*a*), (*b*)) travelling simultaneously in the positive x-direction in a medium be represented by

$$y_1 = A \sin(\omega t - kx) \quad \text{... (1)}$$

$$y_2 = A \sin[(\omega + \delta\omega)t - (k + \delta k)x] \quad \text{... (2)}$$

The resultant displacement y at time t and at position x is given by

$$y = y_1 + y_2$$

$$= A \sin(\omega t - kx) + A \sin[(\omega + \delta\omega)t - (k + \delta k)x]$$

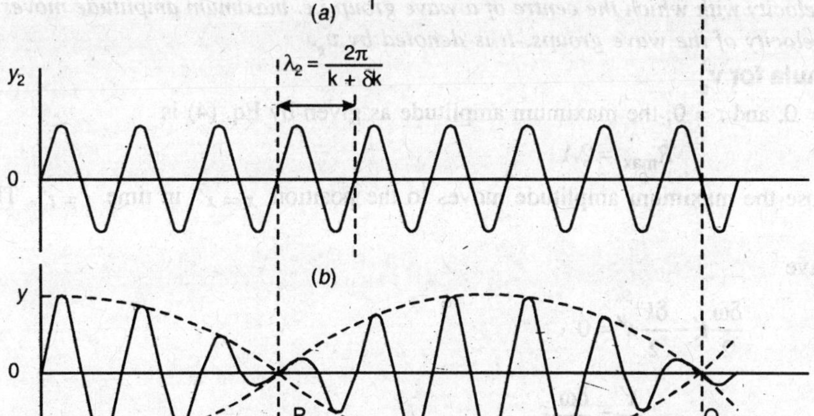

Fig. 2.1

The trigonometric equation for sum of the sines of two angles is

$$\sin C + \sin D = 2\sin\left(\frac{C+D}{2}\right)\cos\left(\frac{C-D}{2}\right)$$

$$= 2\cos\left(\frac{C-D}{2}\right)\sin\left(\frac{C+D}{2}\right)$$

Making use of this equation, we get

$$y = 2A\cos\left(-\frac{\delta\omega}{2}t + \frac{\delta k}{2}x\right)\sin\left[\left(\frac{2\omega+\delta\omega}{2}\right)t - \left(\frac{2k+\delta k}{2}\right)x\right]$$

Since $\delta\omega$ and δk are small compared with ω and k respectively, in the sine term $\delta\omega$ and δk are neglected.

$\therefore$ we get

$$y = 2A\cos\left(\frac{\delta\omega}{2}t - \frac{\delta k}{2}x\right)\sin(\omega t - kx) \quad \text{... (3)}$$

This is the analytical expression for the group of waves, *i.e.*, the wave-packet formed by the two waves.

This equation shows that the resultant wave is an amplitude modulated wave of angular frequency ω and propagation constant k. The phase velocity of the wave is

$$v_p = \frac{\omega}{k}.$$

The amplitude of the wave is

$$R = 2A\cos\left(\frac{\delta\omega}{2}t - \frac{\delta k}{2}x\right) \quad \text{... (4)}$$

which varies sinusoidally as shown by the dashed curve in Fig. 2.1 (*c*). This variation of the amplitude produces successive *wave groups*.

Group velocity

The velocity with which the centre of a wave group i.e. maximum amplitude moves is called the group velocity of the wave groups. It is denoted by v_g.

Formula for v_g

At $x = 0$, and $t = 0$, the maximum amplitude as given by Eq. (4) is

$$R_{max} = 2A$$

Suppose the maximum amplitude moves to the position $x = x'$ in time $t = t'$. Then from Eq. (4),

we have

$$\frac{\delta\omega}{2}t' - \frac{\delta k}{2}x' = 0$$

$$\therefore \quad \frac{x'}{t'} = \frac{\delta\omega}{\delta k}$$

But x'/t' is the group velocity v_g.

$$\therefore \quad v_g = \frac{\delta\omega}{\delta k}.$$

In the limit when $\delta k \to 0$,

$$v_g = \frac{d\omega}{dk} \quad \text{... (5)}$$

Relation Between the Group Velocity (v_g) and the Phase Velocity (v_p)

We have the propagation constant

$$k = \frac{2\pi}{\lambda} \qquad \therefore \qquad \lambda = \frac{2\pi}{k}$$

the phase velocity

$$v_p = \frac{\omega}{k} \qquad \therefore \qquad \omega = v_p\, k$$

and the group velocity

$$v_g = \frac{d\omega}{dk}$$

$$= \frac{d}{dk}(v_p\, k) = v_p + k\frac{dv_p}{dk} \quad \text{... (6)}$$

Now we change the variable k to λ in the second term on the right side of this equation :

$$k\frac{dv_p}{dk} = \underset{\delta k \to 0}{\text{Lt}}\ k\frac{\delta v_p}{\delta k} = \underset{\delta\lambda \to 0}{\text{Lt}}\ \frac{2\pi}{\lambda}\cdot\frac{\delta v_p}{\delta(2\pi/\lambda)}$$

$$= \underset{\delta\lambda \to 0}{\text{Lt}}\ \frac{2\pi}{\lambda}\cdot\frac{\delta v_p}{(-2\pi/\lambda^2)\,\delta\lambda} = -\lambda\frac{dv_p}{d\lambda} \quad \text{... (7)}$$

Hence Eq. (6) becomes :

$$v_g = v_p - \lambda\frac{dv_p}{d\lambda} \quad \text{... (8)}$$

This equation shows that v_g is less than v_p when the medium is dispersive, *i.e.*, when v_p is a function of λ. In a medium in which there is no dispersion, *i.e.*, in which waves of all wavelengths travel with the same speed $dv_p/d\lambda = 0$. Therefore in such a medium $v_g = v_p$. This result is true for electro-magnetic waves in vacuum and elastic waves in a homogeneous medium.

The analysis given above is only an approximate one, because only two components have been considered for the formation of the group of waves.

2.5 VELOCITY OF DE BROGLIE WAVE

(a) Phase velocity, v_p

For a particle of mass m moving with velocity v, the frequency ν of the wave associated with the particle is related to the energy E of the particle by the equation

$$E = h\nu = \frac{h}{2\pi}2\pi\nu = \hbar\omega \quad \text{... (1)}$$

where ω is the angular frequency of the wave.

The momentum p of the particle is related to the de Broglie wavelength λ of the wave by the equation :

$$p = \frac{h}{\lambda} = \frac{h}{2\pi} \cdot \frac{2\pi}{\lambda} = \hbar k \quad \text{... (2)}$$

where k is the propagation constant.

From these equations, we have

$$\omega = \frac{E}{\hbar}, \quad \text{and} \quad k = \frac{p}{\hbar} \quad \text{... (3)}$$

Now the *phase velocity* of the associated wave is given by

$$v_p = \frac{\omega}{k} = \frac{E}{\hbar} \cdot \frac{\hbar}{p} = \frac{E}{p} \quad \text{... (4)}$$

We discuss the following two cases :

(1) When the velocity v of the particle is much less than that of light :

In this case the particle is said to be *nonrelativistic*.

For such a particle

$$E = \frac{p^2}{2m}, \quad \text{and} \quad p = mv \quad \text{... (5)}$$

Therefore,

$$v_p = \frac{E}{p} = \frac{p^2}{2m}\,\frac{1}{p} = \frac{p}{2m} = \frac{mv}{2m}$$

$$= \frac{v}{2} \quad \text{... (6)}$$

Thus for a nonrelativistic particle, the phase velocity is half the particle velocity.

The phase velocity has no physical meaning, and it cannot be measured.

(2) When the velocity v of the particle is comparable with that of light :

In this case the particle is said to be *relativistic*.

For such a particle

$$E = mc^2 \text{ and } p = mv \quad \text{... (7)}$$

Therefore,

$$v_p = \frac{E}{p} = \frac{mc^2}{mv} = \frac{c^2}{v}$$

$$= \frac{c}{v/c} \quad \text{... (8)}$$

Since the term v/c in the denominator is less than unity, v_p must be greater than c.

But a velocity larger than c cannot be measured, because *according to the postulate of the theory of relativity no signal or energy can be transmitted with a speed greater than the speed of light in free space. Therefore, the phase velocity has no physical meaning, and hence a particle in motion cannot be represented by a single wave.*

(*b*) Group Velocity v_g

De Broglie assumed that a particle in motion is represented by a group of waves *i.e.* a wave-packet moving with the group velocity v_g which is given by :

$$v_g = \frac{d\omega}{dk}$$

$$= \lim_{\delta k \to 0} \frac{\delta\omega}{\delta k} \quad \text{... (9)}$$

Now we have

$$\omega = \frac{E}{\hbar}, \quad \text{and} \quad k = \frac{p}{\hbar}$$

$$\therefore \quad \delta\omega = \frac{\delta E}{\hbar}, \quad \text{and} \quad \delta k = \frac{\delta p}{\hbar} \quad \text{... (10)}$$

Substituting these values in Eq. (9), we get

$$v_g = \underset{\delta p \to 0}{\text{Lt}} \frac{\delta E}{\hbar} \frac{\hbar}{\delta p} = \underset{\delta p \to 0}{\text{Lt}} \frac{\delta E}{\delta p}$$

$$= \frac{dE}{dp} \quad \text{... (11)}$$

Now discuss the following two cases :

(*i*) Nonrelativistic particle :

For a non relativistic particle

$$E = \frac{p^2}{2m}, \quad \text{and} \quad p = mv$$

$$\therefore \quad \frac{dE}{dp} = \frac{2p}{2m} = \frac{mv}{m} = v$$

i.e.,
$$v_g = v \quad \text{... (12)}$$

(*ii*) Relativistic particle

For a relativistic particle, we have

$$E^2 = p^2c^2 + m_0^2 c^4 \ , \quad \text{and} \quad p = mv$$

Differentiating the first equation with respect to p, we get

$$2E \frac{dE}{dp} = 2p\, c^2$$

$$\therefore \quad \frac{dE}{dp} = \frac{p c^2}{E} = \frac{(mv)\, c^2}{m c^2} = v$$

i.e.,
$$v_g = v \quad \text{... (13)}$$

Eqs. (12) and (13) show that *the de Broglie group of waves, i.e. wave-packet associated with a nonrelativistic or relativistic particle travels with the same velocity as that of the particle.*

2.6 DIFFRACTION OF PARTICLES

(1) *Diffraction of Electrons and Verification of de Broglie's hypothesis by Davisson and Germer's Experiment :*

Diffraction of electrons was demonstrated experimentally by C. J. Davisson and L. H. Germer in 1927, and also by G. P. Thomson in the same year, and thus de Broglie's hypothesis was confirmed. We shall describe Davisson and Germer's experiment.

Apparatus. The Davisson and Germer apparatus is shown in Fig. 2.2. F is a tungsten filament which emits electrons when it is heated by passing a current from a low tension battery B_1. P is a metal plate having a narrow hole S_1. It is maintained at a positive voltage V with respect to F so that the electrons are *accelerated by the potential difference and emerge as a well collimated beam through the hole S_1.* C is a nickel crystal with its (1 1 1) face normal to the beam of electrons. When the electron beam is incident on the crystal, electrons are scattered in all directions by the atoms in the crystal.

AB is the chamber in which the electron beam scattered in a given direction from the nickel crystal is received. The chamber can be rotated about an axis in the face of C passing through the point of incidence of the electron beam. The electron current is measured by means of a sensitive galvanometer G. The front and back walls of the chamber are insulated from one another and a retarding potential V_r is applied between them so that only those electrons which have energy eV can enter the chamber. The apparatus is enclosed in an evacuated chamber.

Method : A known potential difference is applied between the filament F and the metal plate P. The chamber AB is set at different angles, and for each setting of the chamber, the current

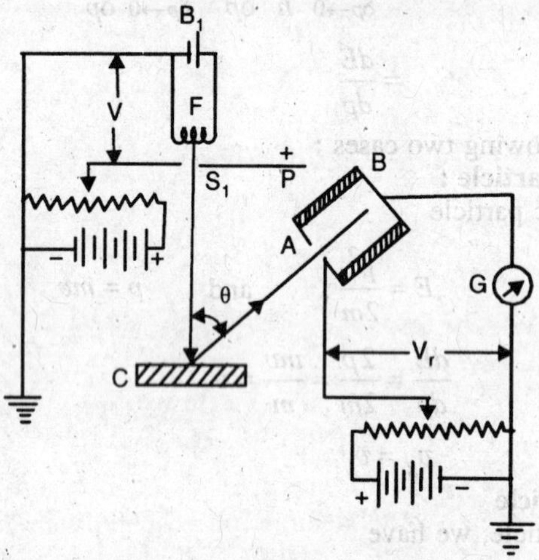

Fig. 2.2

is noted. The current is directly proportional to the number of scattered electrons entering the chamber in 1 sec. Thus the intensity of the scattered beam is measured as a function of the angle of scattering θ. The crystal is held in a fixed position throughout the measurements. This observation is repeated for different known potential differences. For each accelerating potential difference the current is plotted against the angle θ in polar coordinates (r, θ). The polar curves thus obtained are shown in Fig. 2.3. In each graph the length of the radius vector r at an angle θ is directly proportional to the current at that angle.

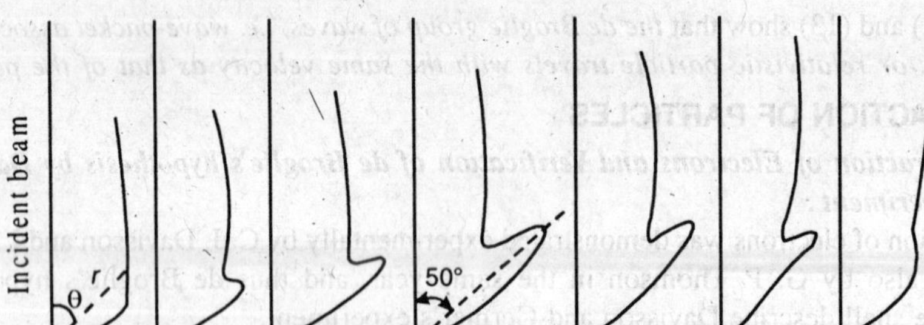

Fig. 2.3

Observations and conclusions

At 40 V tne curve is smooth. At 44 V a slight spur is seen on the curve.

This spur increases with the potential difference V and becomes maximum at $V = 54$ V, and $\theta = 50°$. Beyond 54 V the spur decreases with increasing potential difference and nearly disappears at $V = 68$ V.

The observation of maximum current at the scattering angle $\theta = 50°$ when the potential difference $V = 54$ V confirms that diffraction of the electrons has taken place.

Explanation and verification of the de Broglie relation

When the beam of electrons accelerated by the potential difference is incident normally on the (111) face of the nickel crystal, it enters the crystal without deviation. It is then scattered from regularly spaced atoms in (111) planes in the crystal. The waves associated with the scattered electrons give rise to constructive interference.

The theoretical value of the wavelength of the waves associated with the incident beam of electrons is given by the de Broglie relation

$$\lambda = \frac{h}{mv}$$

If the velocity v acquired by an electron under the action of potential difference V is small in comparison with the speed of light, then its kinetic energy is

$$\frac{1}{2} m v^2 = e V$$

$$\therefore \quad v = \sqrt{\frac{2eV}{m}}$$

Hence $$\lambda = \frac{h}{m\sqrt{\frac{2eV}{m}}} = \frac{h}{\sqrt{2meV}}$$

Substituting the numerical values :

$h = 6.626 \times 10^{-34}$ Js, $m = 9.11 \times 10^{-31}$ kg

$e = 1.6 \times 10^{-19}$ C,

we get,

$$\lambda = \frac{12.27 \times 10^{-10}}{\sqrt{V}} m = \frac{12.27}{\sqrt{V}} \text{Å}$$

In the present case $V = 54$ V

$$\therefore \quad \lambda = \frac{12.27}{\sqrt{54}} = \frac{12.27}{7.348} = 1.67 \text{ Å}$$

The experimental value of λ is calculated using the formula

$$n\lambda = D \sin\theta$$

where θ is the angle of scattering and D is the perpendicular distance between two adjacent rows of atoms in (111) planes of the nickel crystal. The distance D can be calculated from the knowledge of the length of the edge (a = 3.52 Å) of the unit cube of the crystal. The value of D is 2.15 Å.

$\therefore$ for the first order constructive interference of the electron waves

$$\lambda = 2.15 \sin 50° = 2.15 \times 0.7660$$

$$= 1.65 \text{ Å} \quad \text{... (3)}$$

This value is nearly equal to that calculated from the de Broglie relation.

Thus the de Broglie relation is verified.

(2) Demonstration of wave nature of Electrons by Davisson and Germer's Experiment

The wave nature of electrons was directly demonstrated in another series of experiments performed by Davisson and Germer in 1927.

Apparatus : The experimental arrangement is the same as in the previous experiment (See Fig. 2.2)

Method : In this experiment the angle of incidence of the electron beam at the nickel crystal is set at 10°, and the chamber *AB* for receiving the reflected electron-beam from the crystal is kept fixed in the position where the angle of reflection is *equal* to the angle of incidence. The

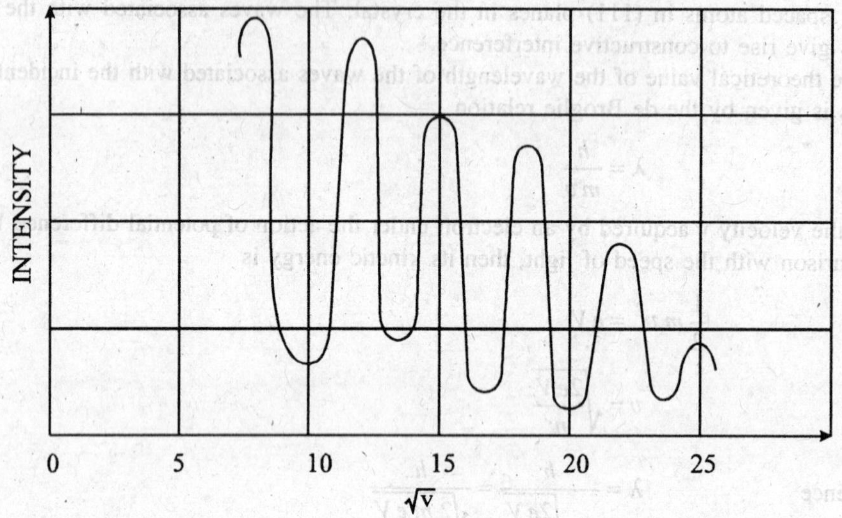

Fig. 2.4

accelerating potential difference V is increased gradually and at each known value of V the intensity of the reflected beam of electrons is determined from the deflection of the galvanometer. The intensity is plotted against the square root of V. The curve obtained shows a series of very nearly equally spaced maxima (Fig. 2.4).

Explanation :

In this experiment the atomic planes which produce the diffraction pattern are parallel to the surface of the crystal.

For a given accelerating potential difference V, the wavelength of the waves associated with the incident beam of electrons is given by :

$$\lambda = \frac{h}{mv} = \frac{h}{\sqrt{2\, m\, e\, V}} \quad \text{... (1)}$$

The occurrence of a series of maxima in the intensity curve (Fig. 2.4), at only certain values of $\sqrt{V}$ is explained on the basis of Eq. (1) and Bragg's law

$$n\lambda = 2\, d \cos\alpha \quad \text{... (2)}$$

where n is the order of diffraction, d is the distance between adjacent atomic planes, and α is the angle between the incident beam and the normal to the atomic planes.

Dividing Eq. (2) by Eq. (1), we get

$$n = (2d\cos\alpha)\left(\frac{\sqrt{2meV}}{h}\right)$$

$$= \frac{2d\cos\alpha\,\sqrt{2me}}{h}V^{1/2} \quad \text{... (3)}$$

Since *h, m, e, d* and α all are constant, we write the above equation as

$$n = k\,V^{1/2}$$

This equation shows that when the accelerating potential difference is varied, the intensity of the reflected beam will be maximum whenever the product $k\sqrt{V}$ is an integer. Thus the occurrence of a series of maxima in the intensity curve is explained.

From Eq. (3) the separation between adjacent maxima should be the same and proportional to $1/2\,d\cos\alpha$. But actual positions of the maxima are slightly different from the calculated positions. This is because of the refraction of the electron beam in the crystal.

2.7 INTERFERENCE OF ELECTRONS

The interference of waves associated with a beam of energetic electrons can be demonstrated by means of a double slit experiment.

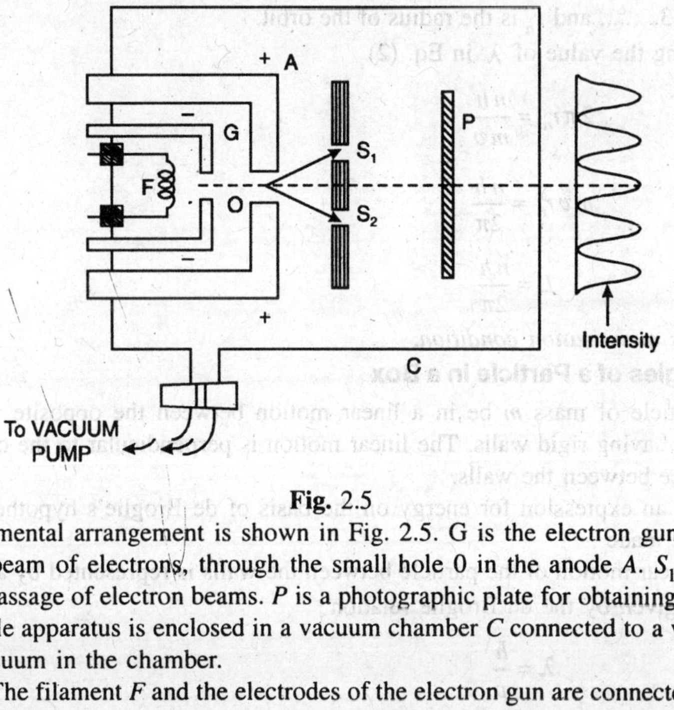

Fig. 2.5

The experimental arrangement is shown in Fig. 2.5. G is the electron gun which supplies mono-energetic beam of electrons, through the small hole 0 in the anode *A*. S_1 and S_2 are two narrow slits for passage of electron beams. *P* is a photographic plate for obtaining the interference pattern. The whole apparatus is enclosed in a vacuum chamber *C* connected to a vacuum pump to produce high vacuum in the chamber.

Method : The filament *F* and the electrodes of the electron gun are connected to the sources of suitable potential differences. The electron beam from the electron gun is incident on the slits S_1 and S_2. Any point on the photographic plate *P* receives electrons from both the slits S_1 and S_2. The superposition of the two beams of electrons gives rise to the interference pattern on the photographic plate, which is observed by means of an electron microscope.

Observation and Conclusion : The distribution of intensity on the photographic plate is shown in the figure.

The interference pattern on the plate shows that a beam of electrons is associated with a wave.

2.8 CONSEQUENCES OF DE BROGLIE'S CONCEPTS

(1) Quantization Condition for the Angular Momentum of the Electron in Hydrogen Atom

In the Bohr theory of the hydrogen atom, the quantization condition

$$L = \frac{nh}{2\pi}$$

for the angular momentum L of the electron, moving in a stationary circular orbit is only arbitrary. On the basis of de Broglie's hypothesis this condition is easily obtained. For this purpose, the following assumptions are made :

(*i*) The motion of the electron in a stationary circular orbit is represented by a standing matter wave (Fig. 2.6) of wavelength λ given by the de Broglie relation

$$\lambda = \frac{h}{mv} \quad \text{... (1)}$$

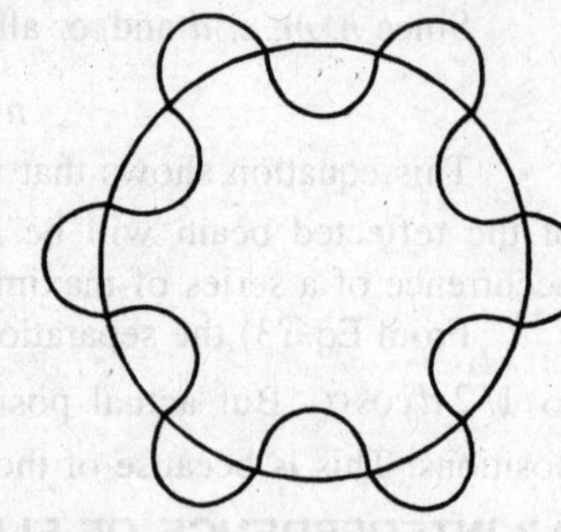

Fig. 2.6

where m is the mass of the electron and v is its velocity in the orbit.

(*ii*) The circular orbit contains an integral number of wavelengths, *i.e.*,

$$2\pi r_n = n\lambda \quad \text{... (2)}$$

where $n = 1, 2, 3, ...$, and r_n is the radius of the orbit.

Substituting the value of λ in Eq. (2)

$$2\pi r_n = \frac{nh}{mv}$$

or

$$mvr_n = \frac{nh}{2\pi}$$

i.e.

$$L = \frac{nh}{2\pi} \quad \text{... (3)}$$

which is Bohr's quantization condition.

(2) Energies of a Particle in a Box

Let a particle of mass m be in a linear motion between the opposite walls of a hollow rectangular box having rigid walls. The linear motion is perpendicular to the opposite walls. Let a be the distance between the walls.

To obtain an expression for energy on the basis of de Broglie's hypothesis, the following assumptions are made :

(*i*) The linear motion of the particle between the walls is represented by a standing wave of wavelength λ given by the de Broglie relation

$$\lambda = \frac{h}{p} \quad \text{... (1)}$$

where p is the linear momentum of the particle.

(*ii*) The distance a between the walls contains an *integral number of half wavelengths*, i.e.

$$a = n\frac{\lambda}{2} \quad \text{... (2)}$$

where $n = 1, 2, 3, ...$

Substituting the value of λ in this equation, we get

$$a = \frac{nh}{2p}$$

$$\therefore \quad p = \frac{nh}{2a} \quad \text{... (3)}$$

Now the energy E_n of the particle is given by :

$$E_n = \frac{p^2}{2m} = \frac{1}{2m}\left(\frac{nh}{2a}\right)^2$$

$$= \frac{n^2 h^2}{8ma^2} \qquad \text{... (4)}$$

Substituting $h = 2\pi\hbar$, we get

$$E_n = \frac{n^2 \pi^2 \hbar^2}{2ma^2} \qquad \text{... (5)}$$

This expression for E_n is the same as that obtained in Sec. 5.1.

(3) Uncertainty Principle

The uncertainty principle of Heisenberg is a direct consequence of de Broglie's hypothesis. We shall study this principle in Chap. 3.

2.9 WAVE PACKET

At any given instant of time, the effect of a particle in motion is localized over a very small region. Therefore, a particle in motion can be represented by a wave packet of very small extension.

Explanation of formation of a wave packet of small extension :

A plane wave travelling in the positive *x*-direction may be represented by

$$\psi(x, t) = A\, e^{i(kx-\omega t)}$$

or

$$\psi(x, t) = A\, e^{-i(kx-\omega t)}$$

The wave has frequency $\nu = \omega / 2\pi$, wavelength $\lambda = 2\pi / k$, and velocity $v = \omega / k$. In our further discussion we choose the first form of the wave equation so that the momentum and energy operators have particular forms (See Sec. 4.4).

If a number of plane waves of propagation number slightly different from the average value k_0 travel simultaneously along the same line in the positive *x*-direction in a medium, a wave packet of small extension Δx is formed [Fig. 2.7 (*a*)]. The wave packet can be expressed, by Fourier's theorem, in the form

$$\psi(x, t) = \frac{1}{\sqrt{2\pi}} \int_{-\infty}^{\infty} A(k)\, e^{i(kx-\omega t)}\, dk \qquad \text{... (1)}$$

where $A(k)$ is a function of *k*. This function is called the Fourier transform of $\psi(x, t)$ and it is given by

$$A(k)\, e^{-i\omega t} = \frac{1}{\sqrt{2\pi}} \int_{-\infty}^{\infty} \psi(x, t)\, e^{-ikx}\, dx \qquad \text{... (2)}$$

or

$$A(k) = \frac{1}{\sqrt{2\pi}} \int_{-\infty}^{\infty} \psi(x, t)\, e^{-i(kx-\omega t)}\, dx \qquad \text{... (3)}$$

Time *t* appears explicitly in the right-hand side of Eq. (3). But $A(k)$ does not depend on *t*, provided the wave packet given by Eq. (1) is a superposition of plane waves. Therefore

$$\frac{\partial A(k)}{\partial t} = 0 \qquad \text{... (4)}$$

Fig. 2.7 (*b*) shows the variation of $A(k)$ with the propagation number k. It can be shown that $\Delta k \geq \frac{1}{\Delta x}$, where Δk is the approximate spread in the propagation number associated with the wave packet.

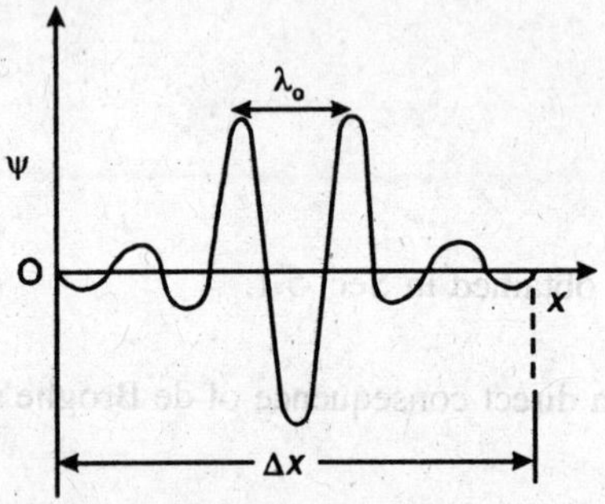

Fig. 2.7 (*a*)

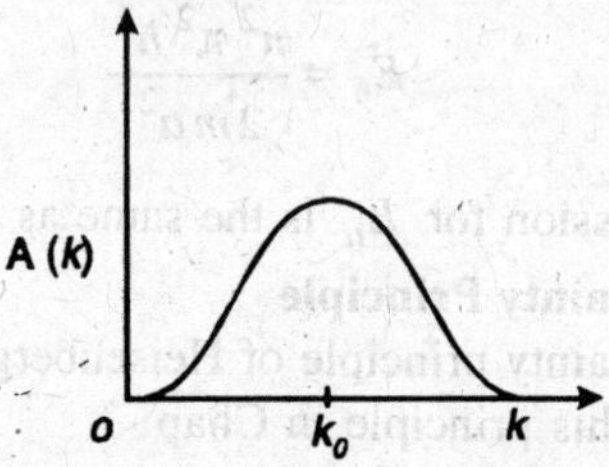

Fig 2.7. (*b*)

Eq. (1) will represent a wave packet of small extension Δx, if $A(k)$ is finite only for a small range of values of k between $k_0 - \frac{\Delta k}{2}$ and $k_0 + \frac{\Delta k}{2}$ about the particular value k_0. It is assumed that for a small range of values of k about k_0, the angular frequency ω varies slowly with k, so that $\omega(k)$ can be expanded in a power series by Taylor's theorem :

$$\omega(k) = \omega(k_0 + k - k_0)$$

$$= \omega(k_0) + (k - k_0)\left(\frac{d\omega}{dk}\right)_{k_0} + \frac{(k-k_0)^2}{2!}\left(\frac{d^2\omega}{dk^2}\right)_{k_0} + \ldots\ldots$$

The second and higher order terms in the expansion can be neglected.

$$\therefore \quad \omega(k) = \omega_0 + (k - k_0)\left(\frac{d\omega}{dk}\right)_{k_0} \quad \ldots (5a)$$

where $\omega_0 = \omega(k_0)$

or

$$\omega = \omega_0 + (k - k_0)\frac{d\omega}{dk} \quad \ldots (5b)$$

Now substituting this value of ω in the expression $(kx - \omega t)$, we get

$$kx - \omega t = kx - \left\{\omega_0 + (k - k_0)\frac{d\omega}{dk}\right\}t$$

$$= -\omega_0 t + kx - (k - k_0)\frac{d\omega}{dk}t$$

$$= k_0 x - \omega_0 t + kx - k_0 x - (k - k_0)\frac{d\omega}{dk}t$$

$$= (k_0 x - \omega_0 t) + (k - k_0)x - (k - k_0)\frac{d\omega}{dk}t$$

$$= (k_0 x - \omega_0 t) + (k - k_0)\left[x - \left(\frac{d\omega}{dk}\right)t\right]$$

Substituting for $(kx - \omega t)$ in Eq. (1) and simplifying we get

$$\psi(x, t) = e^{i(k_0 x - \omega_0 t)} \cdot \frac{1}{\sqrt{2\pi}} \int_{-\infty}^{\infty} A(k)\, e^{i(k-k_0)[x - d\omega/dk)t]} dk \qquad \text{... (6)}$$

This equation represents a wave of wavelength $\lambda_0 = 2\pi/k_0$, and frequency $\omega_0/2\pi$, which is modulated by the integral appearing as a multiplying factor. The value of the integral depends on x and t only, in the expression :

$$x - \frac{d\omega}{dk} t$$

Thus the integral represents a wave packet which moves with the group velocity

$$v_g = \frac{d\omega}{dk} \qquad \text{... (7)}$$

The phase velocity of the wave packet is the velocity of the plane wave represented by $e^{i(k_0 x - \omega_0 t)}$

Thus the phase velocity, $v_p = \dfrac{\omega_0}{k_0}$

SOLVED EXAMPLES

Example 2.1. *Obtain an expression for the de Broglie wavelength for a particle of mass m moving with velocity which is comparable with the velocity of light.*

Solution :

The relativistic kinetic energy K of a particle is related to its total relativistic energy E by the equation :

$$E = K + m_0 c^2$$

$$\sqrt{p^2 c^2 + m_0^2 c^4} = K + m_0 c^2$$

Squaring both the sides of this equation :

$$p^2 c^2 + m_0^2 c^4 = K^2 + 2K\, m_0 c^2 + m_0^2 c^4$$

$$p^2 c^2 = K^2 + 2K\, m_0 c^2$$

$$\therefore \qquad p = \frac{\sqrt{K(K + 2m_0 c^2)}}{c}$$

Hence $$\lambda = \frac{h}{p} = \frac{hc}{\sqrt{K(K + 2m_0 c^2)}}$$

or $$\lambda = \frac{h}{\sqrt{2m_0 K(1 + K/2m_0 c^2)}}$$

Example 2.2. *The most rapidly moving valence electron in metallic sodium, at the absolute zero of temperature, has a kinetic energy 3 eV. Show that its de Broglie wave-length is 7 Å.*

Solution :

$$K = 3\,\text{eV} = 3\times1.6\times10^{-19}\,\text{J}$$

For the electron

$$m_0c^2 = 9.11\times10^{-31}\,(3\times10^8)^2 = 9.11\times9\times10^{-15}\,\text{J}$$

$$= \frac{9.11\times9\times10^{-15}}{1.6\times10^{-19}} = \frac{9.11\times9}{1.6}\times10^4\,\text{eV}$$

$$= 51.2\times10^4\,\text{eV} = 5.12\times10^5\,\text{eV}$$

∴ the kinetic energy of the electron is small compared with m_0c^2.

Hence the de Broglie wavelength is given by :

$$\lambda = \frac{h}{\sqrt{2m_0K}}$$

$$= \frac{6.63\times10^{-34}}{\sqrt{2\times9.11\times10^{-31}\times3\times1.6\times10^{-19}}}$$

$$= \frac{6.63\times10^{-9}}{\sqrt{2\times9.11\times3\times1.6}} = \frac{6.63\times10^{-9}}{9.35}$$

$$= 0.71\times10^{-9} = 7.1\times10^{-10}\,\text{m} = \mathbf{7.1\,\text{Å}}$$

Example 2.3. *Find the wavelength of the waves associated with an electron having energy equal to 1 M eV.*

Solution :

We have, $K = 1\ \text{MeV} = 10^6\ \text{eV} = 10^6\times1.6\times10^{-19}\,\text{J}$

$$= 1.6\times10^{-13}\ \text{J}.$$

The value of m_0c^2 for an electron is (see solved Ex. 2.2).

$$m_0c^2 = 5.12\times10^5\ \text{eV} = 5.12\times10^5\times1.6\times10^{-19}\,\text{J}$$

$$= 1.6\times0.512\times10^{-13}\ \text{J}$$

Since K is comparable with m_0c^2, we use the relativistic expression for λ

∴ $$\lambda = \frac{hc}{\sqrt{K\,(K+2m_0c^2)}}$$

$$= \frac{6.63\times10^{-34}\times3\times10^8}{\sqrt{1.6\times10^{-13}(1.6\times10^{-13}+2\times1.6\times0.512\times10^{-13})}}$$

$$= \frac{6.63\times3\times10^{-26}}{1.6\times0^{-13}\sqrt{(1+1.024)}}$$

$$= \frac{6.63\times3\times10^{-13}}{1.6\times1.4227} = \frac{19.89\times10^{-13}}{2.276} = \mathbf{8.739\times10^{-13}}$$

$$= 0.008739 \times 10^{-10} \text{ m} = 0.008739 \text{ Å}.$$

Example 2.4. *Calculate the de Broglie wavelength of an electron moving with velocity* $\frac{3}{5}c$.

Solution :

We have $v = \frac{3}{5}c$ or $\frac{v}{c} = \frac{3}{5}$

Now $\lambda = \frac{h}{mv}$

Since v is comparable with the speed of the light, m in the formula is the relativistic mass.

Substituting $m = m_0 / \sqrt{1 - v^2/c^2}$ in the formula for λ, we get

$$\lambda = \frac{h}{m_0 v}\sqrt{1 - \frac{v^2}{c^2}}$$

$$= \frac{6.63 \times 10^{-34}}{9.11 \times 10^{-31} \times \frac{3}{5}c}\sqrt{1 - \frac{9}{25}}$$

$$= \frac{6.63 \times 10^{-34} \times 4}{9.11 \times 10^{-31} \times 3 \times 3 \times 10^{8}} = \frac{6.63 \times 4 \times 10^{-11}}{9.11 \times 3 \times 3}$$

$$= 0.323 \times 10^{-11} \text{ m} = \mathbf{0.0323 \text{ Å}}.$$

Example 2.5 *Show that the orbit nearest to the nucleus in the hydrogen atom accommodates one electron wave. Given that the energy of the electron in the orbit is 13.6 eV,* $h = 6.625 \times 10^{-34}$ Js, $m = 9.11 \times 10^{-31}$ kg, *Bohr radius* $r_1 = 5.292 \times 10^{-11}$ m.

Solution :

The circumference of the first orbit is

$$C = 2\pi r_1 = 2 \times 3.14 \times 5.292 \times 10^{-11} \text{ m}$$
$$= 3.323 \times 10^{-10} \text{ m}$$

The kinetic energy of the electron in the orbit is

$$K = 13.6 \text{ eV} = 13.6 \times 1.6 \times 10^{-19} \text{ J}$$

∴ the de Broglie wavelength of the electron is given by :

$$\lambda = \frac{h}{\sqrt{2mK}} = \frac{6.625 \times 10^{-34}}{\sqrt{2 \times 9.11 \times 10^{-31} \times 13.6 \times 1.6 \times 10^{-19}}}$$

$$= \frac{6.625 \times 10^{-9}}{19.91} = 3.327 \times 10^{-10} \text{ m}$$

Thus the circumference of the first orbit is equal to the wavelength of the de Broglie wave. That is, the first orbit accommodates one electron wave.

Example 2.6. *Prove that the length of a group of waves formed by the superposition of simple harmonic plane waves of the propagation constants* k and $k + \delta k$ *is* $2\pi/\delta k$.

Proof : (See Sec. 2.4)

The amplitude of the resultant wave is :

$$R = 2A\cos\left(\frac{\delta\omega}{2}t - \frac{\delta k}{2}x\right) \quad \text{... (1)}$$

At time t, let $P(x_1, 0)$ and $Q(x_2, 0)$ where $x_2 > x_1$ be two successive points at which the amplitude is zero (See Fig. 2.1) :

Then at P and Q, we have

$$\frac{\delta\omega}{2}t - \frac{\delta k}{2}x_1 = (2n+1)\frac{\pi}{2} \quad \text{... (2)}$$

$$\frac{\delta\omega}{2}t - \frac{\delta k}{2}x_2 = (2n-1)\frac{\pi}{2} \quad \text{... (3)}$$

where $n = 0, 1, 2, ...$

The minus sign is used in the factor $(2n - 1)$ because $x_2 > x_1$ and as x increases the phase decreases. Subtracting Eq. (3) from Eq. (2), we get

$$(x_2 - x_1)\frac{\delta k}{2} = \pi$$

$$\therefore \qquad x_2 - x_1 = \frac{2\pi}{\delta k}$$

If $(x_2 - x_1)$ is small and equal to δx, then

$$\delta x = \frac{2\pi}{\delta k} . \quad \text{... (4)}$$

This is the required expression.

QUESTIONS AND PROBLEMS

1. Discuss the nature of de Broglie wave associated with a particle in motion. Obtain an expression for the de Broglie wavelength associated with a particle of mass m moving with the velocity v. (N.U., 2006, Delhi; 2004)
2. Prove that the de Broglie wavelength associated with a particle having kinetic energy E_k which is not negligible compared to its rest energy m_0c^2 is given by :

$$\lambda = \frac{h}{\sqrt{2m_0E_k}}(1 + E_k/2m_0c^2)^{-1/2}$$

3. (*a*) Describe Davisson and Germer's experiment for the study of the diffraction of electrons. (N.U., 2006)

   (*b*) Show that the results of this experiment are closely in agreement with the de Broglie wavelength of electrons in motion.
4. Calculate the de Broglie wavelength of an electron which has energy 12 eV.

   [**Hint :** For the electron $m_0c^2 = 5.12 \times 10^5$ eV

   In this case 12 eV is small compared to m_0c^2

   $\therefore$ use the formula $\lambda = \dfrac{h}{\sqrt{2m_0E_K}}$] (**Ans.** 3.543 Å)

5. What is the wavelength of the wave associated with an electron having kinetic energy 100 eV ? (Kerala, 2005) (**Ans.** 1.228 Å)
6. Find the de Broglie wavelength of 15 keV protons. (Rest mass of the proton = 1.67×10^{-27} kg).

   [**Hint :** For the proton $m_0c^2 = 9.39 \times 10^8$ eV. In this case 1.5×10^4 eV is small compared to m_0c^2.

   $\therefore$ use the formula $\lambda = h/\sqrt{2m_0E_K}$] (**Ans.** 0.002343 Å)
7. An electron initially at rest is accelerated by a potential difference of 5000 V. Find the de Broglie wavelength. (**Ans.** 0.174 Å)
8. A photon of frequency v is scattered by an electron of rest mass m_0. The scattered photon of frequency v' travels in a direction inclined at 90° with the initial direction. Prove that the de Broglie wavelength of the recoil electron is given by :

$$\lambda_r = \frac{c}{\sqrt{v^2 + v'^2}}$$

9. Explain de Broglie's concept of matter waves. Find the de Broglie wavelength of the electron in the first Bohr orbit. (N.M.U. Jalgaon, 2005)
   [**Hint :** The kinetic energy of the electron in the first Bohr orbit = 13.6 *eV*]
   (**Ans.** 3.33 Å)
10. Calculate the momentum of an electron having de Broglie wavelength of 6.6×10^{-11}m (**Ans.** 1.0045×10^{-23} kg. m/s (N.U., 2006)
11. Derive relation between group velocity and phase velocity. (N.U., 2006)

CHAPTER 3

HEISENBERG'S UNCERTAINTY PRINCIPLE

In the previous chapter we have seen that an electron in motion is associated with a wave whose wavelength λ is given by the de Broglie relation, and it can be considered as a wave-packet of small extension formed by the superposition of a large number of waves of wavelengths slightly different from the wavelength of the associated wave. Since a wave packet is of finite width, there will be an uncertainty in specifying the position of the electron. At the same time the spectral distribution of the amplitude of a wave-packet covers a range of wavelengths. By the de Broglie relationship, this means that the momentum of the electron will also be uncertain. Therefore, in general, it is not possible to determine precisely and simultaneously, the position and the momentum of the electron. If the momentum of the electron is accurately known, then by the de Broglie relation, the wavelength of the associated wave has a unique value, *i.e.*, the associated wave is mono-chromatic. In such a case the wave packet has infinite length and hence the position of the electron may be anywhere between minus infinity and plus infinity. On the basis of these considerations, Werner Heisenberg, in 1927, enunciated the principle of *Unbestimmtheit*. This term has been translated as uncertainty, indeterminacy or indefiniteness. In this chapter we discuss the principle of uncertainty and some applications of the principle.

3.1 UNCERTAINTY PRINCIPLE

The principle states that for a particle, of atomic magnitude, in motion, it is impossible to determine both the position and the momentum simultaneously with perfect accuracy. Quantitatively the principle is represented by Heisenberg's uncertainty relation which is as follows :

The product of the uncertainty Δx (or possible error) in the x-coordinate of a particle, in motion, at some instant, and the uncertainty Δp_x in the x-component of the momentum, at the same instant, is of the order of or greater than $\hbar$ ($h/2\pi = 1.054\times10^{-31}$ J. sec.), i.e.,

$$\Delta x \,.\, \Delta p_x \gtrsim \hbar \qquad \text{... (1)}$$

The symbol $\gtrsim$ stands for "*is of the order of, or greater than.*" In three dimensions the uncertainty relations are :

$$\Delta x \,.\, \Delta p_x \gtrsim \hbar$$

$$\Delta y \, . \, \Delta p_y \gtrsim \hbar \qquad \text{... (2)}$$

$$\Delta z \, . \, \Delta p_z \gtrsim \hbar \qquad \text{... (3)}$$

Uncertainty relation for energy and time :

The uncertainty relation for kinetic energy E of a particle in motion and the time t at which it is measured is

$$\Delta E \, . \, \Delta t \gtrsim \hbar \qquad \text{... (4)}$$

where ΔE is the uncertainty in the energy, and Δt the uncertainty in the time.

The uncertainty principle can also be stated in terms of the angular momentum L of the particle and its angular position ϕ in the plane perpendicular to L. The uncertainty relation for these variables is

$$\Delta L \, . \, \Delta \phi \gtrsim \hbar \qquad \text{... (5)}$$

where the symbols have their usual meaning.

Note : In the statement of the uncertainty relation no clear definitions of Δx and Δp_x have been given. These quantities may be defined in various ways, therefore, many expressions for the product $\Delta x \, . \, \Delta p_x$ are possible. If a series of measurements of x and p_x are taken on many identical systems, and if Δx and Δp_x are defined as the root mean square deviations from their mean values, it can be shown that the minimum value of the product of the uncertainties is given by

$$\Delta x \, . \, \Delta p_x = \frac{\hbar}{2}$$

In solving problems in which only one set of values is involved, the minimum value of the product shouled be taken as

$$\Delta x \, . \, \Delta p_x = \hbar$$

This expression will give better estimate of one of the uncertainties, if the other is known.

3.2 ELEMENTARY PROOF OF HEISENBERG'S UNCERTAINTY RELATION

Suppose a particle is in motion along the x-axis. The de Broglie relation between the wavelength λ of the associated wave and the momentum p_x of the particle along the x-axis is

$$\lambda = \frac{h}{p_x}$$

$$\therefore \qquad p_x = \frac{h}{\lambda} = \frac{h}{2\pi} \cdot \frac{2\pi}{\lambda} = \hbar k \qquad \text{... (1)}$$

The particle in motion is represented by a wave-packet formed by the superposition of a number of plane waves of wavelengths different from λ. In our simple consideration we consider the wave-packet as the superposition of two simple harmonic plane waves of propagation constant k and $k + \delta k$. The length of such a wave-packet is given by [See solved Ex. 2.6 : Chap. 2]

$$\Delta x = \frac{2\pi}{\Delta k} \qquad \text{... (2)}$$

Since the particle must be somewhere within the wave-packet, Δx is the uncertainty in the position of the particle, and corresponding to the uncertainty in the position, the uncertainty in the propagation constant of the associated wave is Δk.

From Eq. (1) the uncertainty Δp_x in the momentum is given by

$$\Delta p_x = \hbar \, \Delta k \quad \text{... (3)}$$

Multiplying Eq. (2) by Eq. (3), we get the product of the uncertainties as

$$\Delta x . \Delta p_x = \left(\frac{2\pi}{\Delta k}\right)(\hbar \, \Delta k) = 2\pi\hbar = h$$

If wave-packets have shapes different from that shown in Fig. 2.1 then the sign of equality is replaced by the sign $\gtrsim$

$$\therefore \quad \Delta x . \Delta p_x \gtrsim h \quad \text{... (4)}$$

In obtaining this uncertainty relation, we considered the wave-packet formed by the superposition of two plane waves. But superposition of two plane waves gives rise to series of wave-packets instead of a single wave-packet. A single wave-packet is formed by superposition of an infinite number of plane waves of propagation constants slightly different from one another. By Fourier analysis of a single wave-packet in one dimension, it can be shown that the width Δx of the wave-packet and the range Δk of the propagation constants of the waves which give rise to the wave-packet are related by :

$$\Delta x \gtrsim \frac{1}{\Delta k} \quad \text{(See Sec. 2.9) ... (5)}$$

Multiplying Eq. (3) by relation (5), we get

$$\Delta x . \Delta p_x \gtrsim \hbar \quad \text{... (6)}$$

Physical Significance of Heisenberg's Uncertainty Relation

The uncertainty relation leads to the following conclusions :

(*i*) If the position coordinate x of a particle in motion is accurately determined at some instant, so that $\Delta x = 0$, then at the same instant the uncertainty Δp_x in the determination of the momentum becomes infinite.

(*ii*) If the momentum p_x of a particle is accurately determined at some instant so that $\Delta p_x = 0$, then at the same instant the uncertainty Δx in the determination of the position coordinate becomes infinite.

Thus if an experiment is designed to measure x or p_x accurately, the other quantity will become completely uncertain. We can measure both the quantities by means of an experiment, but only within certain limits of accuracy specified by the uncertainty relation.

(*iii*) For a particle of mass m moving with velocity v the product of the uncertainty Δx and the uncertainty Δv in the velocity is given by

$$\Delta x . \Delta v \gtrsim \frac{\hbar}{m}$$

For a heavy particle $\hbar/m$ is very small and, therefore, the product $\Delta x . \Delta v$ of the two uncertainties becomes very small. For such particles both the position x and the velocity v can be determined accurately.

For very heavy bodies, if m is such that $\frac{\hbar}{m} = 0$, the uncertainties vanish and all quantities can be determined with perfect accuracy. This is the limiting case of classical mechanics. Thus classical mechanics is true for heavy bodies, and the uncertainties are a characteristic of quantum mechanics, which is applicable to light particles, such as electrons, neutrons, protons, etc.

3.3 ELEMENTARY PROOF OF THE UNCERTAINTY RELATION BETWEEN ENERGY AND TIME

The uncertainty relation between energy and time is obtained by considering the motion of a wave-packet. A particle in motion is represented by a wave-packet. The group velocity of the wave-packet is equal to the particle velocity. Let Δx be the width of the wave-packet moving along the x-axis, v_g the group velocity of the wave-packet, and, v_x the particle velocity along x-axis.

Suppose the wave-packet moves through Δx in time Δt.

$$\therefore \quad \Delta t = \frac{\Delta x}{v_g} = \frac{\Delta x}{v_x} \qquad \text{... (1)}$$

Since Δx is the uncertainty in the x-coordinate of the particle, Δt is the uncertainty in time t at which the particle passes through a point with velocity v_g. The kinetic energy of the particle is given by

$$E = \frac{p_x^2}{2m}$$

Taking differential of this equation, the uncertainty ΔE in the kinetic energy is given by

$$\Delta E = \frac{2p_x \, \Delta p_x}{2m} = \frac{p_x}{m} \Delta p_x = \frac{mv_x}{m} \Delta p_x$$

$$= v_x \, \Delta p_x \qquad \text{... (2)}$$

Multiplying Eq. (1) by Eq. (2), we get

$$\Delta E . \Delta t = \Delta x . \Delta p_x \qquad \text{... (3)}$$

According to the uncertainty relation between position and momentum, we have

$$\Delta x . \Delta p_x \gtrsim \hbar$$

$\therefore$ from Eq. (3), we have

$$\Delta E . \Delta t \gtrsim \hbar \qquad \text{... (4)}$$

This is the energy-time uncertainty relation.

Physical Significance of the Energy-time Uncertainty Relation

The physical interpretation of the energy-time uncertainty relation is quite different from that of the position-momentum uncertainty relation. If ΔE is the *maximum* uncertainty in the determination of the energy of a system in a particular state, then according to relation (4) the *minimum* time-interval for which the system remains in the state is given by

$$\Delta t = \frac{\hbar}{\Delta E}$$

And if a system remains in a particular state for a *maximum* time interval Δt, then the minimum uncertainty in the energy of the system in that state is given by

$$\Delta E = \frac{\hbar}{\Delta t}$$

3.4 ILLUSTRATION OF HEISENBERG'S UNCERTAINTY PRINCIPLE BY THOUGHT-EXPERIMENTS

A thought experiment, or a gedanken experiment is an imaginary experiment which does not violate any fundamental law of nature, but which cannot be performed in practice. For example in a thought experiment, we can imagine a man to jump over the planet Jupiter to a height and calculate the required initial velocity.

We now illustrate the principle by considering the following two thought experiments:

(1) Diffraction of Electrons at a slit : Suppose a mono-energic parallel beam of electrons is moving in horizontal direction from left to right. To locate the vertical position y of a particular electron, above a fixed point O, we block the beam by a vertical screen having a slit of width Δy at distance y above O as shown in Fig. 3.1. Then a narrow beam of electrons together with the particular electron passes through the slit.

Since an electron in motion is associated with a wave, the beam passing through the slit undergoes diffraction. Therefore, a Fraunhofer diffraction pattern will be obtained on a photographic plate P placed perpendicular to the direction of the incident beam. The diffraction pattern

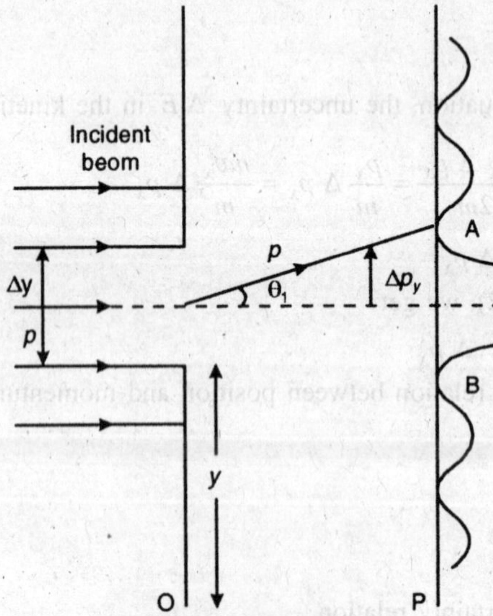

Fig. 3.1

consists of the central band of maximum intensity much wider than the slit, and on both the sides of the central band, there are dark and bright bands of decreasing intensity.

Let p be the momentum of an electron in the incident beam. Then the wavelength of the associated wave is given by :

$$\lambda = \frac{h}{p} \qquad \text{... (1)}$$

Let θ_1 be the angle of diffraction of the electrons in the beam, which form the first minimum *A* of the pattern. This angle is given by,

$$\sin\theta_1 = \frac{\lambda}{\Delta y} \qquad \text{... (2)}$$

From the existence of the diffraction pattern we can conclude that :

(1) Every electron deflected at the slit has passed through the slit ; but the place in the slit at which the passage of an electron takes place remains quite indefinite by the amount Δy.

$\therefore$ the uncertainty in the *y* coordinate of an electron which has passed through the slit $= \Delta y$.

For the electron which is deflected through θ_1 in the upward or downward direction, this uncertainty, from Eqn. (2), is given by

$$\Delta y = \frac{\lambda}{\sin\theta_1} \qquad \text{... (3)}$$

(2) At the instant when an electron is deflected at the slit, its original momentum *p* in the horizontal direction is decreased and it acquires component momentum Δp_y in the *y*-direction (the resultant momentum *p* remaining constant).

The original momentum of an electron in the *y*-direction was accurately known to be zero. Therefore, Δp_y is the uncertainty introduced in the *y* component of the momentum.

For the electron which is deflected through θ_1 in the upward or downward direction, this uncertainty is given by (Fig. 3.1).

$$\Delta p_y = p\sin\theta_1$$

or

$$\Delta p_y = \frac{h}{\lambda}\sin\theta_1 \qquad \text{... (4)}$$

Hence the product of the uncertainties in the simultaneous determination of the *y* coordinate and *y*-component of the momentum of the electron at the instant when it passes through the slit is given by :

$$\Delta y \,.\, \Delta p_y = \frac{\lambda}{\sin\theta_1} \cdot \frac{h}{\lambda}\sin\theta_1$$

$$= h \qquad \text{... (5)}$$

The probability of an electron reaching the centre of the pattern is greatest. Therefore, Eq. (5) gives the maximum uncertainty Δp_y for a given value of Δy. Hence Eq. (5) is consistent with the uncertainty relation

$$\Delta y \,.\, \Delta p_y \geq \hbar$$

In order to decrease the uncertainty in the determination of the *y*-coordinate, we should decrease Δy. But from Eq. (2) we see that decrease in Δy will increase the angle θ_1 and will produce a wider diffraction pattern. Then a wider diffraction pattern will give rise to a larger value of the uncertainty Δp_y.

(2) Gamma Ray Microscope Thought Experiment : This thought experiment was first proposed by Heisenberg. It is usually called γ-ray microscope experiment. Suppose we want to locate the position, *i.e.*, the *x*-coordinate of an electron of an atom by means of a microscope. The radius of the atom is of the order of 10^{-11} m. Therefore, in order to determine the position of an electron with an uncertainty of about 10% of the radius of the atom we must employ radiation of wavelength of the order of 10^{-12} m, *i.e.*, 0.01 Å. It means that we must illuminate the electron with γ-rays of wavelength of the order of 0.01 Å.

Suppose initially the electron at *O* (Fig. 3.2) is at rest and to locate its position suppose it is illuminated by a narrow beam of monochromatic γ-rays proceeding in the *x*-direction.

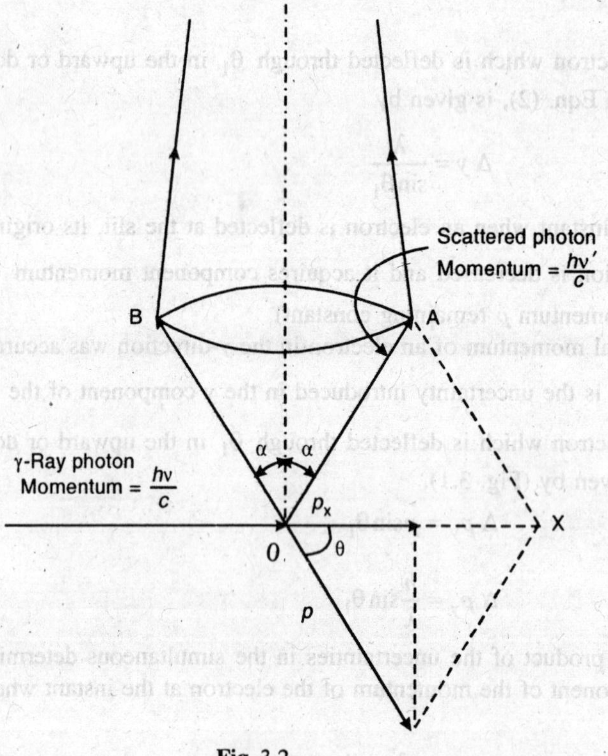

Fig. 3.2

Let ν be the frequency and λ the wavelength of the incident γ-rays. Then the momentum of an incident γ-ray photon in the *x*-direction

$$= \frac{h\nu}{c} = \frac{h}{\lambda}, \text{ where } c \text{ is the speed of light in free space.}$$

At least one photon should be scattered by the electron into the microscope, so that the electron is visible. In this process the frequency and wavelength of the scattered photon is changed and the electron suffers a Compton recoil due to gain of momentum.

At the instant when the electron is observed in the microscope let 2α be the angle subtended at the electron by the diameter *AB* of the instrument's aperture.

The scattered photon may enter the microscope along the surface of the cone whose semi-vertical angle is α, or along any other direction within the cone. Suppose the photon enters the microscope along *OA*. Let ν' be the frequency and λ' the wavelength of the scattered photon. Then the momentum of the scattered photon along *OA* :

$$= \frac{h\nu'}{c} = \frac{h}{\lambda'}$$

The image of the electron formed by the microscope will be a diffraction pattern which consists of a central bright disc surrounded by alternate dark and bright rings. Since the position of the electron may be anywhere within the central bright disc, the uncertainty in the position of the electron is the diameter of the central disc. Let Δx be the diameter of the central disc. Then the uncertainty in the position $= \Delta x$.

According to Rayleigh's criterion in optics, the *resolving power of an optical instrument is the distance between the peak intensity and the first minimum of the diffraction pattern*, and its expression is

$$R.P. = \frac{\lambda'}{2\sin\alpha}$$

In this case $R.P. = \frac{\Delta x}{2}$

$$\therefore \quad \frac{\Delta x}{2} = \frac{\lambda'}{2\sin\alpha}$$

or $$\Delta x = \frac{\lambda'}{\sin\alpha} \quad \text{... (1)}$$

This is the expression for the uncertainty in the position. Let *p* be the gain of momentum by the electron in the direction of recoil θ.

Resolving the mementa along *OX*, we get,

$$\frac{h\nu}{c} = \frac{h\nu'}{c}\cos(90° - \alpha) + p\cos\theta$$

or $$\frac{h}{\lambda} = -\frac{h}{\lambda'}\sin\alpha + p\cos\theta$$

or $$p\cos\theta = \frac{h}{\lambda} - \frac{h}{\lambda'}\sin\alpha \quad \text{... (2)}$$

In this equation $p\cos\theta$ is the *x*-component p_x of the momentum *p*.

Since the term h/λ on the right hand side of this equation is accurately known and since the scattered photon can enter the microscope along any other direction making angle less than α with the axis of the microscope, the second term on the right hand side of Eq. (2) represents maximum uncertainty in p_x.

Let Δp_x be this uncertainty in p_x. Then

$$\Delta p_x = \frac{h}{\lambda'}\sin\alpha \quad \text{... (3)}$$

Multiplying Eq. (1) by Eq. (3), we get,

$$\Delta x . \Delta p_x = h$$

Since the value of Δp_x is maximum, this equation is consistent with the uncertainty relation :

$$\Delta x \,.\, \Delta p_x \gtrsim \hbar$$

3.5 CONSEQUENCES OF THE UNCERTAINTY RELATION

(1) Ground – state energy of a particle in a box :

We consider the one dimensional motion along *x*-axis of a particle of mass *m* in a hollow rectangular box having perfectly rigid walls. Let the origin be at one corner of the box and the *x*-axis be perpendicular to the parallel opposite walls. Let *a* be the distance between the walls so that the motion is confined between $x = 0$ and $x = a$.

Suppose that inside the box there is no force acting on the particle, so that in this region the potential energy is zero.

The particle can be anywhere within the distance *a* from the origin. Therefore, the *maximum* uncertainty in the determination of its position with respect to the origin is *a, i.e.*,

$$(\Delta x)_{\max} = a$$

From the uncertainty relation in the form

$$\Delta x \,.\, \Delta p_x \gtrsim h$$

where *h* is Planck's constant, the *minimum* uncertainty in the momentum is given by

$$\Delta p_x = \frac{h}{(\Delta x)_{\max}} = \frac{h}{a}$$

The particle may be moving in the positive or negative direction of *x*.

Therefore, the minimum uncertainty in the momentum in either direction

$$= \frac{h}{2a}$$

The magnitude p_x of the momentum in either direction cannot be less than the uncertainty $h/2a$. Therefore, the *minimum possible momentum* in the + *x* or – *x* direction is :

$$p_x = \frac{h}{2a}$$

Hence the lowest possible kinetic energy of the particle is given by

$$E = \frac{p_x^2}{2m} = \frac{1}{2m}\left(\frac{h}{2a}\right)^2 = \frac{h^2}{8ma^2} \qquad \text{... (1)}$$

$$= \frac{1}{8ma^2}(2\pi)^2\left(\frac{h}{2\pi}\right)^2 = \frac{\pi^2\hbar^2}{2ma^2} \qquad \text{... (2)}$$

where $\hbar = \dfrac{h}{2\pi}$

Eq. (2) gives the required expression.

(2) Position of the electron in a Bohr orbit

Suppose the electron in the hydrogen atom moves round the proton in a circular orbit of radius *r*. Then the maximum uncertainty in the determination of its position with respect to the proton can be taken to be equal to *r, i.e.*,

$$(\Delta x)_{\max} = r$$

From the uncertainty relation

$$\Delta x . \Delta p \gtrsim \hbar$$

the *minimum* uncertainty in the simultaneous determination of its momentum *p* in the plane of the orbit is given by

$$\Delta p = \frac{\hbar}{(\Delta x)_{max}} = \frac{\hbar}{r}$$

The momentum *p* cannot be less than the uncertainty Δp; therefore, the minimum possible momentum at distance *r* from the nucleus is

$$p = \frac{\hbar}{r}$$

$\therefore$ the minimum kinetic energy of the electron in the orbit of radius *r* is given by

$$E_k = \frac{p^2}{2m} = \frac{\hbar^2}{2mr^2} \quad \text{... (1)}$$

and the electrostatic potential energy is given by

$$E_p = -\frac{e^2}{4\pi\varepsilon_0 r} \quad \text{... (2)}$$

$\therefore$ the total energy of the electron in the hydrogen atom is given by

$$E = \frac{\hbar^2}{2mr^2} - \frac{e^2}{4\pi\varepsilon_0 r} \quad \text{... (3)}$$

The ground state energy must be a minimum value of *E*. For a minimum value of *E* :

$$\frac{dE}{dr} = -\frac{\hbar^2}{mr^3} + \frac{e^2}{4\pi\varepsilon_0 r^2} = 0 \quad \text{... (4)}$$

i.e.,

$$-\frac{\hbar^2}{mr^3} + \frac{e^2}{4\pi\varepsilon_0 r^2} = 0$$

or

$$\frac{e^2}{4\pi\varepsilon_0} = \frac{\hbar^2}{mr} \quad \text{... (5)}$$

$\therefore$

$$r = \frac{4\pi\varepsilon_0 \hbar^2}{me^2} = \frac{4\pi\varepsilon_0}{me^2}\left(\frac{h}{2\pi}\right)^2$$

$$= \frac{\varepsilon_0 h^2}{\pi m e^2} \quad \text{... (6)}$$

This is the well known expression for the radius of the first Bohr orbit. This is usually called the Bohr radius and is denoted by r_1.

Thus the total energy of the electron is minimum when it is in the first Bohr orbit of radius r_1:

$$r_1 = \frac{\varepsilon_0 h^2}{\pi m e^2}$$

The calculated value of r_1 is 5.3×10^{-11} m.

Expression for the ground state energy :

The minimum value of the total energy is given by

$$E_1 = \frac{\hbar^2}{2mr_1^2} - \frac{e^2}{4\pi\varepsilon_0 r_1}$$

$$= \frac{1}{2r_1}\left(\frac{\hbar^2}{mr_1} - \frac{e^2}{2\pi\varepsilon_0}\right)$$

Using Eq. (5), we get

$$E_1 = \frac{1}{2r_1}\left(\frac{e^2}{4\pi\varepsilon_0} - \frac{e^2}{2\pi\varepsilon_0}\right) = -\frac{e^2}{8\pi\varepsilon_0 r_1}$$

$$= -\frac{e^2}{8\pi\varepsilon_0} \times \frac{\pi m e^2}{\varepsilon_0 h^2} = -\frac{me^4}{8\varepsilon_0^2 h^2} \quad \text{... (7)}$$

This is the expression for the minimum energy or the ground state energy. The calculated value of this energy is

$$E_1 = -13.6\,\text{eV}.$$

SOLVED EXAMPLES

Example 3.1 *An electron has a speed of 300* m/s *accurate to 0.01%. With what fundamental accuracy can we locate the position of the electron ?* (Poona, 2005)

Solution :

We have

$$\Delta v = 0.01\% = 300 \times \frac{0.01}{100} = 3 \times 10^{-2}\ \text{m/s}$$

The uncertainty relation is

$$\Delta x \,.\, \Delta p_x \gtrsim h$$

∴ for the given uncertainty in the speed, the *minimum* uncertainty in the position is given by

$$\Delta x = \frac{\hbar}{\Delta p_x} = \frac{\hbar}{m\Delta v} = \frac{h}{2\pi m\Delta v}$$

$$= \frac{6.63 \times 10^{-34}}{2 \times 3.14 \times 9.11 \times 10^{-31} \times 3 \times 10^{-2}}$$

$$= \frac{6.63 \times 10^{-1}}{2 \times 3.14 \times 9.11 \times 3} = \frac{663 \times 10^{-3}}{171.6}$$

$$= \mathbf{3.86 \times 10^{-3}\ m}$$

Example 3.2. *Find the smallest possible uncertainty in the position of an electron moving with velocity 3 × 10⁷ m/sec.* (Given : $\hbar = 1.054 \times 10^{-34}$ Js, $m_0 = 9.11 \times 10^{-31}$ kg)

Solution :
The maximum uncertainty in the momentum is

$$\Delta p_x = p_x = mv = \frac{m_0 v}{\sqrt{1 - v^2/c^2}}$$

From the uncertainty relation $\Delta x . \Delta p_x \gtrsim \hbar$, the minimum uncertainty in the position is given by

$$\Delta x = \frac{\hbar}{\Delta p_x} = \frac{\hbar}{m_0 v}\sqrt{1 - v^2/c^2}$$

But $\sqrt{1 - v^2/c^2} = \sqrt{1 - (3\times 10^7 / 3\times 10^8)^2} = \frac{\sqrt{99}}{10} = 0.995$

$$\therefore \quad \Delta x = \frac{\hbar \times 0.995}{m_0 v} = \frac{1.054\times 10^{-34} \times 0.995}{9.11\times 10^{-31} \times 3\times 10^7}$$

$$= \frac{1.054\times 9.95\times 10^{-11}}{9.11\times 3} = 0.384\times 10^{-11}\,\text{m}$$

$$= 0.0384 \times 10^{-10}\ \text{m}$$

$$= \mathbf{0.0384\ Å}$$

Example 3.3. *The average period that elapses between the excitation of an atom and the time it emits radiation is 10^{-8} sec. Find the uncertainty in the energy emitted and the uncertainty in the frequency of light emitted. (Given : $\hbar = 1.054\times 10^{-34}$ Js, $h = 6.63 \times 10^{-34}$ Js)*

Solution :
The maximum uncertainty in the interval of time is

$$\Delta t = 10^{-8}\,\text{s}$$

From the uncertainty relation $\Delta E . \Delta t \gtrsim \hbar$, the minimum uncertainty in the energy is given by

$$\Delta E = \frac{\hbar}{\Delta t} = \frac{1.054\times 10^{-34}}{10^{-8}} = 1.054\times 10^{-26}\,\text{J}$$

Now $\quad hv = E$

$\therefore$ the uncertainty in the frequency is given by

$$h\Delta v = \Delta E$$

$$\Delta v = \frac{\Delta E}{h} = \frac{1.054\times 10^{-26}}{6.63\times 10^{-34}} = \mathbf{1.59\times 10^7\,Hz}$$

QUESTIONS AND PROBLEMS

1. State and explain Heisenberg's uncertainty principle. Using the following data, show that there is no existence of free electrons in the nucleus of an atom : the radius of the nucleus = 10^{-14} m, the mass of the electron = 9.11×10^{-31} kg, the maximum kinetic energy of an electron in an atom = 4 M eV, and 1 eV = 1.602×10^{-19} J.

2. State and prove Heisenberg's uncertainty principle. Discuss its physical importance.
3. State Heisenberg's uncertainty principle and illustrate it by any thought experiment.
4. A microscope can locate an electron within a distance of 1 Å. Calculate the uncertainty in the measurement of its momentum. (Delhi, 2005) (**Ans.** 1.054×10^{-24} kg. m/s)
5. Prove that for rotational motion of a particle the uncertainty principle can be stated in the form

$$\Delta L \,.\, \Delta \phi \gtrsim \hbar$$

where ΔL is the uncertainty in the angular momentum of the particle and $\Delta \phi$ is the uncertainty in its angular position.

[**Proof :** The kinetic energy E due to rotational motion about the axis of rotation is given by

$$E = \frac{1}{2} I\omega^2$$

$$\therefore \quad \Delta E = \frac{1}{2} \times 2\omega \, \Delta I\omega = \omega \, \Delta L$$

or $$\omega \Delta L = \Delta E \qquad \text{... (1)}$$

where L is the angular momentum $I\omega$.

The angular position ϕ of the particle at time t is given by

$$\phi = \omega t$$

$$\therefore \quad \frac{\Delta \phi}{\omega} = \Delta t \qquad \text{... (2)}$$

Multiplying Eq. (1) by Eq. (2), we get

$$\Delta L \,.\, \Delta \phi = \Delta E \,.\, \Delta t$$

But $$\Delta E \,.\, \Delta t \gtrsim \hbar$$

Hence $$\Delta L \,.\, \Delta \phi \gtrsim \hbar \text{]}.$$

6. A particle is diffracted at a certain angle and the uncertainty in the measurement of angle is one second of arc. Estimate the error in the measurement of its angular momentum. (N.U., 2006) (**Ans.** 2.186×10^{-29} J.S
7. Does the concept of Bohr orbit violate Heisenberg's uncertainty principle ? (N.U., 2006

CHAPTER 4

SCHRÖDINGER'S WAVE EQUATION

In classical mechanics, a wave equation is a second order differential equation in space and time. Solutions of this equation represent wave disturbances in a medium. Therefore, a wave equation is the usual basis of mathematical theory of wave motion. For example an electromagnetic wave, travelling in the x-direction, is described by the wave equation

$$\frac{\partial^2 E_y}{\partial x^2} = \frac{1}{c^2}\frac{\partial^2 E_y}{\partial t^2}$$

where E_y is the y-component of the electric intensity.

A differential equation for the wave associated with a particle in motion cannot be derived from first principles. The equation may be developed by any one of the following procedures :

(1) The equations of motion of classical mechanics are transformed into a wave equation in accordance with wave properties of matter based on de Broglie's hypothesis.

(2) A complex variable quantity, called the wave function, is assumed to represent a plane simple harmonic wave associated with a free particle, and the classical expression for the total energy is used.

(3) A particle at a given position and at a given time is represented by a wave packet which is obtained by superposition of a group of plane waves of nearly the same wavelength, which interfere destructively everywhere except at the wave packet, and the classical expression for the total energy is used.

(4) In the classical expression for the total energy of a particle, the dynamical quantities are replaced by their corresponding operators. These operators are allowed to operate upon the wave function.

In this chapter we will follow procedure (2) to develop the Schrodinger equation.

4.1. SCHRODINGER'S ONE DIMENSIONAL TIME-DEPENDENT WAVE EQUATION

Wave Function for a Free Particle

Let a particle of mass m be in motion in the positive x-direction with velocity v, accurately known momentum p_x and total energy E. The position of the particle would be completely undetermined. The wave associated with such a particle should be a plane continuous simple harmonic wave travelling in the positive x-direction.

In wave mechanics it is assumed that the wave is represented by a complex variable quantity $\psi(x, t)$ given by

$$\psi(x, t) = A\, e^{-i\omega(t - x/v)} \qquad \text{... (1)}$$

where $i = \sqrt{-1}$, A is the amplitude and ω is the angular frequency of the wave.

The right side of Eq. (1) can be expressed in terms of p_x and E.

The wavelength λ of the associated wave is given by de Broglie's hypothesis :

$$\lambda = \frac{h}{p_x}$$

$$\therefore \quad p_x = \frac{h}{\lambda} = \frac{h}{2\pi} \cdot \frac{2\pi}{\lambda} = \hbar \cdot \frac{2\pi}{v/\nu} \quad \text{, where } \nu \text{ is the frequency}$$

$$= \hbar \cdot \frac{2\pi\nu}{v} = \hbar \cdot \frac{\omega}{v}$$

$$\therefore \quad \frac{\omega}{v} = \frac{p_x}{\hbar} \qquad \text{... (2)}$$

The frequency ν of the associated wave is given by Planck's hypothesis :

$$E = h\nu = \frac{h}{2\pi} \cdot 2\pi\nu = \hbar\omega$$

$$\therefore \quad \omega = \frac{E}{\hbar} \qquad \text{... (3)}$$

Now from Eq. (1),

$$\psi(x, t) = A\, e^{-i(\omega t - \omega x/v)}$$

Substituting the expressions for ω and ω/v in this equation we get

$$\psi(x, t) = A\, e^{-i(Et/\hbar - p_x x/\hbar)}$$

$$= A\, e^{i/\hbar\,(p_x x - Et)} \qquad \text{... (4)}$$

This is the expression for the wave function $\psi(x, t)$ of a particle in motion in the positive x-direction with momentum p_x and total energy E.

One-dimensional time-dependent wave equation

If the speed of the particle is small compared with that of light, the total energy E is the sum of its kinetic energy $p_x^2/2m$ and its potential energy V, *i.e.*

$$\frac{p_x^2}{2m} + V = E \qquad \text{... (5)}$$

If the motion of the particle is due to the action of a force $F(x)$ which is a function of x, then V will be a function only of x. Multiplying both the sides of Eq. (5) by the wave function $\psi(x, t)$, we get

$$\frac{p_x^2\,\psi}{2m} + V\psi = E\psi \qquad \text{... (6)}$$

We write Eq. (4) as

$$\psi = A\, e^{i/\hbar\,(p_x x - Et)} \qquad \text{... (4)}$$

Differentiating Eq. (4) with respect to x,

$$\frac{\partial \psi}{\partial x} = A\left(\frac{i}{\hbar}\right) p_x\, e^{i/\hbar\,(p_x x - Et)} = \left(\frac{i}{\hbar}\right) p_x\, A\, e^{i/\hbar\,(p_x x - Et)}$$

$$= \left(\frac{i}{\hbar}\right) p_x \, \psi \quad \text{... (7)}$$

and
$$\frac{\partial^2 \psi}{\partial x^2} = \left(\frac{i}{\hbar}\right) p_x \frac{\partial \psi}{\partial x} = \left(\frac{i}{\hbar}\right) p_x \left(\frac{i}{\hbar}\right) p_x \, \psi$$

$$= -\frac{1}{\hbar^2} p_x^2 \, \Psi$$

From this equation, we have

$$p_x^2 \psi = -\hbar^2 \frac{\partial^2 \psi}{\partial x^2} \quad \text{... (8)}$$

Differentiating Eq. (4) with respect to t

$$\frac{\partial \psi}{\partial t} = A\left(\frac{i}{\hbar}\right)(-E)\, e^{i/\hbar (p_x x - Et)} = -\left(\frac{i}{\hbar}\right) E\, A\, e^{i/\hbar (p_x x - Et)}$$

$$= -\frac{i}{\hbar} E\psi$$

$$\therefore \qquad E\psi = -\frac{\hbar}{i} \frac{\partial \psi}{\partial t} \quad \text{... (9)}$$

Substituting these expressions for $p_x^2 \psi$ and $E\psi$ in Eq. (6), we get

$$-\frac{\hbar^2}{2m} \frac{\partial^2 \psi}{\partial x^2} + V\psi = -\frac{\hbar}{i} \frac{\partial \psi}{\partial t} \quad \text{... (10)}$$

This is the *one dimensional time-dependent wave equation*, first derived by Schrodinger in 1926.

In three dimensions the time-dependent Schrodinger's wave equation is

$$-\frac{\hbar^2}{2m}\left(\frac{\partial^2 \psi}{\partial x^2} + \frac{\partial^2 \psi}{\partial y^2} + \frac{\partial^2 \psi}{\partial z^2}\right) + V\psi = -\frac{\hbar}{i} \frac{\partial \psi}{\partial t} \quad \text{... (11)}$$

This equation is written as

$$-\frac{\hbar^2}{2m} \nabla^2 \psi + V\psi = -\frac{\hbar}{i} \frac{\partial \psi}{\partial t} \quad \text{... (12)}$$

or
$$\left[-\frac{\hbar^2}{2m} \nabla^2 + V\right] \psi = -\frac{\hbar}{i} \frac{\partial \psi}{\partial t} \quad \text{... (13)}$$

where ∇^2 is the Laplacian operator defined by

$$\nabla^2 \equiv \frac{\partial^2}{\partial x^2} + \frac{\partial^2}{\partial y^2} + \frac{\partial^2}{\partial z^2}$$

4.2. ONE DIMENSIONAL TIME-INDEPENDENT SCHRODINGER'S WAVE EQUATION

The one-dimensional time-dependent Schrodinger's wave equation is

$$-\frac{\hbar^2}{2m} \frac{\partial^2 \psi}{\partial x^2} + V\psi = -\frac{\hbar}{i} \frac{\partial \psi}{\partial t} \quad \text{... (1)}$$

Eq. (1) is a partial differential equation in two variables *(x, t)*. The equation is separable into the time-independent part and time dependent part, if the potential energy *V* is a function of *x* only and the total energy E is constant.

Let $u(x)$ and $f(t)$ be the time-independent and time-dependent parts respectively of the wave function. Then

$$\psi(x, t) = u(x)\, f(t) \quad \text{... (2)}$$

Substituting this equation in Eq. (1), we get

$$-\frac{\hbar^2}{2m} f \frac{d^2u}{dx^2} + Vuf = -\frac{\hbar}{i} u \frac{df}{dt}$$

We have used ordinary derivatives in place of partial derivatives because each of the functions, u and f depends on only one variable.

Dividing both the sides by uf, we get

$$-\frac{\hbar^2}{2m}\frac{1}{u}\frac{d^2u}{dx^2} + V = -\frac{\hbar}{i}\frac{1}{f}\frac{df}{dt} \quad \text{... (3)}$$

The right-hand side of this equation is a function only of time t, and the left-hand side is a function only of the coordinate x. Therefore, the right-hand side is the *time-dependent part* and the left-hand side is the *time-independent* part of Eq. (1).

Now we make use of Eq. (9) of Sec. 4.1 :

$$-\frac{\hbar}{i}\frac{\partial \psi}{\partial t} = E\psi$$

Substituting Eq. (2) into this equation, we obtain

$$-\frac{\hbar}{i} u \frac{df}{dt} = E\, uf$$

$$\therefore \quad -\frac{\hbar}{i}\frac{1}{f}\frac{df}{dt} = E \quad \text{... (4)}$$

This is time-dependent part of Schrodinger's equation.

Now from Eqs. (3) and (4), we get

$$-\frac{\hbar^2}{2m}\frac{1}{u}\frac{d^2u}{dx^2} + V = E$$

Multiplying through by u and rearranging the terms, we obtain

$$\frac{d^2u}{dx^2} + \frac{2m}{\hbar^2}(E - V)\, u = 0 \quad \text{... (5)}$$

This is the one-dimensional time-independent (*i.e.* the steady state) Schrodinger's equation. In three dimensions the steady state Schrodinger's equation is

$$\nabla^2 u + \frac{2m}{\hbar^2}(E - V)\, u = 0 \quad \text{... (6)}$$

where $u(x, y, z)$ is the position-dependent wave function.

4.3 PHYSICAL INTERPRETATION OF THE WAVE FUNCTION Ψ

We have assumed that the wave associated with a particle in motion is represented by a complex variable quantity $\psi(x, y, z, t)$ called the wave function. Therefore, it cannot have a direct physical meaning. Since it is a complex quantity, it may be expressed in the form

$$\psi(x, y, z, t) = a + ib \quad \text{... (1)}$$

where a and b are real functions of the variables (x, y, z, t), and $i = \sqrt{-1}$.

The complex conjugate of ψ which is denoted by ψ^* is obtained by changing i to $-i$. Therefore, we have

$$\psi^* (x, y, z, t) = a - ib \quad \text{... (2)}$$

Multiplying Eq. (1) by Eq. (2)

$$\psi (x, y, z, t)\, \psi^* (x, y, z, t) = a^2 + b^2 \quad \text{... (3)}$$

On the left-hand side of this equation the product is denoted by

$$|\varphi (x, y, z, t)|^2$$

$$\therefore \quad |\psi (x, y, z, t)|^2 = a^2 + b^2 \quad \text{... (4)}$$

Thus the product of ψ and ψ^* is real and positive if $\psi \neq 0$. Its positive square root is denoted by $|\psi(x, y, z, t)|$ and it is called the modulus of ψ.

The fact expressed by Eq. (4) has been used by Max Born to give *interpretation* of $\psi (x, y, z, t)$ which is as follows :

For the motion of a paticle in three dimensions the product

$$\psi (x, y, z, t)\, \psi^* (x, y, z, t) = |\psi (x, y, z, t)|^2 \quad \text{... (5)}$$

is the probability density P (x, y, z) (i.e. probability per unit volume) for the particle at position (x, y, z), at time t.

Hence the product of the probability density and the volume element $d\tau = dx\, dy\, dz$*, i.e.,*

$$P (x, y, z)\, d\tau = \psi (x, y, z, t)\, \psi^* (x, y, z, t)\, d\tau = |\psi (x, y, z, t|^2\, d\tau \quad \text{... (6)}$$

is the probability that the particle will be found in a volume element $d\tau = dxdydz$ surrounding the point at position (x, y, z) at time t

For the motion of a particle in one dimension the quantity

$$P(x)\, dx = \psi (x, t)\, \phi^* (x, t)\, dx = |\phi (x, t)|^2\, dx$$

is the probability that the particle will be found over a small distance dx at position x, at time t. In this case $|\psi (x, t)|^2$ is called the probability per unit distance.

Since $\quad \psi (x, y, z, t) = u (x, y, z)\, e^{-i\omega t}$

and $\quad \psi^* (x, y, z, t) = u^* (x, y, z)\, e^{+i\omega t}$

for a particular value of the constant energy E, we get

$$P (x, y, z)\, d\tau = u (x, y, z)\, u^* (x, y, z)\, d\tau = |u (x, y, z)|^2\, d\tau$$

Thus for the wave function satisfying the time-independent Schrödinger equation, the probability is always independent of time.

Dimensions of ψ (x, y, z, t)

We have

$$|\psi(x, y, z, t|^2 = \frac{\text{probability}}{\text{volume}}$$

$$\therefore \quad |\psi(x, y, z, t)| = (\text{probability})^{1/2}\ (\text{volume})^{-1/2}$$

Probability is a dimensionless quantity and the dimensions of volume = $[L^3]$

$\therefore$ dimensions of $|\psi(x,y,z,t)| = [L^3]^{-1/2} = [L^{-3/2}]$

Similarly we can show that for the motion of a particle in one dimension,

the dimensions of $|\psi(x,t)| = [L^{-1/2}]$

Limitations on ψ

Because of the above interpretation of $|\psi|^2$ as a probability density, the solutions that can be allowed for ψ from the Schrödinger equation are subjected to certain limitations. The most important limitations are :

(*i*) ψ must be finite for all values of *x, y, z*.

(*ii*) ψ must be single-valued, *i.e.*, for each set of values of *x, y, z,* ψ must have one value only.

(*iii*) ψ must be continuous in all regions except in those regions where the potential energy $V(x, y, z) = \infty$.

(*iv*) the partial derivatives $\partial\psi/\partial x, \partial\psi/\partial y, \partial\psi/\partial z$ must be continuous everywhere. A wave function which satisfies these conditions is called a well-behaved function.

Normalization of Wave Function

Since $|\psi(x,y,z,t)|^2\, d\tau$ is the probability that the particle will be found in a volume element $d\tau$ surrounding the point at the position (*x, y, z*) at the time *t*, the total probability that the particle will be somewhere in space at the time *t* must be equal to 1. Thus we have

$$\int_{-\infty}^{\infty} |\psi(x, y, z, t)|^2\, d\tau = 1 \qquad \text{... (7)}$$

where the integration is to be taken over all space. Eq. (7) may also be written as

$$\int_{-\infty}^{\infty} \psi^*(x, y, z, t)\, \psi(x, y, z, t)\, d\tau = 1 \qquad \text{... (8)}$$

A wave function which satisfies the above condition is said to be *normalized* to unity, (or simply normalized). The normalization condition for the wave function for the motion of a particle in one dimension is

$$\int_{-\infty}^{\infty} \psi^*(x, t)\, \psi(x, t)\, dx = 1 \qquad \text{... (9)}$$

For any wave function that is a solution of the time-dependent Schrödinger equation [Eq. (11) Sec. 4.1], the integral $\int_{-\infty}^{\infty} \psi^*(x, y, z, t)\, \psi(x, y, z, t)\, d\tau$ is independent of time.

$$\therefore \quad \int_{-\infty}^{\infty} \psi^* (x, y, z, t)\, \psi (x, y, z, t)\, d\tau = \int_{-\infty}^{\infty} \psi^* (x, y, z), \psi (x, y, z)\, d\tau$$

Hence the normalization condition becomes

$$\int_{-\infty}^{\infty} \psi^* (x, y, z)\, \psi (x, y, z)\, d\tau = 1 \qquad \text{... (10)}$$

and for one dimensional motion the condition is

$$\int_{-\infty}^{\infty} \psi^*(x)\, \psi (x)\, dx = 1\,. \qquad \text{... (11)}$$

4.4. OPERATORS IN QUANTUM MECHANICS, EIGEN FUNCTION, EIGEN VALUE AND EIGEN VALUE EQUATION

An operator is a rule which changes a function into another function. For example, the operator $\frac{d}{dx}$ represents differentiation with respect to x. When it operates on a function, *e.g.*

$$f(x) = x^n$$

then

$$\frac{df}{dx} = nx^{n-1}$$

If a function $f(x)$ is such that an operator A which operates on $f(x)$ gives

$$Af(x) = af(x) \qquad \text{... (1)}$$

or

$$\frac{1}{f(x)} |Af(x)| = a$$

where a is constant, then

(*i*) $f(x)$ is called *eigen-function* of the operator (the German word *eigen* means proper or characteristic),

(*ii*) the constant a is called the eigen-value of the operator belonging to the eigen-function $f(x)$, and

(*iii*) the equation, such as Eq. (1) is called the *eigen-value* equation.

Thus an eigen value equation states that an operator, acting on a function, reproduces the same function multiplied by a constant factor.

Now we derive some operators of quantum mechanics for a free particle. The operators will also be valid for a bound particle. *All operators of quantum mechanics have eigen-functions and eigen values.*

Operator for Momentum

The wave function for a free particle moving in the positive x-direction is

$$\psi (x, t) = A\, e^{i/\hbar\, (p_x x - Et)} \qquad \text{... (2)}$$

Differentiating this equation with respect to x, we get

$$\frac{\partial \psi}{\partial x} = A \left(\frac{i}{\hbar} \right) p_x\, e^{i/\hbar\, (p_x x - Et)} = \frac{i}{\hbar}\, p_x \Psi$$

or

$$\frac{\hbar}{i} \frac{\partial \psi}{\partial x} = p_x \Psi \qquad \text{... (3)}$$

This is the eigen value equation for the x-component of the momentum. The equation shows that :

(*i*) $\frac{\hbar}{i}\frac{\partial}{\partial x}$ is the operator, (*ii*) $\psi(x,t)$ is the eigen function of the operator, and

(*iii*) p_x is the eigen value of the operator. Hence $\frac{\hbar}{i}\frac{\partial}{\partial x}$ is the momentum operator for the x-component of the momentum. The operator is denoted by $\hat{p}_x$. Thus

$$\hat{p}_x = \frac{\hbar}{i}\frac{\partial}{\partial x} \quad \text{... (4)}$$

[The symbol ^ ('hat') is used above the quantity to distinguish the operator from the physical quantity.]

Similarly for the y and z-components of the momentum, the operators are

$$\hat{p}_y = \frac{\hbar}{i}\frac{\partial}{\partial y} \quad \text{... (5)}$$

$$\hat{p}_z = \frac{\hbar}{i}\frac{\partial}{\partial z} \quad \text{... (6a)}$$

The momentum operator is defined as the operator which, operating on the wave function, reproduces the wave function multiplied by the momentum.

In three dimensions, the operator for the momentum $\vec{p}$ is

$$\hat{p} = \frac{\hbar}{i}\vec{\nabla} \quad \text{... (6b)}$$

Operator for Kinetic Energy

From the momentum operator, we have

$$\frac{\hbar}{i}\frac{\partial\psi}{\partial x} = p_x\psi$$

Differentiating this equation with respect to x,

$$\frac{\hbar}{i}\frac{\partial^2\psi}{\partial x^2} = p_x\frac{\partial\psi}{\partial x}$$

But,

$$\frac{\partial\psi}{\partial x} = \frac{i}{\hbar}p_x\psi$$

$\therefore$

$$\frac{\hbar}{i}\frac{\partial^2\psi}{\partial x^2} = p_x\frac{i}{\hbar}p_x\psi$$

or

$$\frac{\hbar^2}{i^2}\frac{\partial^2\psi}{\partial x^2} = p_x^2\psi$$

or

$$-\hbar^2\frac{\partial^2\psi}{\partial x^2} = p_x^2\psi$$

Dividing this equation by $2m$

$$-\frac{\hbar^2}{2m}\frac{\partial^2\psi}{\partial x^2} = \frac{p_x^2}{2m}\psi \quad \text{... (7)}$$

or

$$-\frac{\hbar^2}{2m}\frac{\partial^2\psi}{\partial x^2} = K\psi \quad \text{... (8)}$$

where,

$$K = \frac{p_x^2}{2m} = \text{kinetic energy of the particle.}$$

Eq. (8) is the eigen value equation for the kinetic energy of the particle moving in the x-direction. The equation shows that :

(*i*) $-\frac{\hbar^2}{2m}\frac{\partial^2}{\partial x^2}$ is the operator, (*ii*) $\psi(x, t)$ is the eigen function of the operator,

and (*iii*) $K = \frac{p_x^2}{2m}$ is the eigen value of the operator. Hence $-\frac{h^2}{2m}\frac{\partial^2}{\partial x^2}$ is the kinetic energy operator for the motion of the particle in the x-direction. The operator is denoted by $\hat{K}$. Thus,

$$\hat{K} = -\frac{\hbar^2}{2m}\frac{\partial^2}{\partial x^2} \quad \text{... (9a)}$$

In three dimensions the operator for K is

$$\hat{K} = -\frac{\hbar^2}{2m}\nabla^2 \quad \text{... (9b)}$$

Operator for Total Energy

The total energy of the particle moving in the x-direction is given by

$$E = \frac{p_x^2}{2m} + V(x)$$

where $V(x)$ is the potential energy.

or

$$\frac{p_x^2}{2m} + V = E$$

Multiplying through by $\psi(x, t)$, we get

$$\frac{p_x^2}{2m}\psi + V\psi = E\psi$$

But

$$\frac{p_x^2}{2m}\psi = -\frac{\hbar^2}{2m}\frac{\partial^2\psi}{\partial x^2}$$

$\therefore$

$$-\frac{\hbar^2}{2m}\frac{\partial^2\psi}{\partial x^2} + V\psi = E\psi$$

$$\left[-\frac{\hbar^2}{2m}\frac{\partial^2}{\partial x^2} + V\right]\psi = E\psi \quad \text{... (10)}$$

This is the eigen value equation for the total energy E of the particle moving in the x-direction. The equation shows that (*i*) $-\frac{\hbar^2}{2m}\frac{\partial^2}{\partial x^2}+V$ is the operator, (*ii*) $\psi(x,t)$ is the eigen function of the operator, and (*iii*) E is the eigen value of the operator. Hence

$$-\frac{\hbar^2}{2m}\frac{\partial^2}{\partial x^2}+V$$

is the total energy operator for the motion of the particle along the x-direction. This operator is denoted by $\hat{H}_x$ and is called the Hamiltonian operator for the one-dimensional motion. Thus :

$$\hat{H}_x=-\frac{\hbar^2}{2m}\frac{\partial^2}{\partial x^2}+V$$

For the three-dimensional motion, the total energy operator will be

$$-\frac{\hbar^2}{2m}\left(\frac{\partial^2}{\partial x^2}+\frac{\partial^2}{\partial y^2}+\frac{\partial^2}{\partial z^2}\right)+V$$

or $$-\frac{\hbar^2}{2m}\nabla^2+V$$

where $$\nabla^2=\frac{\partial^2}{\partial x^2}+\frac{\partial^2}{\partial y^2}+\frac{\partial^2}{\partial z^2}$$

The total energy operator is denoted by $\hat{H}$, and is called the *Hamiltonian operator*. Thus

$$\hat{H}=-\frac{\hbar^2}{2m}\nabla^2+V \quad \text{... (11)}$$

Thus the Hamiltonian operator $\hat{H}$ is the differential operator which, operating on the wave function, reproduces the same wave function multiplied by the total energy. (For the total energy operator we write $\hat{H}$ and not $\hat{E}$ because the total energy is assumed to be expressed in terms of the momentum, similar to the Hamiltonian function H, which stands for the total energy in terms of the position and momentum coordinates).

Importance of the Hamiltonian Operator

Let u (x, y, z) be the wave function associated with a particle in motion. The three-dimensional time-independent Schrödinger equation is :

$$-\frac{\hbar^2}{2m}\nabla^2 u+Vu=Eu$$

or $$\left[-\frac{\hbar^2}{2m}\nabla^2+V\right]u=Eu \quad \text{... (12)}$$

or $$\hat{H}u=Eu$$

In Eq. (12) we find :

(*i*) On the left-side, the operator is the Hamiltonian operator which operates on the wave function $u\,(x, y, z)$.

(*ii*) On the right-side, Eu is the product of the total energy E and the wave function u.

Thus the Hamiltonian operator operating on the wave function reproduces the same function multiplied by the total energy E.

Therefore, the solutions of the time-independent Schrödinger equation are the eigen-functions of the Hamiltonian operator, and the eigen-values E of the operator are the only possible values of the total energy that a quantum mechanical system may possess.

Operator for the Total Energy in terms of the Differential with respect to Time

Differentiating Eq. (2) with respect to t, we get

$$\frac{\partial \psi}{\partial t} = A\left(\frac{i}{\hbar}\right)(-E)\,e^{i/h\,(p_x x - Et)}$$

$$= -\frac{i}{\hbar}E\psi = \frac{1}{i\hbar}E\psi$$

or

$$i\hbar\frac{\partial \psi}{\partial t} = E\psi \qquad \text{... (13)}$$

This equation shows that the total energy operator is

$$i\hbar\frac{\partial}{\partial t}$$

This operator is denoted by $\hat{E}$

$$\therefore \qquad \hat{E} = i\hbar\frac{\partial}{\partial t} \qquad \text{... (14)}$$

The total energy operator is defined as the operator, which, operating on the wave function, reproduces the wave function multiplied by the total energy.

Operators for Angular Momentum

In classical mechanics the angular momentum $\vec{L}$ of a particle is defined by

$$\vec{L} = \vec{r} \times \vec{p} \qquad \text{... (15)}$$

where $\vec{r}$ is the position vector of the particle relative to some arbitrary origin and $\vec{p}$ is its linear momentum. From Eq. (15) the components L_x, L_y and L_z of $\vec{L}$, along x, y and z axes, are respectively given by

$$L_x = yp_z - zp_y$$

$$L_y = zp_x - xp_z \qquad \text{... (16)}$$

$$L_z = xp_y - yp_x$$

Now using the expressions for the linear momentum operators, the operators for L_x, L_y and L_z are given by

$$\hat{L}_x = \frac{\hbar}{i}\left[y\frac{\partial}{\partial z} - z\frac{\partial}{\partial y}\right]$$

$$\hat{L}_y = \frac{\hbar}{i}\left[z\frac{\partial}{\partial x} - x\frac{\partial}{\partial z}\right] \quad \text{... (17)}$$

$$\hat{L}_z = \frac{\hbar}{i}\left[x\frac{\partial}{\partial y} - y\frac{\partial}{\partial x}\right]$$

These operators can be transformed into spherical polar coordinates (r, θ, ϕ). We do not give the details of the mathematical transformation, we state only the following expressions for the operators :

$$\hat{L}_x = \frac{\hbar}{i}\left[-\sin\phi\frac{\partial}{\partial\theta} - \cot\theta\cos\phi\frac{\partial}{\partial\phi}\right]$$

$$\hat{L}_y = \frac{\hbar}{i}\left[\cos\phi\frac{\partial}{\partial\theta} - \cot\theta\sin\phi\frac{\partial}{\partial\phi}\right] \quad \text{... (18)}$$

$$\hat{L}_z = \frac{\hbar}{i}\frac{\partial}{\partial\phi}$$

The operator for the square of the total angular momentum can be obtained from the above expressions as :

$$\hat{L}^2 = \hat{L}_x^2 + \hat{L}_y^2 + \hat{L}_z^2$$

$$= -\hbar^2\left[\frac{1}{\sin\theta}\frac{\partial}{\partial\theta}\left(\sin\theta\frac{\partial}{\partial\theta}\right) + \frac{1}{\sin^2\theta}\frac{\partial^2}{\partial\phi^2}\right] \quad \text{... (19)}$$

4.5 EXPECTATION VALUES

The expression for the wave function $\psi(x, y, z, t)$, which we get as a solution of Schrödinger's wave equation for a particle under given conditions contains all the information about the variables of the particle subject to the uncertainty principle. Except for those variables for which the solution gives quantized values, the information is in the form of probabilities and not definite values. The interpretation of $\psi^*(x, t).\psi(x, t)\,dx$ as the probability that the particle will be found over a small distance dx at position x, at time t makes it possible to find the *average or the expectation* value $< x >$ of the position of the particle along the x-axis. First we define the expectation value of a dynamical quantity.

The expectation value of a dynamical quantity is the mathematical expectation for the result of a single measurement. Or it is defined as the average of the results of a large number of measurements on independent identical systems, i.e., the systems represented by identical wave functions.

As an example, let us find the expectation value $< x >$ at time t of the position of an electron along the x-axis in an experimental arrangement such as the electron-diffraction experiment. Suppose we study the positions of a large number of electrons, N, all of which are described by the same wave function $\psi(x, t)$. Suppose at time t, for each electron, we make an observation for the electron's position and find the number of electrons with positions between x and $x + dx$. Then the probability that an electron will be in the position between x and $x + dx$

$$= \frac{\text{number of electrons in the positions between } x \text{ and } x + dx}{N}$$

But according to the interpretation of the wave function this probability is $\psi^*(x,t).\psi(x,t)\,dx$, where $\psi(x,t)$ is normalized.

$\therefore$ the number of electrons in the positions between x and $x + dx$

$$= N\psi^*(x,t)\,\psi(x,t)\,dx$$

Hence the sum of all the measured values $x_1, x_2, x_3, \ldots\ldots, x_N$ for all the N electrons is given by :

$$x_1 + x_2 + x_3 + \ldots\ldots + x_N = \int_{-\infty}^{+\infty} x\,N\,\psi^*(x,t)\,\psi(x,t)\,dx$$

$$\therefore \quad \frac{x_1 + x_2 + \ldots\ldots + x_N}{N} = \int_{-\infty}^{+\infty} x\,\psi^*(x,t)\,\psi(x,t)\,dx$$

The left-hand side of this equation is the expectation value $< x >$.

$$\therefore \quad < x > = \int_{-\infty}^{+\infty} \psi^*(x,t)\,x\,\psi(x,t)\,dx \quad \ldots (1)$$

where the function $\psi(x,t)$ is normalized.

In a similar way the expectation value of any function $f(x)$ is given by :

$$< f(x) > = \int_{-\infty}^{+\infty} \psi^*(x,t)\,f(x)\,\psi(x,t)\,dx \quad \ldots (2)$$

Thus, if the potential energy is a function of x, *i.e.* $V(x)$, its expectation value is given by:

$$< V > = \int_{-\infty}^{+\infty} \psi^*(x,t)\,V(x)\,(x,t)\,dx \quad \ldots (3)$$

To obtain the expectation value of the momentum p_x, we should express p_x in terms of x. But we cannot find p_x and x exactly and simultaneously. Therefore to find $<p_x>$, the function $f(x)$ in Eq. (2) is replaced by the operator $\hat{p}_x$. Thus :

$$< p_x > = \int_{-\infty}^{+\infty} \psi^*(x,t)\,\hat{p}_x\,\psi(x,t)\,dx$$

Since $\quad \hat{p}_x = \dfrac{\hbar}{i}\dfrac{\partial}{\partial x}$

$$\therefore \quad < p_x > = \int_{-\infty}^{+\infty} \psi^*(x,t)\,\frac{\hbar}{i}\frac{\partial}{\partial x}\,\psi(x,t)\,dx \quad \ldots (4)$$

In the same way the expectation value $<K>$ of the kinetic energy is given by

$$< K > = \int_{-\infty}^{+\infty} \psi^*(x,t)\,\hat{K}\,\psi(x,t)\,dx$$

$$= \int_{-\infty}^{+\infty} \psi^*(x,t)\left(-\frac{\hbar^2}{2m}\frac{\partial^2}{\partial x^2}\right)\psi(x,t)\,dx \quad \ldots (5)$$

This equation can be expressed in a simple form :

$$< K > = -\frac{\hbar^2}{2m}\int_{-\infty}^{+\infty} \psi^*\,\frac{\partial}{\partial x}\left(\frac{\partial \psi}{\partial x}\right)dx$$

Integrating by parts :

$$<K> = -\frac{\hbar^2}{2m}\left[\left\{\psi^*\frac{\partial\psi}{\partial x}\right\}_{-\infty}^{+\infty} - \int_{-\infty}^{+\infty}\frac{\partial\psi^*}{\partial x}\cdot\frac{\partial\psi}{\partial x}\,dx\right]$$

The first term on the right hand is zero, because according to the normalization condition: $\int_{-\infty}^{+\infty}\psi^*\psi\,dx = 1$, the function ψ^* is zero at $x = \pm\infty$

Hence
$$<K> = \frac{\hbar^2}{2m}\int_{-\infty}^{+\infty}\frac{\partial\psi^*}{\partial x}\cdot\frac{\partial\psi}{\partial x}\,dx \qquad \text{... (6a)}$$

$$= \frac{\hbar^2}{2m}\int_{-\infty}^{+\infty}\left|\frac{\partial\psi}{\partial x}\right|^2 dx \qquad \text{... (6b)}$$

4.6 POSTULATES OF QUANTUM MECHANICS

We have seen that in Schrödinger's formulation of quantum mechanics, a complex variable quantity $\psi(x, y, z, t)$, called the wave-function, is introduced to represent the wave associated with a particle in motion. Based on our discussion in the earlier sections, now we give five postulates which are sufficient to describe a single-particle system.

(1) For a system consisting of a particle moving in a field of conservative force, there is an associated complex wave function $\psi(x, y, z, t)$, where x, y, z are the space coordinates and t is the time. This function enables us to obtain a description of the behaviour of the system, consistent with the principle of uncertainty.

(2) With every observable dynamical quantity there is an operator. The operators corresponding to the pertinent dynamical quantities are :

Dynamical variable	*Symbol*	*Quantum Mechanical Operator*
Position	x y z	x y z
Momentum	p_x	$\frac{\hbar}{i}\frac{\partial}{\partial x}$
	p_y	$\frac{\hbar}{i}\frac{\partial}{\partial y}$
	p_z	$\frac{\hbar}{i}\frac{\partial}{\partial z}$
	$\vec{p}$	$\frac{\hbar}{i}\vec{\nabla}$
Total energy	E	$i\hbar\frac{\partial}{\partial t}$
Total energy	E	$-\frac{\hbar^2}{2m}\nabla^2 + V$
Kinetic energy	K	$-\frac{\hbar^2}{2m}\nabla^2$
Potential energy	$V(x, y, z)$	$V(x, y, z)$

All the operators have eigen-functions and eigen-values. The method of forming the Schrödinger wave equations is explained below :

(*i*) To obtain the three-dimensional time-dependent Schrödinger wave equation, we equate the two operators for the total energy E :

$$-\frac{\hbar^2}{2m}\nabla^2 + V = i\hbar\frac{\partial}{\partial t}$$

Now we multiply the identity $\psi(x, y, z, t) = \psi(x, y, z, t)$ by the above equation and we get,

$$-\frac{\hbar^2}{2m}\nabla^2\psi + V\psi = i\hbar\frac{\partial\psi}{\partial t}$$

This is the required equation.

(*ii*) To obtain the three-dimensional time-independent Schrödinger equation, we assume u (x, y, z) to be the eigen-function of the total energy operator $\left[-\frac{\hbar^2}{2m}\nabla^2 + V\right]$. Therefore we get

$$\left[-\frac{\hbar^2}{2m}\nabla^2 + V\right]u = Eu$$

This is the required equation.

(*iii*) To obtain the time-dependent part of the Schrödinger equation, we assume $f(t)$ to be the eigen-function of the total energy operator $i\hbar\frac{\partial}{\partial t}$. Therefore, we get, $i\hbar\frac{\partial f}{\partial t} = Ef$

This is the required equation.

(3) The wave function $\psi(x, y, z, t)$ and its partial derivatives $\frac{\partial\psi}{\partial x}, \frac{\partial\psi}{\partial y}, \frac{\partial\psi}{\partial z}$ must be finite, continuous and single valued for all values of x, y, z and t.

(4) The product $\psi(x, y, z, t)\,\psi^*(x, y, z, t)$, where ψ^* is the complex conjugate of ψ, is always a real quantity. The product is called the probability density and $\psi\psi^* d\tau$ is interpreted as the probability that the particle will be found in the volume element $d\tau$ at x, y, z and time t. Since the total probability that the particle will be somewhere in space must be equal to 1, we have:

$$\int_{-\infty}^{+\infty} \psi\,\psi^* d\tau = 1$$

The integral is taken over all space.

(5) The average or expectation value of an observable quantity α with which an operator $\hat{\alpha}$ is associated is defined by :

$$<\alpha> = \int_{-\infty}^{\infty} \psi^*\hat{\alpha}\,\psi\, d\tau,$$

where ψ is normalized, the integral being taken over all space.

4.7. TRANSITION PROBABILITY

For an atom which undergoes a transition from an intial excited state (*i.e.* higher energy state) ψ_k to a final state (*i.e.* lower energy state) ψ_i the transition probability is defined as follows :

Let an atom be in an initial excited state ψ_k. Let τ be the *mean lifetime* of the excited state. This is the time for which the atom would remain in the excited state. Let N be the number of photons generated by the atom in *time* τ. In the time τ when there is transition of atom from the state ψ_k to the state ψ_i, there is spontaneous emission of photons.

The probability per unit time of the transition of the atom from the initial excited state to the final state is called the transition probability A_{ik} and is defined as follows :

$$A_{ik} = \frac{\text{number of photons emitted per unit time}}{\text{number of photons generated in time } \tau}$$

$$= \frac{N/\tau}{N} = \frac{1}{\tau}$$

Thus, in this case the transition probability per unit time is the reciprocal of the mean lifetime of the atom in the excited state.

SOLVED EXAMPLES

Example 4.1. *A particle moving along the positive direction of the x-axis in a region of potential energy V (x) is represented by a wave-packet given by :*

$$\psi(x, t) = \frac{1}{\sqrt{2\pi\hbar}} \int A(p)\, e^{i/\hbar\,(p_x x - Et)}\, dp$$

Using the expression for non-relativistic total energy, obtain the one-dimensional time-dependent Schrödinger wave equation.

Solution :

The total energy E of the particle is given by :

$$\frac{p_x^2}{2m} + V(x) = E \qquad \text{... (1)}$$

Now we have :

$$\psi(x, t) = \frac{1}{\sqrt{2\pi\hbar}} \int A(p)\, e^{i/\hbar\,(p_x x - Et)} \cdot dp \qquad \text{... (2)}$$

Differentiating this equation partially w.r. to x :

$$\frac{\partial\psi}{\partial x} = \frac{1}{\sqrt{2\pi\hbar}} \int A(p) \left(\frac{i}{\hbar}\right) p_x\, e^{i/\hbar\,(p_x x - Et)} \cdot dp$$

And

$$\frac{\partial^2\psi}{\partial x^2} = \frac{1}{\sqrt{2\pi\hbar}} \int A(p) \left(\frac{i}{\hbar}\right)^2 p_x^2\, e^{i/\hbar\,(p_x x - Et)} \cdot dp$$

$$\therefore \quad -\frac{\hbar^2}{2m} \frac{\partial^2\psi}{\partial x^2} = \frac{1}{\sqrt{2\pi\hbar}} \int \frac{p_x^2}{2m} A(p)\, e^{i/\hbar\,(p_x x - Et)} \cdot dp \qquad \text{... (3)}$$

Differentiating Eq. (2) partially w.r. to t

$$\frac{\partial\psi}{\partial t} = \frac{1}{\sqrt{2\pi\hbar}} \int A(p) \left(\frac{i}{\hbar}\right) (-E)\, e^{i/\hbar\,(p_x x - Et)} \cdot dp$$

$$\therefore \qquad i\hbar \frac{\partial \psi}{\partial t} = \frac{1}{\sqrt{2\pi\hbar}} \int E\, A(p)\, e^{i/\hbar (p_x x - Et)} \cdot dp \qquad \text{... (4)}$$

Subtracting Eq. (4) from (3)

$$-\frac{\hbar}{2m} \frac{\partial^2 \psi}{\partial x^2} - i\hbar \frac{\partial \psi}{\partial t} = \frac{1}{\sqrt{2\pi\hbar}} \int \left(\frac{p_x^2}{2m} - E \right) A(p)\, e^{i/\hbar (p_x x - Et)} \cdot dp$$

Now using Eq. (1),

$$-\frac{\hbar^2}{2m} \frac{\partial^2 \psi}{\partial x^2} - i\hbar \frac{\partial \psi}{\partial t} = -V(x)\, \psi$$

or

$$-\frac{\hbar}{2m} \frac{\partial^2 \psi}{\partial x^2} + V\psi = i\hbar \frac{\partial \psi}{\partial t} \qquad \text{... (5)}$$

This is the one-dimensional time-dependent Schrödinger wave equation.

Example 4.2. *A particle is in motion along a line between $x = 0$ and $x = a$ with zero potential energy, and at points for which $x < 0$ and $x > a$ the potential energy is infinite. The wave function for the particle in the nth state is given by :*

$$\psi_n = A \sin \frac{n\pi x}{a}$$

Find the expression for the normalized wave function.

Solution :

For the nth state the probability that the particle will be between x and $x + dx$ is :

$$P_n(x)\, dx = |\psi_n(x)|^2\, dx$$

$$= A^2 \sin^2 \frac{n\pi x}{a}\, dx$$

There is only one particle in the region from $x = 0$ to $x = a$ and at all times it is somewhere in this region.

Therefore,

$$\int P_n(x)\, dx = \int_0^a |\psi_n(x)|^2\, dx = 1$$

or

$$\int_0^a A^2 \sin^2 \frac{n\pi x}{a}\, dx = 1$$

$$A^2 \int_0^a \frac{1}{2} \left[1 - \cos \frac{2n\pi x}{a} \right] dx = 1$$

$$\frac{A^2}{2} \left[x - \frac{a}{2\pi n} \sin \frac{2n\pi x}{a} \right]_0^a = 1$$

The second term of the integrated expression is zero at both the limits. Therefore

$$\frac{A^2}{2} a = 1$$

so $$A=\sqrt{\frac{2}{a}}$$

$\therefore$ the normalized wave function is :

$$\psi_n(x)=\sqrt{\frac{2}{a}}\sin\frac{n\pi x}{a}$$

Example 4.3. *Show that :*

$$(\Delta x)^2 = <(x-<x>)^2> = <x^2> - <x>^2$$

where Δx is the uncertainty in the position and $<f(x)>$ denotes the average of $f(x)$ in a state described by the wave function $\psi(x)$.

Solution :

The uncertainty Δx in the x-coordinate of a particle in motion is defined as the *square root of the mean square deviation* in the position.

Let $x_1, x_2, x_3, ..., x_N$ be the N individual observations of the position of the particle along the positive direction of x. The *mean value* $<x>$ of these observations is given by :

$$<x> = \frac{x_1+x_2+x_3+.....+x_N}{N} \quad ...(1)$$

The deviations of the individual values from the mean value are :

$$(x_1-<x>),\ (x_2-<x>),\ ....,\ (x_N-<x>)$$

The mean square deviation is denoted by $<(x-<x>)^2>$ and it is given by

$$<(x-<x>)^2> = \frac{(x_1-<x>)^2+(x_2-<x>)^2+.....+(x_N-<x>)^2}{N}$$

$$= \frac{(x_1^2+x_2^2+....+x_N^2)-2(x_1+x_2+...+x_N)<x>+N<x>^2}{N}$$

$$= \frac{x_1^2+x_2^2+...+x_N^2}{N} - \frac{2(x_1+x_2+...+x_N)<x>}{N} + <x>^2$$

$$= <x^2> - 2<x><x> + <x>^2$$

$$= <x^2> - <x>^2 \quad ...(2)$$

Now according to the definition of Δx :

$$\Delta x = <(x-<x>)^2>^{1/2}$$

$$\therefore \quad (\Delta x)^2 = <(x-<x>)^2> \quad ...(3)$$

Hence from Eqs. (2) and (3), we have

$$(\Delta x)^2 = <(x-<x>)^2> = <x^2> - <x>^2$$

Example 4.4. *Show that :*

$$<p_x x> - <x\, p_x> = \frac{\hbar}{i}$$

Solution : The expectation value $<p_x x>$ is given by :

$$< p_x x > = \int_{-\infty}^{\infty} \psi^* \hat{p}_x \hat{x} \psi \, dx$$

$$= \int_{-\infty}^{\infty} \psi^* \frac{\hbar}{i} \frac{\partial}{\partial x} (x \psi) \, dx$$

$$= \frac{\hbar}{i} \int_{-\infty}^{\infty} \psi^* \left(x \frac{\partial \psi}{\partial x} + \psi \right) dx$$

$$= \frac{\hbar}{i} \left[\int_{-\infty}^{\infty} x \psi^* \frac{\partial \psi}{\partial x} dx + \int_{-\infty}^{\infty} \psi^* \psi \, dx \right]$$

$$= \frac{\hbar}{i} \left[\int_{-\infty}^{\infty} x \psi^* \frac{\partial \psi}{\partial x} dx + 1 \right] \quad \text{... (1)}$$

The expectation value $< x\, p_x >$ is given by :

$$< x\, p_x > = \int_{-\infty}^{\infty} \psi^* \hat{x} \hat{p}_x \psi \, dx$$

$$= \int_{-\infty}^{\infty} \psi^* x \frac{\hbar}{i} \frac{\partial}{\partial x} (\psi) \, dx$$

$$= \frac{\hbar}{i} \int_{-\infty}^{\infty} \psi^* x \frac{\partial \psi}{\partial x} dx = \frac{\hbar}{i} \int_{-\infty}^{\infty} x \psi^* \frac{\partial \psi}{\partial x} dx \quad \text{... (2)}$$

Subtracting Eq. (2) from Eq. (1), we get :

$$< p_x\, x > - < x\, p_x > = \frac{\hbar}{i}$$

QUESTIONS AND PROBLEMS

1. Deduce the time-independent Schrödinger equation. Give the significance of the wave function. (N.U., 2006)
2. (*a*) Derive the time-independent Schrödinger wave equation for a particle. (Arunachal, 2005)

   (*b*) Give the physical meaning of the wave function. What do you understand by normalized wave function ?
3. (*a*) Obtain the time-dependent Schrödinger wave equation for a particle. (Madras, 2004)

   (*b*) Separate the wave function into time-dependent and time-independent parts and obtain the steady state Schrödinger equation.
4. Show that the dimensions of $|\psi (x, y, z, t)|$ are $[L^{-3/2}]$, where L stands for unit of length.
5. A particle moving along the positive direction of the x-axis in a region of potential energy $V(x)$ is represented by a wave-packet given by :

   $$\psi (x, t) = \frac{1}{\sqrt{2\pi\hbar}} \int_{-\infty} A(p)\, e^{i/\hbar (px - Et)} dp$$

   by differentiating this equation and using the expression for non-relativistic total energy, obtain the one-dimensional time-dependent Schrödinger wave equation.

6. If $\psi_1(x,t)$ and $\psi_2(x,t)$ are both solutions of the time-dependent Schrödinger equation for the motion of a particle with potential energy $V(x)$, prove that the linear combination,

$$\psi(x,t) = A_1\,\psi_1(x,t) + A_2\psi_2(x,t),$$

where A_1 and A_2 are constants, is also a solution.

7. For one-dimensional motion of a particle of mass m, prove that the expectation value of its kinetic energy is given by :

$$<K> = \frac{\hbar^2}{2m}\int_{-\infty}^{\infty}\frac{\partial\psi}{\partial x}\frac{\partial\psi^*}{\partial x}\,dx$$

8. Using the operator representation of the x-component of the momentum of a particle prove that :

$$(x\,\hat{p}_x - \hat{p}_x\,x)\,\psi = i\hbar\psi$$

where ψ is an arbitrary function.

Solution :

$$(x\,\hat{p}_x - \hat{p}_x\,x)\,\psi = \left[x\frac{\hbar}{i}\frac{\partial\psi}{\partial x} - \frac{\hbar}{i}\frac{\partial(x\,\psi)}{\partial x}\right]$$

$$= \frac{\hbar}{i}\left[x\frac{\partial\psi}{\partial x} - x\frac{\partial\psi}{\partial x} - \psi\right]$$

$$= -\frac{\hbar}{i}\psi = i\hbar\,\psi$$

9. State any two postulates of quantum mechanics. (N.U., 2006)

10. Using time dependent form of the wave-function deduce operators for momentum and energy. (N.U., 2006)

11. What is eigen value and eigen function ? (N.U., 2006)

CHAPTER 5

APPLICATIONS OF QUANTUM MECHANICS

In this chapter we shall study application of Schrödinger's wave equation to the following cases :

(1) particle in a one-dimensional box,
(2) particle in a three-dimensional box,
(3) harmonic oscillator,
(4) reflection at a step potential, and
(5) transmission across a potential barrier.

5.1. PARTICLE IN A ONE-DIMENSIONAL BOX

Particle in an Infinitely Deep One-Dimensional Potential Well

We consider the one-dimensional motion along x-axis of a particle of mass m in a hollow rectangular box having perfectly rigid walls. Let the origin be at one corner of the box and the x-axis be perpendicular to the parallel opposite walls (Fig. 5.1). Let a be the distance between the walls so that the motion along the x-axis is confined between $x = 0$ and $x = a$.

Suppose inside the box, *i.e.*, in the region.

$$0 < x < a$$

there is no force acting on the particle so that in this region the potential energy $V(x)$ is zero. When the particle collides with the perfectly rigid walls, there is no loss of energy so that the total energy E of the particle remains constant. In order to leave the region, the particle will have to do an infinite amount of work. Since this is not possible, it cannot exist outside the box. Hence for,

$$x \leq 0 \quad \text{and} \quad x \geq a$$

the wave-function $\psi(x) = 0$.

The potential energy curve for the particle is shown in Fig. 5.2 ; because of its appearance it is called a *square well potential of infinite depth*.

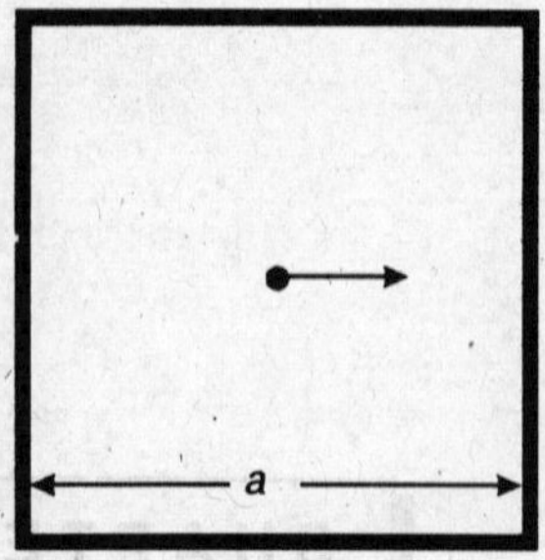

Fig. 5.1

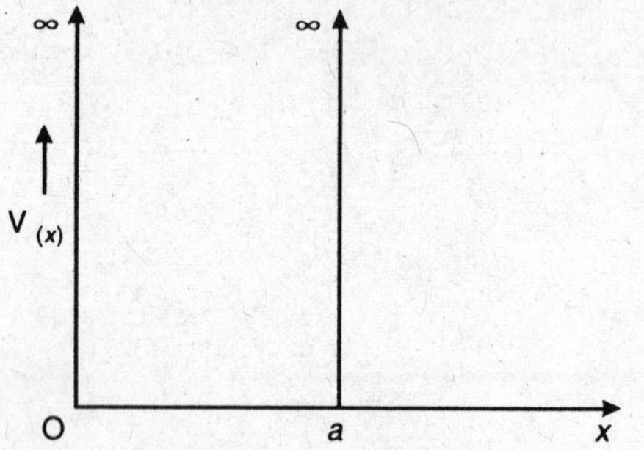

Fig 5.2

Wave Equation for the Particle

For the motion of the particle along the x-axis inside the box, where $V(x) = 0$, the time-independent Schrödinger wave equation is :

$$-\frac{\hbar^2}{2m}\frac{d^2\psi}{dx^2} = E\psi$$

where E is the total energy of the particle,

or $$\frac{d^2\psi}{dx^2} + \frac{2mE}{\hbar^2}\psi = 0 \quad \text{... (1)}$$

or $$\frac{d^2\psi}{dx^2} + k^2\psi = 0 \quad \text{... (2)}$$

where, $$k = \sqrt{\frac{2mE}{\hbar^2}} \quad \text{... (3)}$$

For a paticular value of the energy E, k is constant.

Solution of the Equation

The general solution of Eq. (2) is :

$$\psi(x) = A\sin kx + B\cos kx \quad \text{... (4)}$$

where, A and B are constants of integration. We have the boundary conditions :

(*i*) at $x = 0$, $\psi(x) = 0$, and

(*ii*) at $x = a$, $\psi(x) = 0$

From the first condition, we get,

$$B = 0$$

Therefore, from Eq. (4) we have,

$$\psi(x) = A\sin kx \quad \text{... (5)}$$

Now using the second condition, we have,

$$\psi(a) = A\sin ka = 0 \quad \text{... (6)}$$

We cannot take $A = 0$, because there will then be no solution. Hence Eq. (6) is satisfied only when,

$$ka = n\pi$$

or $$k = \frac{n\pi}{a} \quad \text{... (7)}$$

where, $n = 1, 2, 3, ...$

We cannot take $n = 0$, because for $n = 0$, $k = 0$, $E = 0$ and hence $\psi(x) = 0$ everywhere in the box. This means that a particle with zero energy cannot be present in the box. That is, a particle in the box, cannot have zero energy. Hence the wave-functions for the motion in the region $0 < x < a$ are given by :

$$\psi_n(x) = A \sin \frac{n\pi x}{a} \quad \text{... (8)}$$

Eigen Values of Energy

Substituting the value of k in Eq. (7), we get :

$$\sqrt{\frac{2mE}{\hbar^2}} = \frac{n\pi}{a}$$

From this equation we get :

$$E = \frac{n^2\pi^2\hbar^2}{2ma^2}$$

or $$E_n = \frac{n^2\pi^2\hbar^2}{2ma^2} \quad \text{... (9)}$$

This equation shows that the eigen-values of the energy are discrete (not continuous). These values are called the energy-levels of the particle.

Since, $\hbar = \frac{h}{2\pi}$, we also have

$$E_n = \frac{n^2h^2}{8ma^2}$$

From Eq. (9), we get the following conclusions :

(1) The lowest energy of the particle is obtained by putting $n = 1$ in Eq. (9) and it is

$$E_1 = \frac{\pi^2\hbar^2}{2ma^2} \quad \text{... (10)}$$

It is called the *ground state energy-level of the particle.* The values of E_n, in terms of E_1, are given by :

$$E_n = n^2 E_1 \quad \text{... (11)}$$

(2) The possible values of energy of the particle in the potential box are discrete corresponding to $n = 1, 2, 3, ...$

(3) The spacing between the nth energy-level and the next higher level increases as $(n+1)^2 E_1 - n^2 E_1 = (2n+1) E_1$.

The wave-functions ψ_n corresponding to E_n are called *eigen-functions* of the particle. The integer n corresponding to the energy E_n is called the quantum number of the energy-level E_n. Fig. 5.3 shows the energy-level diagram for the particle.

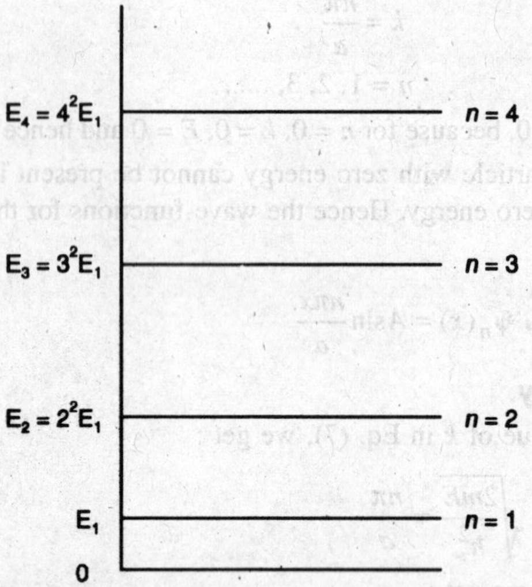

Fig. 5.3

Normalization of the Wave-Functions

The wave-functions for the motion of the particle are :

$$\psi_n(x) = A \sin \frac{n\pi x}{a}, \quad \text{... (8)}$$

in the region $0 < x < a$

and $\psi_n(x) = 0$, in the region $x < 0; x > a$.

The total probability that the particle is somewhere in the box must be unity. Therefore, we have :

$$\int_0^a |\psi_n(x)|^2 \, dx = 1 \quad \text{... (12)}$$

$$\int_0^a A^2 \sin^2 \frac{n\pi x}{a} \, dx = 1$$

$$A^2 \int_0^a \frac{1}{2}\left[1 - \cos \frac{2n\pi x}{a}\right] dx = 1$$

$$\frac{A^2}{2}\left[x - \frac{a}{2\pi n} \sin \frac{2n\pi x}{a}\right]_0^a = 1$$

The second term of the integrated expression becomes zero at both limits. Therefore,

$$\frac{A^2 a}{2} = 1 \quad \text{... (13)}$$

or

$$A = \sqrt{\frac{2}{a}} \quad \text{... (14)}$$

Hence the normalized wave function is

$$\psi_n(x) = \sqrt{\frac{2}{a}} \sin \frac{n\pi x}{a}$$

The wave-functions for the first three values of n are shown in Fig. 5.4. It is evident that the wave-function ψ_1 has two nodes at $x = 0$ and at $x = a$. The wave-function ψ_2 has three nodes at $x = 0$, $x = \frac{a}{2}$ and at $x = a$. The wave-function ψ_3 has four nodes at $x = 0$, $x = \frac{a}{3}$, $x = \frac{2a}{3}$ and at $x = a$. Thus, the wave-function ψ_n will have $(n + 1)$ nodes.

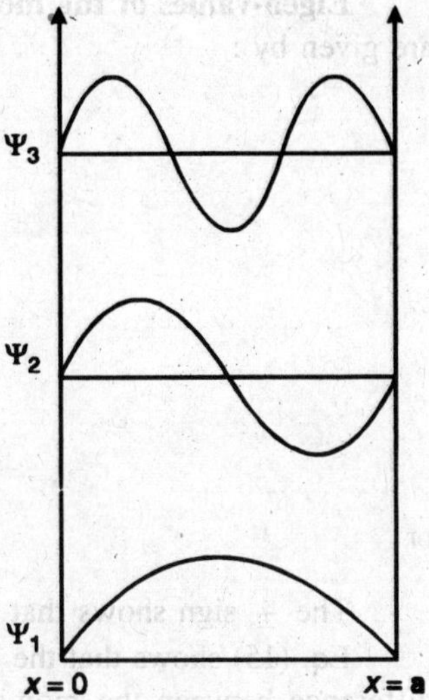

Fig. 5.4

Orthogonality of the Wave-Functions

Two eigenfunctions Ψ_m and Ψ_n of one-dimensional schrodinger's equation are said to be orthogonal if they satisfy the equation

$$\int \Psi_m^* \Psi_n dx = 0, \qquad \text{when} \quad m \neq n$$

$$= 1, \qquad \text{when} \quad m = n$$

Let $\psi_n(x)$ and $\psi_m(x)$ be the normalized wave-functions of the particle in the interval $(0, a)$ corresponding to the different energy-levels E_n and E_m respectively. These wave-functions are :

$$\psi_n(x) = \sqrt{\frac{2}{a}} \cdot \sin \frac{n\pi x}{a}$$

$$\psi_m(x) = \sqrt{\frac{2}{a}} \sin \frac{m\pi x}{a}$$

where m and n are integers.

In this case the functions are real, therefore :

$$\psi_n^*(x) = \psi_n(x),$$

and
$$\psi_m^*(x) = \psi_m(x)$$

Now we have, when $m \neq n$

$$\int_0^a \psi_m^* \psi_n \, dx = \frac{2}{a} \int_0^a \sin \frac{m\pi x}{a} \sin \frac{n\pi x}{a} \, dx$$

$$= \frac{1}{a} \int_0^a \left[\cos \frac{(m-n)\pi x}{a} - \cos \frac{(m+n)\pi x}{a} \right] dx$$

$$= \frac{1}{2a} \left[\frac{a}{\pi(m-n)} \sin \frac{(m-n)\pi x}{a} - \frac{a}{\pi(m+n)} \sin \frac{(m+n)\pi x}{a} \right]_0^a = 0$$

$\therefore$ both the terms are zero at $x = 0$, and at $x = a$.

Hence, the functions are mutually orthogonal in the interval $(0, a)$. These functions are also normalized in this interval. The wave-functions which, are normalized and mutually orthogonal in an interval, are said to form an orthogonal set in this interval. Since the wave-functions are zero outside the interval $(0, a)$, they are also orthogonal in the whole range of x, *i.e.*, in the interval $(-\infty, \infty)$.

Eigen-values of the momentum : The eigen values of the momentum p_n along the x-axis are given by :

$$p_n^2 = 2mE_n = 2m\frac{n^2\pi^2\hbar^2}{2ma^2}$$

$$= \frac{n^2\pi^2\hbar^2}{a^2}$$

$$\therefore \qquad p_n = \pm\frac{n\pi\hbar}{a} \qquad \text{... (15)}$$

or

$$p_n = \pm\frac{nh}{2a} \qquad \text{... (16)}$$

The $\pm$ sign shows that the particle is moving back and forth in the potential box.

Eq. (15) shows that the eigen-values of the momentum of the particle are discrete, and the difference between the momenta corresponding to two consecutive energy-levels is constant, equal to $\frac{h}{2a}$.

Probability of Location of the Particle over a Small Range between x and $x + dx$

According to quantum mechanics, the probability $P(x)\,dx$ that the particle be found over a small distance dx at the position x is given by :

$$P(x)\,dx = |\psi_n(x)|^2\,dx$$

$$= \frac{2}{a}\sin^2\frac{n\pi x}{a}\,dx \qquad \text{... (17)}$$

so that the probability-density for the one dimensional motion is :

$$P(x) = \frac{2}{a}\sin^2\frac{n\pi x}{a} \qquad \text{... (18)}$$

The probability-density is maximum when :

$$\frac{n\pi x}{a} = \frac{\pi}{2}, \frac{3\pi}{2}, \frac{5\pi}{2}$$

or

$$x = \frac{a}{2n}, \frac{3a}{2n}, \frac{5a}{2n}, \qquad \text{... (19)}$$

Thus for the state defined by $n = 1$, the most probable position of the particle is at $x = \frac{a}{2}$.

For $n = 2$, the most probable positions are at :

$$x = \frac{a}{4} \quad \text{and} \quad x = \frac{3a}{4}.$$

For $n = 3$, the most probable positions are at :

$$x = \frac{a}{6}, x = \frac{3a}{6}, x = \frac{5a}{6}$$

The variation of the probability densities with x for first three values of n are shown in Fig. 5.5.

Thus the quantum mechanical result is quite different from the classical one. According to classical mechanics, a particle in such a potential box would travel with a uniform velocity from one wall to the other, and at the walls it would be perfectly reflected. Therefore, the probability of finding the particle within a small distance dx anywhere in the box is the same and is equal to $\frac{dx}{a}$. The probability-density $\frac{1}{a}$ is represented by a straight line at height $\frac{1}{a}$ above the x-axis as shown in Fig. 5.5.

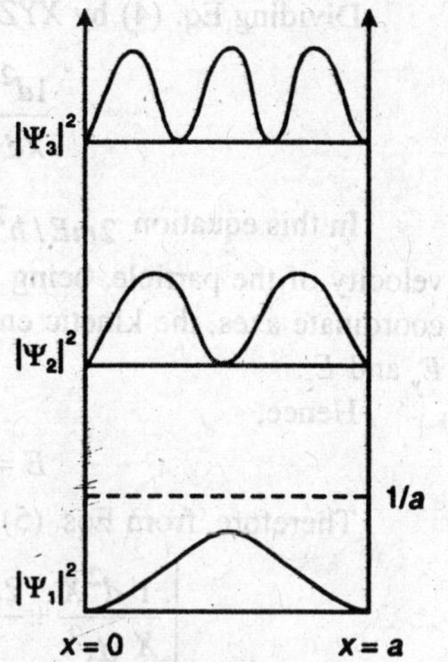

Fig. 5.5

5.2. PARTICLE IN A RECTANGULAR THREE-DIMENSIONAL BOX

Let a particle of mass m be in motion in a rectangular potential box (Fig. 5.6) with sides of lengths a, b, c, parallel to the x, y and z-axes respectively. Suppose there is no force acting on the particle inside the box, so that in the region,

$$0 < x < a$$
$$0 < y < b$$
$$0 < z < c$$

the potential energy $V(x, y, z) = 0$

and outside the box $V(x, y, z) = \infty$

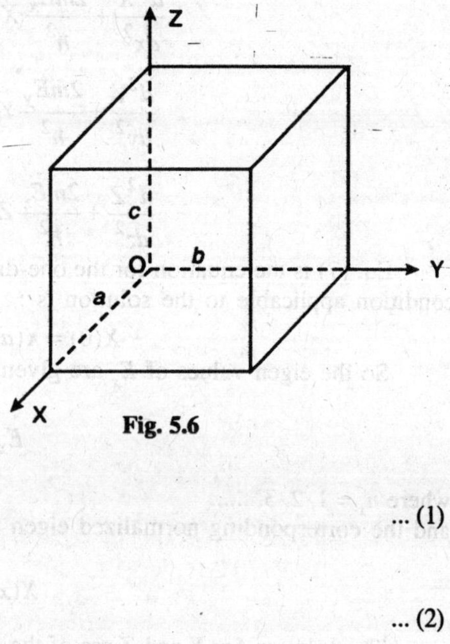

Fig. 5.6

Wave Equation for the Particle

For the motion of the particle inside the box, the Schrödinger time-independent wave equation is :

$$-\frac{\hbar^2}{2m}\nabla^2\psi = E\psi \qquad \text{... (1)}$$

or
$$\frac{\partial^2\psi}{\partial x^2}+\frac{\partial^2\psi}{\partial y^2}+\frac{\partial^2\psi}{\partial z^2}+\frac{2m}{\hbar^2}E\psi = 0 \qquad \text{... (2)}$$

We assume that the wave-function $\psi(x, y, z)$ is equal to the product of three functions X, Y, and Z each of which is a function of one variable only.

Thus we have :

$$\psi(x, y, z) = X(x)\,Y(y)\,Z(z) \qquad \text{... (3)}$$

Substituting this equation in Eq. (2), we get,

$$YZ\frac{d^2X}{dx^2}+ZX\frac{d^2Y}{dy^2}+XY\frac{d^2Z}{dz^2}+\frac{2mE}{\hbar^2}XYZ = 0 \qquad \text{... (4)}$$

We have used ordinary derivatives instead of partial derivatives because each of the functions X, Y and Z is a function of one variable only.

Dividing Eq. (4) by *XYZ*, we get :

$$\frac{1}{X}\frac{d^2X}{dx^2}+\frac{1}{Y}\frac{d^2Y}{dy^2}+\frac{1}{Z}\frac{d^2Z}{dz^2}+\frac{2mE}{\hbar^2}=0 \quad \text{... (5)}$$

In this equation $2mE/\hbar^2$ is a constant for a particular value of the kinetic energy. Since the velocity of the particle, being a vector quantity, can be resolved into three components along the coordinate axes, the kinetic energy *E* can be expressed as the sum of the corresponding terms E_x, E_y and E_z.

Hence,

$$E = E_x + E_y + E_z \quad \text{... (6)}$$

Therefore, from Eqs. (5) and (6), we get

$$\left[\frac{1}{X}\frac{d^2X}{dx^2}+\frac{2mE_x}{\hbar^2}\right]+\left[\frac{1}{Y}\frac{d^2Y}{dy^2}+\frac{2mE_y}{\hbar^2}\right]+\left[\frac{1}{Z}\frac{d^2Z}{dz^2}+\frac{2mE_z}{\hbar}\right]=0$$

This equation gives three independent equations :

$$\frac{d^2X}{dx^2}+\frac{2mE_x}{\hbar^2}X=0 \quad \text{... (7)}$$

$$\frac{d^2Y}{dy^2}+\frac{2mE_y}{\hbar^2}Y=0 \quad \text{... (8)}$$

$$\frac{d^2Z}{dz^2}+\frac{2mE_z}{\hbar^2}Z=0 \quad \text{... (9)}$$

Eq. (7) is the equation for the one-dimensional case discussed in Section 5.1. The boundary condition applicable to the solution is :

$$X(0) = X(a) = 0$$

So the eigen values of E_x are given by :

$$E_x = \frac{\pi^2\hbar^2}{2ma^2}n_x^2 \quad \text{... (10)}$$

where $n_x = 1, 2, 3, ...$
and the corresponding normalized eigen functions are given by :

$$X(x) = \sqrt{\frac{2}{a}}\sin\frac{n_x\pi x}{a} \quad \text{... (11)}$$

The solution for *Y* and *Z* are of the same form, therefore, we have :

$$E_y = \frac{\pi^2\hbar^2}{2mb^2}n_y^2 \quad \text{... (12)}$$

$$Y(y) = \sqrt{\frac{2}{b}}\sin\frac{n_y\pi y}{b} \quad \text{... (13)}$$

and

$$E_z = \frac{\pi^2\hbar^2}{2mc^2}n_z^2 \quad \text{... (14)}$$

$$Z(z) = \sqrt{\frac{2}{c}}\sin\frac{n_z\pi z}{c} \quad \text{... (15)}$$

EIGEN VALUES OF ENERGY

Substituting the expressions for E_x, E_y and E_z in Eq. (6), we get :

$$E_{n_x, n_y, n_z} = \frac{\pi^2 \hbar^2}{2m}\left[\frac{n_x^2}{a^2}+\frac{n_y^2}{b^2}+\frac{n_z^2}{c^2}\right] \qquad \text{... (16)}$$

where $n_x = 1, 2, 3, ...$
$n_y = 1, 2, 3, ...$
$n_z = 1, 2, 3, ...$

This equation gives the eigen values of the energy of the particle. These values are called the energy-levels of the particle.

Wave-Function

The total normalized wave-function inside the box for the stationary states is given by :

$$\psi_{n_x, n_y, n_z}(x, y, z) = X(x)\,Y(y)\,Z(z)$$

$$= \sqrt{\frac{8}{abc}}\sin\frac{n_x \pi x}{a}\cdot\sin\frac{n_y \pi y}{b}\cdot\sin\frac{n_z \pi z}{c}, \qquad \text{... (17)}$$

where n_x, n_y and n_z are integers.

The wave-function is zero outside the box. It may easily be proved that the wave-function is normalized, because :

$$\frac{8}{abc}\int_0^a\left(\sin\frac{n_x \pi x}{a}\right)^2 dx\cdot\int_0^b\left(\sin\frac{n_y \pi y}{b}\right)^2 dy\cdot\int_0^c\left(\sin\frac{n_z \pi z}{c}\right)^2 dz = 1$$

From Eqs. (17) and (16) we *get the following conclusions :*

(1) Three integers n_x, n_y, and n_z, which are called *quantum numbers*, are required to describe each stationary state. If we change the sign of the quantum numbers, there is no change in the energy and in the wave-function except that the minus sign will appear on the right hand side of Eq. (17). Therefore, all the stationary states are given by the positive integral values of n_x, n_y and n_z. No quantum number can be zero, because if any one of them is taken zero, then $\psi(x, y, z) = 0$, which would mean that the particle does not exist in the box.

(2) The lowest possible energy, *i.e.*, the energy in the ground state, occurs when $n_x = n_y = n_z = 1$ and it depends on the values of *a, b* and *c*.

(3) If the particle is confined in a cubical box in which *a* = *b* = *c* = *L*, the eigen-values of energy are given by :

$$E_{n_x, n_y, n_z} = \frac{\pi^2 \hbar^2}{2mL^2}(n_x^2 + n_y^2 + n_z^2) \qquad \text{... (18)}$$

In this case the energy of the particle in the ground state is given by :

$$E_{111} = \frac{3\pi^2 \hbar^2}{2mL^2} \qquad \text{... (19)}$$

No other state will have this energy, and this state has only one wave-function. Therefore, the ground state and the energy-level are said to be *non-degenerate*.

(4) In a cubical box, the energy depends on the sum of the squares of the quantum numbers. Consequently the particle having the same energy in an excited state will have several different stationary states, or different wave-functions. Such states and energy-levels are said to be *degenerate*.

For example for the first excited state, the values of the quantum number are :

n_x	n_y	n_z
2	1	1
1	2	1
1	1	2

Thus there are three different eigen functions and hence three different stationary states

Each state has the same energy $\frac{6\pi^2\hbar^2}{2mL^2}$. Therefore the first excited state is said to be triply degenerate or three-fold degenerate.

Degree of Degeneracy : The number of independent wave-functions for the stationary states of an energy-level is called the degree of degeneracy of the level.

For a particle in a cubical box a number of energy-levels with the corresponding quantum numbers and the degree of degeneracy are given in the following table :

Energy Levels	*Quantum Numbers (n_x, n_y, n_z)*	*Degree of Degeneracy*
$\frac{3\pi^2\hbar^2}{2mL^2}$	(111)	Non-degenerate
$\frac{6\pi^2\hbar^2}{2mL^2}$	(211), (121), (112)	Three-fold degenerate
$\frac{9\pi^2\hbar^2}{2mL^2}$	(221), (212), (122)	Three-fold degenerate
$\frac{11\pi^2\hbar^2}{2mL^2}$	(311), (131) (113)	Three-fold degenerate
$\frac{12\pi^2\hbar^2}{2mL^2}$	(222)	Non-degenerate
$\frac{14\pi^2\hbar^2}{2mL^2}$	(123), (132), (213) (231), (312), (321)	Six-fold degenerate
$\frac{17\pi^2\hbar^2}{2mL^2}$	(322), (232), (223)	Three-fold degenerate
$\frac{18\pi^2\hbar^2}{2mL^2}$	(411), (141), (114).	Three-fold degenerate
$\frac{19\pi^2\hbar^2}{2mL^2}$	(331), (313), (133)	Three-fold degenerate
$\frac{21\pi^2\hbar^2}{2mL^2}$	(421), (412), (241) (214), (124), (142)	Six-fold degenerate

5.3. SIMPLE HARMONIC OSCILLATOR

When a particle oscillates about its means position along a straight line under the action of a force which (*i*) is directed towards the mean position and (*ii*) is proportional to the displacement at any instant from this position, the motion of the particle is said to be simple harmonic, and the oscillating particle is called a simple harmonic oscillator, or a linear harmonic oscillator.

The harmonic oscillator is an important example of periodic motion because it serves as an exact or an approximate model for many problems in classical or quantum physics. At temperatures above 0° K, the atoms in a crystal are temporarily displaced from their normal positions in the structure, due to absorption of thermal energy. Consequently, interatomic forces obeying Hooke's law act on the displaced atoms. Under the action of such restoring forces each atom vibrates about its normal position which is the correct position in the ideal structure. Thus the vibrations of each atom are similar to those of a simple harmonic oscillator.

5.3. (*a*) One-Dimensional Simple Harmonic Oscillator in Classical Mechanics

Let the equilibrium position of a linear harmonic oscillator of mass m be the origin 0, and the straight line of its motion be the x-axis. When x is its displacement from 0, the restoring force F is given by :

$$F = -kx$$

where k is a positive constant.

According to the second law of motion :

$$F = m\frac{d^2x}{dt^2}$$

Therefore, its Newtonian equation of motion is :

$$m\frac{d^2x}{dt^2} = -kx$$

or
$$\frac{d^2x}{dt^2} = -\left(\frac{k}{m}\right)x = -\omega^2 x$$

where
$$\omega = \sqrt{\frac{k}{m}}$$

The general solution of this equation is :

$$x = A\sin(\omega t + \theta) \qquad \text{... (1)}$$

where A and θ are constants, which may be determined from the initial conditions. Eq. (1) shows that the particle performs simple harmonic oscillations with frequency :

$$\nu = \frac{\omega}{2\pi} = \frac{1}{2\pi}\sqrt{\frac{k}{m}} \qquad \text{... (2)}$$

where ω is called the angular frequency of oscillations.

The potential energy $V(x)$ at the displacement x is given by :

$$V = \int_0^V dV = \int_0^x \frac{dV}{dx}\,dx$$

But
$$\frac{dV}{dx} = -F = -(-kx) = kx$$

$$\therefore \quad V = \int_0^x kx\,dx = \frac{1}{2}kx^2 = \frac{1}{2}m\omega^2x^2 \qquad \text{... (3)}$$

And the kinetic energy K at the displacement x is given by :

$$K = \frac{1}{2} m \left(\frac{dx}{dt} \right)^2 = \frac{1}{2} m A^2 \omega^2 \cos^2 (\omega t + \theta)$$

$$= \frac{1}{2} m\omega^2 A^2 [1 - \sin^2 (\omega t + \theta)]$$

$$= \frac{1}{2} m\omega^2 (A^2 - x^2) \quad \text{... (4)}$$

Therefore, according to classical mechanics the total energy E of the oscillator is given by :

$$E = K + V$$

$$= \frac{1}{2} m\omega^2 (A^2 - x^2) + \frac{1}{2} m\omega^2 x^2$$

$$= \frac{1}{2} m\omega^2 A^2 \quad \text{... (5)}$$

Eq. (3) shows that the potential energy has a parabolic form. It means that the particle moves in a potential well of parabolic form. Eq. (5) shows that the total energy of a particle oscillating with a constant frequency $\nu = \frac{\omega}{2\pi}$ is proportional to the square of the amplitude. According to classical mechanics the particle can oscillate with any amplitude, consequently the total energy increases continuously with increase in the amplitude.

Probability of finding the Linear Simple Harmonic Oscillator within a Small Distance dx according to Classical Mechanics

The classical probability of finding the particle performing a linear simple harmonic motion within the distance between x and $x + dx$ from its equilibrium position is the ratio of the time which the particle takes to pass over the distance dx during the course of its *one* oscillation to the period of oscillation, $T (= 2\pi / \omega)$.

Thus, if the particle passes through the distance dx in one direction in time dt, then the probability $P(x)\,dx$ of finding it within dx is given by :

$$P(x)\,dx = \frac{2dt}{T} = \frac{2dt}{2\pi / \omega} = \frac{\omega dt}{\pi} \quad \text{... (6)}$$

But $\qquad x = A \sin (\omega t + \theta)$

$\therefore \qquad dx = A\omega \cos (\omega t + \theta)\, dt$

Hence

$$dt = \frac{dx}{A\omega \cos (\omega t + \theta)} = \frac{dx}{A\omega \sqrt{1 - x^2 / A^2}}$$

$$= \frac{dx}{\omega \sqrt{A^2 - \omega^2}}$$

But

$$A^2 = \frac{2E}{m\omega^2} \quad \text{[See Eq. (5)]}$$

$\therefore$

$$dt = \frac{dx}{\omega \sqrt{\frac{2E}{m\omega^2} - x^2}}$$

Substituting this value of dt in Eq. (6), we get :

$$P(x)\,dx = \frac{dx}{\pi\sqrt{\dfrac{2E}{m\omega^2} - x^2}} \qquad \text{... (7)}$$

5.3. (*b*) ONE-DIMENSIONAL SIMPLE HARMONIC OSCILLATOR IN QUANTUM MECHANICS

Wave Equation for the Oscillator

The time-independent Schrödinger wave equation for linear motion of a particle along the x-axis is :

$$-\frac{\hbar^2}{2m}\frac{d^2\psi}{dx^2} + V\psi = E\psi$$

or

$$\frac{d^2\psi}{dx^2} + \frac{2m}{\hbar^2}(E - V)\,\psi = 0 \qquad \text{... (1)}$$

where E is the total energy of the particle, V the potential energy, and ψ the wave-function for the particle, which is a function of x alone.

For a linear oscillator along the x-axis with the angular frequency ω under a restoring force proportional to the displacement x, the potential energy is given by :

$$V = \frac{1}{2}m\omega^2 x^2 \qquad \text{... (2)}$$

Substituting the value of V in Eq. (1) we get :

$$\frac{d^2\psi}{dx^2} + \frac{2m}{\hbar^2}\left(E - \frac{1}{2}m\omega^2 x^2\right)\psi = 0 \qquad \text{... (3)}$$

or

$$\frac{d^2\psi}{dx^2} + \left(\frac{2mE}{\hbar^2} - \frac{m^2\omega^2}{\hbar^2}x^2\right)\psi = 0 \qquad \text{... (4)}$$

This is the Schrödinger wave equation for the oscillator.

Simplification of the Wave Equation

To simplify Eq. (4), we introduce a dimensionless independent variable y which is related to x by the equation :

$$y = ax \qquad \text{... (5)}$$

so that

$$x = \frac{y}{a},$$

where

$$a = \sqrt{\frac{m\omega}{\hbar}}$$

Now we have,

$$\frac{d\psi}{dx} = \frac{d\psi}{dy}\frac{dy}{dx} = \frac{d\psi}{dy}a$$

and

$$\frac{d^2\psi}{dx^2} = \frac{d^2\psi}{dy^2}\frac{dy}{dx}a = \frac{d^2\psi}{dy^2}a^2$$

$$= a^2 \frac{d^2\psi}{dy^2} \quad \text{... (6)}$$

Substituting the values of $d^2\psi / dx^2$ and x^2 in Eq. (4), we get

$$a^2 \frac{d^2\psi}{dy^2} + \left(\frac{2mE}{\hbar^2} - a^4 \frac{y^2}{a^2} \right) \psi = 0$$

Dividing through by a^2

$$\frac{d^2\psi}{dy^2} + \left(\frac{2mE}{a^2 \hbar^2} - y^2 \right) \psi = 0$$

or

$$\frac{d^2\psi}{dy^2} + \left(\frac{2E}{\hbar\omega} - y^2 \right) \psi = 0 \quad \text{... (7)}$$

or

$$\frac{d^2\psi}{dy^2} + (\lambda - y^2)\, \psi = 0 \quad \text{where } \lambda = \frac{2E}{\hbar\omega} \quad \text{... (8)}$$

Though Eq. (7) is in a simplified form, it is not easy to solve it. Therefore, its solution in detail is not given here.

In the following paragraphs, we discuss the results of its solution.

Eigen-values of the total energy E_n

The wave equation for the oscillator is satisfied only for discrete values of total energies given by

$$\frac{2E}{\hbar\omega} = (2n+1)$$

or

$$E_n = \frac{1}{2}(2n+1)\, \hbar\omega$$

$$E_n = \left(n + \frac{1}{2} \right) \hbar\omega \quad \text{... (9)}$$

Substituting $\hbar = \frac{h}{2\pi}$ and $\omega = 2\pi\nu$, this expression has the form :

$$E_n = \left(n + \frac{1}{2} \right) h\nu \quad \text{... (10)}$$

where, $n = 0, 1, 2, \ldots\ldots$, ω is the angular frequency and ν is the frequency of the classical harmonic oscillator, given by

$$\nu = \frac{\omega}{2\pi} = \frac{1}{2\pi} \sqrt{\frac{k}{m}}$$

From Eq. (9), we get the *following conclusions* :

(1) The lowest energy of the oscillator is obtained by putting $n = 0$ in Eq. (9) and it is :

$$E_0 = \frac{1}{2} \hbar\omega \quad \text{... (11)}$$

This is called the ground state energy or the *zero point* vibrational energy of the harmonic oscillator. The zero-point energy is the characteristic result of quantum mechanics. The values of E_n in terms of E_0 are given by :

$$E_n = (2n+1)\,E_0 \qquad \text{... (12)}$$

where $n = 0, 1, 2, 3, ...$

(2) The eigen-values of the total energy depend only on one quantum number *n*. Therefore all the energy-levels of the oscillator are non-degenerate.

(3) The successive energy-levels are equally spaced; the separation between two adjacent energy-levels being $\hbar\omega$. The energy-level diagram for the harmonic oscillator is shown in Fig. 5.7.

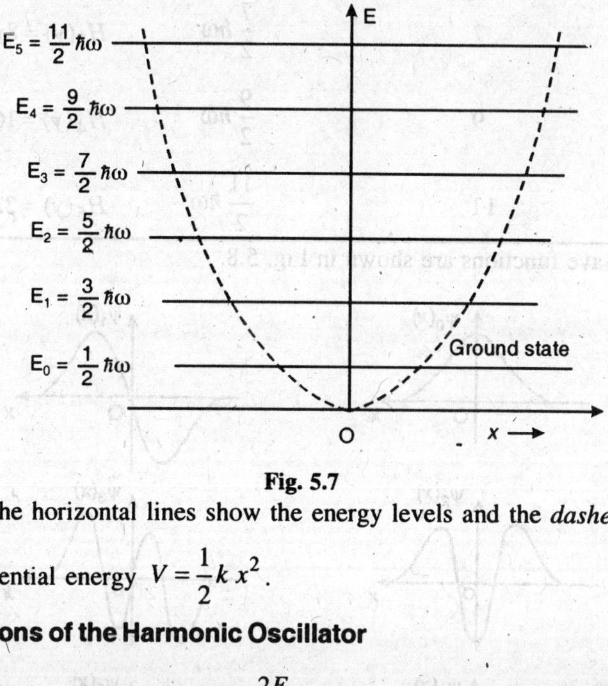

Fig. 5.7

In the figure the horizontal lines show the energy levels and the *dashed curve* is parabola representing the potential energy $V = \frac{1}{2} k\, x^2$.

Wave Functions of the Harmonic Oscillator

For each value of the parameter $\lambda = \frac{2E}{\hbar\omega} = 2n+1$, there is a different wave function ψ_n which consists of :

(*i*) the normalization constant N_n given by :

$$N_n = \left(\frac{m\,\omega}{\pi\,\hbar}\right)^{1/4} (2^n\; n!)^{-1/2},$$

(*ii*) the exponential factor $e^{-y^2/2}$, and

(*iii*) a polynomial $H_n(y)$, called Hermite polynomial in either odd or even powers of *y*.

Thus the general formula for the *n*th wave function is :

$$\psi_n = \left(\frac{m\omega}{\pi\hbar}\right)^{1/4} (2^n\; n!)^{-1/2} e^{-y^2/2}\, H_n(y)$$

The first six Hermite polynomials are given in the following table :

n	$\lambda = 2n+1$	E_n	$H_n(y)$
0	1	$\frac{1}{2}\hbar\omega$	$H_0(y) = 1$
1	3	$\frac{3}{2}\hbar\omega$	$H_1(y) = 2y$
2	5	$\frac{5}{2}\hbar\omega$	$H_2(y) = 4y^2 - 1$
3	7	$\frac{7}{2}\hbar\omega$	$H_3(y) = 8y^3 - 12y$
4	9	$\frac{9}{2}\hbar\omega$	$H_4(y) = 16y^4 - 48y^2 + 12$
5	11	$\frac{11}{2}\hbar\omega$	$H_5(y) = 32y^5 - 160y^3 + 120y$

The first six wave functions are shown in Fig. 5.8.

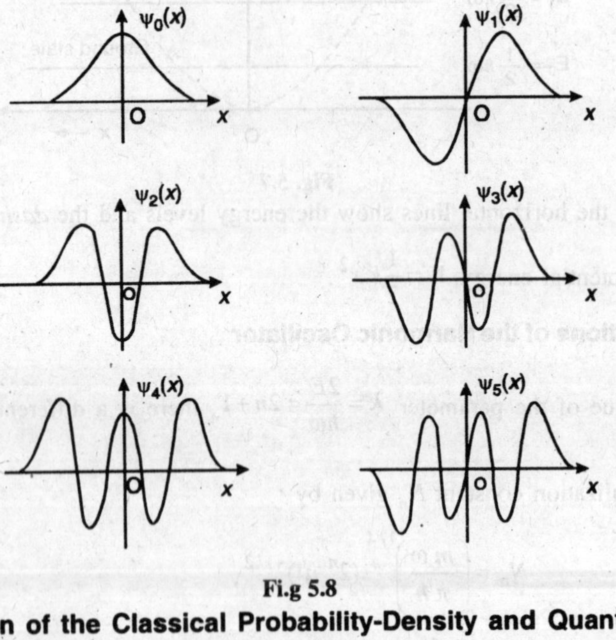

Fi.g 5.8

Comparison of the Classical Probability-Density and Quantum Mechanical Probability-Density

According to classical mechanics the probability-density of a linear simple harmonic oscillator, having amplitude A and energy $E_n = (n+1/2)\,\hbar\omega$, is given by

$$P(x) = \frac{1}{\pi\sqrt{A^2 - x^2}} = \frac{1}{\pi\sqrt{\frac{2E_n}{m\omega^2} - x^2}}$$ [See Sec. 5.3. (*a*) Eq. (7)]

This equation shows that the probability of finding the particle is maximum at $x = \pm A$, *i.e.*, at the extremities of the path, and it is minimum at $x = 0$, *i.e.*, at the equilibrium position. The classical probability-density for $n = 0$ and $n = 10$ is shown by dashed curves in Fig. 5.9 and Fig. 5.10.

According to quantum mechanics the probability-density of the particle in the nth energy-state is given by :

$$P(x) = \psi_n(x)\,\psi^*(x)$$

Calculations show that for $n = 0$, $|\psi_0|^2$ is maximum at $x = 0$ and decreases on either side of $x = 0$ along the continuous curve (Fig. 5.9). For $n = 10$, $|\psi_{10}|^2$ has 5 peaks on either side of $x = 0$ (Fig. 5.10). This means that the disagreement between two probability-densities becomes less and less when n increases.

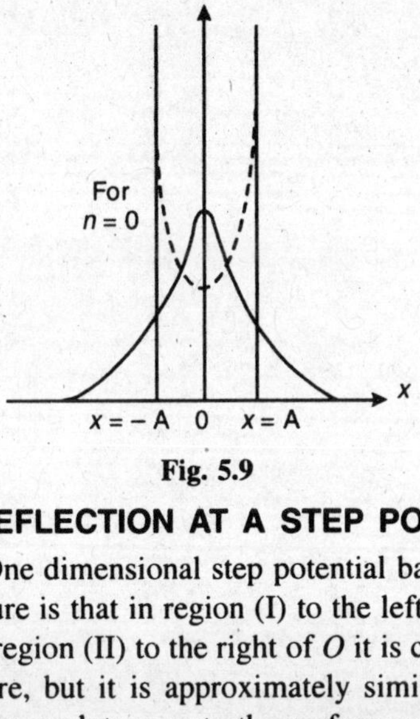

Fig. 5.9

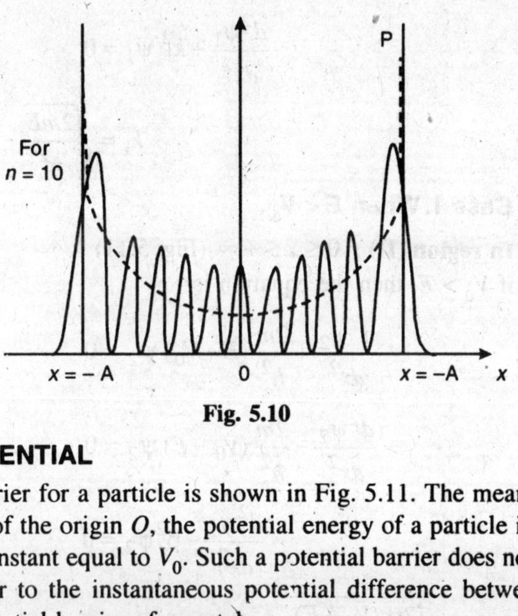

Fig. 5.10

5.4. REFLECTION AT A STEP POTENTIAL

One dimensional step potential barrier for a particle is shown in Fig. 5.11. The meaning of the figure is that in region (I) to the left of the origin O, the potential energy of a particle is zero, and in region (II) to the right of O it is constant equal to V_0. Such a potential barrier does not exist in nature, but it is approximately similar to the instantaneous potential difference between the dees of a cyclotron or to the surface potential barrier of a metal.

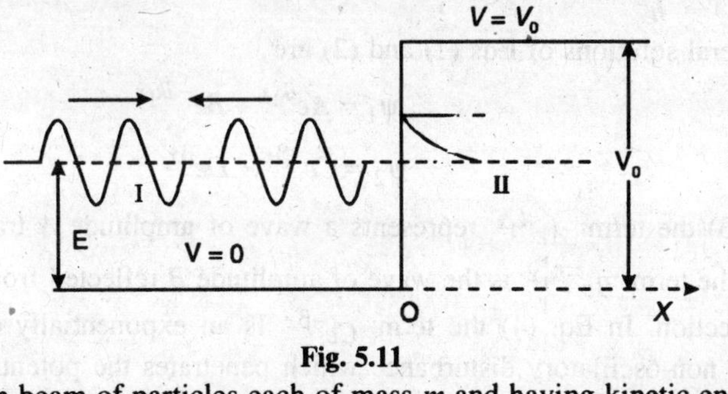

Fig. 5.11

Suppose a uniform beam of particles each of mass m and having kinetic energy E is travelling parallel to the x-axis from left to right in region (I), and is incident on the potential step. In region (I) the energy E of a particle is wholly kinetic, and in region (II) it is partly kinetic and partly potential. If $E < V_0$, then according to classical mechanics, no particle can enter region (II).

However according to quantum mechanics although the wave function for an incident particle has a finite value in region (II) there is no steady transmission of the particles in that region, all the particles are reflected back from the potential step ($V_0 > E$). In the following discussion, we investigate this behaviour of the particles.

Let $\psi_1(x)$ and $\psi_2(x)$ be the wave functions for the motion of a particle in the beam in regions (I) and (II) respectively.

In region (I) : $-\infty \le x < 0$, the time-independent Schrödinger wave equation is :

$$-\frac{\hbar^2}{2m}\frac{d^2\psi_1}{dx^2} = E\psi_1$$

or
$$\frac{d^2\psi_1}{dx^2} + \frac{2mE}{\hbar^2}\psi_1 = 0$$

or
$$\frac{d^2\psi_1}{dx^2} + k_1^2\,\psi_1 = 0 \qquad \text{... (1)}$$

where
$$k_1 = \sqrt{\frac{2mE}{\hbar^2}}$$

Case 1. When $E < V_0$

In region (II) : $0 \le x \le +\infty$ (Fig. 5.11)

if $V_0 > E$, then the equation is :

$$\frac{d^2\psi_2}{dx^2} + \frac{2m}{\hbar^2}(E - V_0)\,\psi_2 = 0$$

or
$$\frac{d^2\psi_2}{dx^2} - \frac{2m}{\hbar^2}(V_0 - E)\,\psi_2 = 0$$

or
$$\frac{d^2\psi_2}{dx^2} - \beta^2\psi_2 = 0 \qquad \text{... (2)}$$

where $\beta = \sqrt{\frac{2m\,(V_0 - E)}{\hbar^2}}$

The general solutions of Eqs (1) and (2) are

$$\psi_1 = Ae^{ik_1x} + Be^{-ik_1x} \qquad \text{... (3)}$$

$$\psi_2 = Ce^{-\beta x} + De^{\beta x} \qquad \text{... (4)}$$

In Eq. (3) the term Ae^{ik_1x} represents a wave of amplitude A travelling in the positive x-direction and the term Be^{-ik_1x} is the wave of amplitude B reflected from the potential step in the negative x-direction. In Eq. (4) the term $Ce^{-\beta x}$ is an exponentially decreasing wave function representing a non-oscillatory disturbance which penetrates the potential barrier for some finite distance in the positive x-direction (Fig. 5.11) ; and the term $De^{\beta x}$ is an exponentially increasing wave function in the positive x-direction. According to the physical interpretation, ψ must remain finite when x approaches ∞. From this condition it follows that $D = 0$. Hence in region (II), the valid solution of the wave equation is :

$$\psi_2 = Ce^{-\beta x} \quad \text{... (5)}$$

Expressions for the amplitudes *B* and *C* in terms of the amplitude *A*

(*i*) At $x = 0$, we have

$$\psi_1(0) = \psi_2(0)$$

∴ from Eqns. (3) and (5), we have

$$A + B = C \quad \text{... (6)}$$

(*ii*) We also have

$$\left(\frac{d\psi_1}{dx}\right)_{x=0} = \left(\frac{d\psi_2}{dx}\right)_{x=0}$$

$$\therefore \quad Aik_1 - Bik_1 = -C\beta$$

$$A - B = -\frac{\beta}{ik_1}C = \frac{i\beta}{k_1}C \quad \text{... (7)}$$

Adding Eqs. (6) and (7) :

$$2A = \left(1 + \frac{i\beta}{k_1}\right)C = \left(\frac{k_1 + i\beta}{k_1}\right)C$$

$$\therefore \quad C = \left(\frac{2k_1}{k_1 + i\beta}\right)A \quad \text{... (8)}$$

Subtracting Eq. (7) from Eq. (6),

$$2B = \left(1 - \frac{i\beta}{k_1}\right)C = \left(\frac{k_1 - i\beta}{k_1}\right)C$$

$$= \left(\frac{k_1 - i\beta}{k_1}\right)\left(\frac{2k}{k_1 + i\beta}\right)A$$

$$\therefore \quad B = \left(\frac{k_1 - i\beta}{k_1 + i\beta}\right)A \quad \text{... (9)}$$

Eqs. (9) and (8) can be expressed in polar form.

Let $\quad k_1 = r\cos\delta$ and $\beta = r\sin\delta$

Then $\quad r = \sqrt{k_1^2 + \beta^2}$, and $\tan\delta = \beta / k_1 = \sqrt{\frac{V_0 - E}{E}}$

Substituting for k_1 and β in Eq. (9),

$$B = \frac{re^{-i\delta}}{re^{i\delta}}A = e^{-2i\delta}A \quad \text{... (10)}$$

Now Eq. (8) is,

$$C = \left(\frac{2k_1}{k_1 + i\beta}\right)A = \left(\frac{2k_1}{k_1 + i\beta} - 1 + 1\right)A$$

$$= \left(\frac{k_1 - i\beta}{k_1 + i\beta} + 1\right)A = (e^{-2i\delta} + 1)\,A$$

$$= (1 + e^{-2i\delta})\,A \quad \text{... (11)}$$

Wave Functions in regions (I) and (II)

In region (I) : $x < 0$

Substituting the expression for B in Eq. (3), we get :

$$\psi_1 = Ae^{ik_1x} + e^{-2i\delta}Ae^{-ik_1x}$$

$$= Ae^{-i\delta}(e^{i\delta}e^{ik_1x} + e^{-i\delta}e^{-ik_1x})$$

$$= 2Ae^{-i\delta}\left[\frac{e^{i(k_1x+\delta)} + e^{-i(k_1x+\delta)}}{2}\right]$$

$$= 2Ae^{-i\delta}\cos(k_1x+\delta) \qquad \ldots (12)$$

where $\quad k_1 = \sqrt{\dfrac{2mE}{\hbar^2}}$, and $\delta = \tan^{-1}\left(\sqrt{\dfrac{V_0 - E}{E}}\right)$

In region (II) : $x > 0$

Substituting the expression for C in Eq. (5), we get :

$$\Psi_2 = (1 + e^{-2i\delta})Ae^{-\beta x}$$

$$= Ae^{-i\delta}(e^{i\delta} + e^{-i\delta})e^{-\beta x}$$

$$= 2Ae^{-i\delta}\left(\frac{e^{i\delta} + e^{-i\delta}}{2}\right)e^{-\beta x}$$

$$\psi_2 = (2Ae^{-i\delta}\cos\delta)\,e^{-\beta x} \qquad \ldots (13)$$

Conclusions

From the foregoing discussion we draw the following inferences :

(1) Eq. (12) represents a standing wave in which equal numbers of particles are passing per second normally through unit area of incident and reflected waves in opposite directions. Therefore, in this case the reflection coefficient $R = 1$.

(2) Eq. (13) shows that to the right of the potential step the wave function, because of the factor $e^{-\beta x}$, is exponentially damped. So there is a finite probability of finding particles in this region, but there is no transmission of particles in this region. Therefore, in this case the transmission coefficient $T = 0$.

Case 2. When $E > V_0$

In region (II). $0 \le x \le +\infty$ (Fig. 5.12)

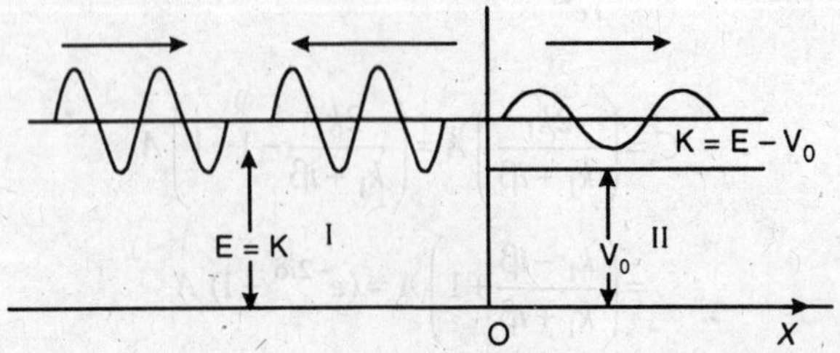

Fig. 5.12

If $E > V_0$, then the time-independent Schrödinger wave equation is :

$$\frac{d^2\psi_2}{dx^2} + \frac{2m}{\hbar^2}(E - V_0) = 0$$

or
$$\frac{d^2\psi_2}{dx^2} + k_2^2\,\psi_2 = 0 \qquad \text{... (14)}$$

where
$$k_2 = \sqrt{\frac{2m\,(E - V_0)}{\hbar^2}}$$

The general solution of Eq. (14) is

$$\psi_2 = Ge^{ik_2x} + He^{-ik_2x} \qquad \text{... (15)}$$

In this equation the term Ge^{ik_2x} represents a wave travelling from the potential step in the positive x-direction, and the term He^{-ik_2x} a wave travelling in the negative x-direction towards the potential step. Since the particles are incident only from the left of the potential step, H must be zero. Hence in region (II), the valid solution of the wave equation is :

$$\psi_2 = Ge^{ik_2x} \qquad \text{... (16)}$$

Expressions for the amplitudes B and G in terms of the amplitude A

Applying the conditions of continuity as explained in Case 1, we shall get the following expressions for B and G :

$$B = \left(\frac{k_1 - k_2}{k_1 + k_2}\right)A \qquad \text{... (17)}$$

$$G = \left(\frac{2k_1}{k_1 + k_2}\right)A \qquad \text{... (18)}$$

Wave Functions in regions (I) and (II)

In region (I) : $x < 0$

$$\psi_1 = Ae^{ik_1x} + Be^{-ikx}$$

$$= A\left[e^{ik_1x} + \left(\frac{k_1 - k_2}{k_1 + k_2}\right)e^{-ikx}\right] \qquad \text{... (19)}$$

In region (II) : $x > 0$

$$\psi_2 = Ge^{ik_2x}$$

$$= \left(\frac{2k_1}{k_1 + k_2}\right)Ae^{ik_2x} \qquad \text{... (20)}$$

Reflection and transmission coefficients

The reflection coefficient R is the ratio of the probability current density for the reflected beam of particles to the probability current density for the incident beam. Thus :

$$R = \frac{S_r}{S_i} = \frac{\frac{\hbar k_1}{m}.|B|^2}{\frac{\hbar k_1}{m}.|A|^2} = \frac{|B|^2}{|A|^2}$$

Now using Eq. (17) we get :

$$R = \frac{(k_1 - k_2)^2}{(k_1 + k_2)^2} \qquad \text{... (21)}$$

The transmission coefficient T is the ratio of the probability current density for the transmitted beam of particles to the probability current density for the incident beam. Thus :

$$T = \frac{S_t}{S_i} = \frac{\frac{\hbar k_2}{m}|G|^2}{\frac{\hbar k_1}{m}|A|^2} = \frac{k_2 |G|^2}{k_1 |A|^2}$$

Now using Eq. (18) , we get :

$$T = \frac{k_2}{k_1}\left(\frac{2k_1}{k_1 + k_2}\right)^2 = \frac{4k_1 k_2}{(k_1 + k_2)^2} \qquad \text{... (22)}$$

Adding Eqns. (21) and (22) it is easily verified that :

$$R + T = 1 \qquad \text{... (23)}$$

5.5. TRANSMISSION ACROSS A POTENTIAL BARRIER :

The Tunnel Effect

A rectangular potential barrier of height V_0 and width a for a particle is shown in Fig. 5.13. It extends over the region (II) from $x = 0$ to $x = a$ in which the potential energy V of the particle will be constant equal to V_0. On both sides of the barrier, in regions (I) and (III) $V = 0$; this means that when the particle is in these regions, no forces act on it.

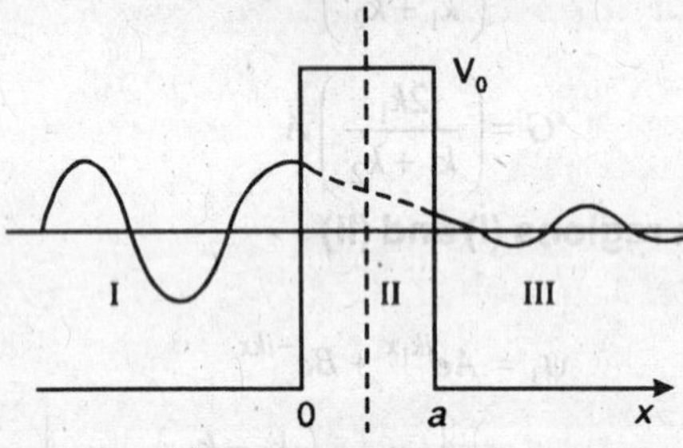

Fig. 5.13

Suppose a beam of particles travelling parallel to the x-axis from left to right is incident on the potential barrier. In the regions (I) and (III), the energy E of a particle is wholly kinetic, and in the region (II) it is partly kinetic and partly potential. If $E < V_0$, then according to classical mechanics, the probability of any particle reaching the region (III) after crossing the region (II) is zero. However, according to quantum mechanics, the transmission probability has a small but defnite value. This behaviour is called the *tunnel effect.*

Let $\psi_1(x)$, $\psi_2(x)$ and $\psi_3(x)$ be the wave functions for the motion of particle in regions (I), (II) and (III) respectively.

In region (I) : $-\infty < x < 0$, the time-independent Schrödinger wave equation is :

$$-\frac{\hbar^2}{2m}\frac{d^2\psi_1}{dx^2} = E\psi_1$$

or $$\frac{d^2\psi_1}{dx^2}+\frac{2mE}{\hbar^2}\psi_1=0$$

or $$\frac{d^2\psi_1}{dx^2}+k^2\psi_1=0 \qquad \text{... (1)}$$

where $$k=\sqrt{\frac{2mE}{\hbar^2}}$$

Case 1. When $E < V_0$

In region (II) : $0 \le x \le a$

If $E < V_0$, then the equation is

$$\frac{d^2\psi_2}{dx^2}+\frac{2m}{\hbar^2}(E-V_0)\psi_2=0$$

or $$\frac{d^2\psi_2}{dx^2}-\frac{2m}{\hbar^2}(V_0-E)\psi_2=0$$

or $$\frac{d^2\psi_2}{dx^2}-\beta^2\psi_2=0 \qquad \text{... (2)}$$

where $$\beta=\sqrt{\frac{2m(V_0-E)}{\hbar^2}}$$

In region (III) : $a \le x < \infty$

$$\frac{d^2\psi_3}{dx^2}+\frac{2mE}{\hbar^2}\psi_3=0$$

or $$\frac{d^2\psi_3}{dx^2}+k^2\psi_3=0 \qquad \text{... (3)}$$

The general solutions of Eqs. (1), (2) and (3) are :

$$\psi_1=Ae^{ikx}+Be^{-ikx} \qquad \text{... (4)}$$

$$\psi_2=Ce^{\beta x}+De^{-\beta x} \qquad \text{... (5)}$$

$$\psi_3=Ge^{ikx}+He^{-ikx}$$

Since there is no particle coming from the right in the region (III), we must have $H = 0$. Therefore,

$$\psi_3=Ge^{ikx} \qquad \text{... (6)}$$

The interpretation of the terms in the above solutions is as follows :

In Eq. (4) the term Ae^{ikx} is a wave of amplitude A travelling in the positive x-direction and the term Be^{-ikx} is the wave of amplitude B reflected in the negative x-direction from the potential barrier, when the incident wave falls on the barrier. In Eq. (5), the term $De^{-\beta x}$ is an exponentially decreasing wave function representing a non-oscillatory disturbance which moves through the barrier in the positive x-direction, and the term $Ce^{\beta x}$ is the reflected disturbance within the barrier; it is an exponentially decreasing wave function. Eq. (6) represents the *transmitted* wave in the region (III). This wave travels in the positive x-direction.

Applying the conditions that ψ and its derivatives are continuous at $x = 0$ and $x = a$, we get the following equations :

$$A + B = C + D \quad \text{... (7)}$$

$$Aik - Bik = C\beta - D\beta \quad \text{... (8)}$$

$$C\,e^{\beta a} + D\,e^{-\beta a} = G\,e^{ika} \quad \text{... (9)}$$

$$C\,\beta\,e^{\beta a} - D\,\beta\,e^{-\beta a} = G\,i\,k\,e^{ika} \quad \text{... (10)}$$

Solving these equations for A in terms of G, and for B in terms of G, we will get :

$$A = \left[\cosh\beta a + \frac{i}{2}\left(\frac{\beta}{k} - \frac{k}{\beta}\right)\sinh\beta a\right] G\,e^{ika} \quad \text{... (11)}$$

and

$$B = -\frac{i}{2}\left(\frac{\beta}{k} + \frac{k}{\beta}\right)\sinh\beta a\,G\,e^{ika} \quad \text{... (12)}$$

Reflection Coefficient:

The reflection coefficient R is given by :

$$R = \frac{BB^*}{AA^*} = \frac{\frac{1}{4}\left(\frac{\beta}{k} + \frac{k}{\beta}\right)^2 \sinh^2\beta a}{\cosh^2\beta a + \frac{1}{4}\left(\frac{\beta}{k} - \frac{k}{\beta}\right)^2 \sin^2\beta a}$$

$$= \frac{\frac{V_0^2}{4E\,(V_0 - E)}\sinh^2\beta a}{1 + \frac{V_0^2}{4E\,(V_0 - E)}\sinh^2\beta a} \quad \text{... (13)}$$

Transmission Coefficient:

The transmission coefficient T is given by :

$$\frac{1}{T} = \frac{AA^*}{GG^*} = 1 + \frac{V_0^2}{4E\,(V_0 - E)}\cdot\sinh^2\beta a$$

$$\therefore \quad T = \frac{1}{1 + \frac{V_0^2}{4E\,(V_0 - E)}\cdot\sinh^2\beta a} \quad \text{... (14)}$$

From Eqs. (13) and (14) it is seen that :

$$R + T = 1$$

In this case when $E < V_0$, the expression for T leads to the following conclusions :

(1) The transmission coefficient is zero if E is zero, and it has a finite value less than 1 for an incident beam of particles having initial kinetic energy. That is, there is a finite probability for a particle *to tunnel through a potential barrier* of height V_0 even when its initial kinetic energy is less than V_0.

(2) If the energy E is increased, $(V_0 - E)$ decreases and $\beta = \sqrt{\frac{2m(V_0 - E)}{\hbar^2}}$ also decreases, but $\sinh^2 \beta a$ for a fixed value of the width of the potential barrier decreases more rapidly than $(V_0 - E)$. Therefore T increases steadily with E.

(3) If the width a of the potential barrier is increased $\sinh^2 \beta a$ increases rapidly and therefore T decreases rapidly.

The tunnel effect provides explanations for the following phenomena :

(1) the field emission of electrons from a cold metallic surface,
(2) the electrical breakdown of insulators,
(3) the reverse breakdown of semi-conductor diodes,
(4) the switching action of a tunnel diode and
(5) the emission of α-particles from a radio-active element.

SOLVED EXAMPLES

Example 5.1. *Find the lowest energy of an electron confined to move in a one-dimensional potential box of length 1 Å.*

Given $m = 9.11 \times 10^{-31}$ kg, $\hbar = 1.054 \times 10^{-34}$ J. *sec.*, *1* eV = *1.6* × 10^{-19} J

Solution :

We have $a = 1\,Å = 10^{-10}$ m

$$E_1 = \frac{1^2 \pi^2 \hbar^2}{2ma^2} = \frac{\pi^2 \times (1.054 \times 10^{-34})^2}{2 \times 9.11 \times 10^{-31} \times (10^{-10})^2}$$

$$= \frac{1.054^2 \pi^2 \times 10^{-17}}{2 \times 9.11} = \frac{10.95 \times 10^{-17}}{18.22} = 6 \times 10^{-18}\,\text{J}$$

$$= \frac{6 \times 10^{-18}}{1.6 \times 10^{-19}} = \frac{600}{16} = \mathbf{37.5\ eV}$$

Example 5.2. *Find the lowest energy of a neutron confined to a nucleus of size* 10^{-14} m. *Given : mass of the neutron* = *1.67* × 10^{-27} kg.

Solution :

We have $a = 10^{-14}$ m

$$E_1 = \frac{1^2 \pi^2 \hbar^2}{2ma^2} = \frac{\pi^2 \times (1.054 \times 10^{-34})^2}{2 \times 1.67 \times 10^{-27} \times (10^{-14})^2}$$

$$= \frac{1.054^2 \pi^2 \times 10^{-13}}{3.34} = \frac{10.95 \times 10^{-13}}{3.34}$$

$$= 3.28 \times 10^{-13}\,\text{J}$$

$$= \frac{3.28 \times 10^{-13}}{1.6 \times 10^{-19}} = \frac{32.8}{16} \times 10^6\,\text{eV} = \mathbf{2.05 MeV}$$

Example 5.3. (*a*) *Find the lowest energy of an electron confined in a cubical box of each side 1 Å.*

(*b*) *Find the temperature at which the average energy of the molecules of a perfect gas would be equal to the lowest energy of the electron. (Given k = 1.38 × 10^{-23} J/°K).*

Solution :

(*a*) We have $a = 10^{-10}$ m.

The possible energies of a particle in a cubical box of each side a are given by :

$$E = \frac{\pi^2 \hbar^2}{2ma^2}\left(n_x^2 + n_y^2 + n_z^2\right)$$

For the lowest energy $n_x = n_y = n_z = 1$

$$\therefore \quad E_1 = \frac{3\pi^2 \hbar^2}{2ma^2} = \frac{3\pi^2 \times (1.054 \times 10^{-34})^2}{2 \times 9.11 \times 10^{-31} \times (10^{-10})^2}$$

$$= \frac{3 \times 1.054^2 \pi^2 \times 10^{-17}}{2 \times 9.11} = \frac{32.85 \times 10^{-17}}{18.22} \text{J}$$

$$= \mathbf{18.03 \times 10^{-18}\ J}$$

(*b*) Let T °K be the required temperature. Then :

$$\frac{3}{2} kT = \frac{3\pi^2 \hbar^2}{2ma^2}, \text{ where } k \text{ is Boltzmann's constant}$$

$$= 18.03 \times 10^{-18} \text{ J}$$

$$\therefore \quad T = \frac{2 \times 18.03 \times 10^{-18}}{3 \times 1.38 \times 10^{-23}}$$

$$= \frac{2 \times 18.03 \times 10^{5}}{3 \times 1.38} \text{K}$$

$$= \mathbf{8.71 \times 10^5\ K}$$

Example 5.4. *The potential energy of a simple harmonic oscillator of mass m, oscillating with angular frequency ω is*

$$V(x) = \frac{1}{2} m\omega^2 x^2$$

(*a*) *Write the time-independent Schrödinger equation for a simple harmonic oscillator.*

(*b*) *Given the eigen-function of the Hamiltonian operator for the ground state as :*

$$\psi_0 = \left(\frac{m\omega}{\pi\hbar}\right)^{1/4} e^{-\alpha^2 x^2/2}$$

where $\alpha = \sqrt{\frac{m\omega}{\hbar}}$, *calculate the energy eigen value in the ground state.*

Solution :

(*a*) The Hamiltonian operator for the oscillator is

$$\hat{H} = -\frac{\hbar^2}{2m}\frac{d^2}{dx^2} + \frac{1}{2} m\omega^2 x^2$$

Therefore, the time-independent Schrödinger equation is :

$$\left[-\frac{\hbar^2}{2m}\frac{d^2}{dx^2}+\frac{1}{2}m\omega^2x^2\right]\psi(x)=E\psi(x)$$

(*b*) For the ground state the Schrödinger equation is :

$$\left[-\frac{\hbar^2}{2m}\frac{d^2}{dx^2}+\frac{1}{2}m\omega^2x^2\right]\psi_0=E_0\psi_0 \qquad \text{... (1)}$$

Now

$$\psi_0=\left(\frac{m\omega}{\pi\hbar}\right)^{1/4}e^{-\alpha^2x^2/2}$$

$$\therefore \qquad \frac{d\psi_0}{dx}=\left(\frac{m\omega}{\pi\hbar}\right)^{1/4}e^{-\alpha^2x^2/2}(-\alpha^2x)$$

$$=-\alpha^2x\,\psi_0 \qquad \text{... (2)}$$

and

$$\frac{d^2\psi_0}{dx^2}=-\alpha^2x\frac{d\psi_0}{dx}-\alpha^2\psi_0$$

$$=-\alpha^2x(-\alpha^2x\,\psi_0)-\alpha^2\psi_0$$

$$=\alpha^2\left(\alpha^2x^2-1\right)\psi_0$$

or

$$\frac{d^2\psi_0}{dx^2}-\alpha^4x^2\psi_0=-\alpha^2\psi_0$$

or

$$\frac{d^2\psi_0}{dx^2}-\frac{m^2\omega^2}{\hbar^2}x^2\psi_0=-\frac{m\omega}{\hbar}\psi_0$$

Multiplying through by $-\hbar^2/2m$,

$$-\frac{\hbar^2}{2m}\cdot\frac{d^2\psi_0}{dx^2}+\frac{\hbar^2}{2m}\left(\frac{m^2\omega^2}{\hbar^2}\right)x^2\psi_0=\frac{\hbar^2}{2m}\cdot\frac{m\omega}{\hbar}\psi_0$$

Simplifying we get,

$$\left[-\frac{\hbar^2}{2m}\frac{d^2}{dx^2}+\frac{1}{2}m\omega^2x^2\right]\psi_0=\frac{1}{2}\hbar\omega\,\psi_0 \qquad \text{... (3)}$$

Comparing Eqs. (1) and (3), we get,

$$E_0=\frac{1}{2}\hbar\omega$$

Example 5.5. *Derive an approximate expression for the transmission coefficient for a rectangular potential barrier for which* $\frac{a}{\hbar}\sqrt{2m(V_0-E)}>>1$

Ans. The transmission coefficient in the case $E<V_0$ is given by

$$\frac{1}{T}=1+\frac{V_0^2}{4E(V_0-E)}\cdot\sinh^2\beta a \qquad \text{... (1)}$$

where $\beta = \sqrt{\dfrac{2m(V_0 - E)}{\hbar^2}}$, and a is the width of the barrier.

When $\beta a >> 1$, $e^{\beta a}$ is large but $e^{-\beta a}$ is very small. Therefore, $e^{-\beta a}$ in the expression for $\sinh \beta a$ can be neglected compared to $e^{\beta a}$.

Hence $$\sinh^2 \beta a = \left(\frac{e^{\beta a} - e^{-\beta a}}{2}\right)^2 = \frac{1}{4} e^{2\beta a}$$

Substituting this value in Eq. (1) and neglecting 1 compared to the second term, we get :

$$\frac{1}{T} \approx \frac{V_0^2}{4E(V_0 - E)} \frac{1}{4} e^{2\beta a}$$

$$\therefore \quad T \approx \frac{16E}{V_0^2}(V_0 - E)\, e^{-2\beta a}$$

$$\approx \frac{16E}{V_0}\left(1 - \frac{E}{V_0}\right) e^{-2\beta a} \qquad \text{... (2)}$$

$$\approx \frac{16E}{V_0}\left(1 - \frac{E}{V_0}\right) e^{-2a/\hbar\left(\sqrt{2m(V_0 - E)}\right)} \qquad \text{... (3)}$$

This is the required expression.

Example 5.6. *A stream of electrons, each of energy $E = 3eV$ is incident on a potential barrier of height $V_0 = 4$ eV. The width of the barrier is 20 Å. Calculate the percentage transmission of the beam through this barrier.*

Solution :

We have
$$E = 3 \text{ eV} = 3 \times 1.6 \times 10^{-19} \text{ J}$$
$$V_0 = 4 \text{ eV} = 4 \times 1.6 \times 10^{-19} \text{ J}$$
$$a = 20 \text{ Å} = 20 \times 10^{-10} = 2 \times 10^{-9} \text{ m}$$

The coefficient of transmisson is given by :

$$T = \frac{16E}{V_0}\left(1 - \frac{E}{V_0}\right) e^{-2\beta a}$$

Now,
$$2\beta a = 2a\sqrt{\frac{2m(V_0 - E)}{\hbar^2}}$$

$$= \frac{2a}{\hbar}\sqrt{2m(V_0 - E)}$$

$$= \frac{2 \times 2 \times 10^{-9}}{1.054 \times 10^{-34}}\sqrt{2 \times 9.11 \times 10^{-31} \times 1.6 \times 10^{-19}}$$

$$= \frac{2 \times 2}{1.054}\sqrt{2 \times 9.11 \times 1.6}$$

$$= \frac{4 \times 5.4}{1.054} = 20.49$$

$$\therefore \quad T = \frac{16\,E}{V_0}\left(1 - \frac{E}{V_0}\right)e^{-2\beta a}$$

$$= \frac{16 \times 3}{4}\left(1 - \frac{3}{4}\right)\frac{1}{2.718^{20.49}}$$

$$= \frac{3}{7.9 \times 10^8} = \frac{30}{7.9} \times 10^{-9} = 3.797 \times 10^{-9}$$

$\therefore$ percentage transmission = $\mathbf{3.797 \times 10^{-7}\,\%}$

QUESTIONS AND PROBLEMS

1. A particle of mass m is confined in a field free region between impenetrable walls at $x = 0$ and $x = a$. Show that the stationary energy levels of the particle are given by

$$E_n = \frac{n^2 \pi^2 \hbar^2}{2ma^2} \qquad \text{(Agra, 2005)}$$

Obtain the corresponding wave-functions.

2. (*a*) Write down the time-dependent and time-independent Schrödinger wave equations for a particle.
(*b*) Solve the Schrödinger wave equation for a particle moving in a rectangular potential box and obtain its energy levels. Show that the eigen-values of energy are discrete.

3. Find the energies of the six lowest energy-levels of a particle in a cubical box. Which of the levels are degenerate ?

(**Ans.** 3, 6, 9, 11, 12 and $14 \times \dfrac{\pi^2 \hbar^2}{2mL^2}$, 1st and 5th levels are non-degenerate; 2nd, 3rd and 4th are three-fold degenerate and the 6th is six-fold degenerate).

4. Determine the degree of degeneracy of the energy-level $\dfrac{38\pi^2 \hbar^2}{2mL^2}$ of a particle in a cubical potential box.
(**Ans.** The quantum numbers (611), (161), (116), (532), (523), (352), (325), (253) and (235) give the same energy level; therefore, the level is nine-fold degenerate).

5. Write down the Schrödinger equation for a linear harmonic oscillator and obtain the eigen-values of the energy of the oscillator. (Delhi, 2004, Meerut, 2005)

6. (*a*) Solve the Schrödinger equation for the linear harmonic oscillator and obtain its energy-levels.
(*b*) Compare the energy-values obtained quantum mechanically with those obtained by classical mechanics and old quantum theory. (Punjab, 2003)

7. (*a*) Explain the meaning of the eigen-functions and eigen-values of an operator.
(*b*) Establish the time-independent Schrödinger equation for a linear harmonic oscillator and obtain its energy-levels.

8. Calculate the probability of finding a simple harmonic oscillator within the classical limits, if the oscillator is in its normal state. (Arunachal, 2003)

9. Show that the lowest or ground-state energy level of a particle in one dimensional potential box with rigid walls is in agreement with the uncertainty principle.

(**Ans.** The ground-state energy is $E_1 = \frac{\pi^2 \hbar^2}{2ma^2}$ the maximum uncertainty in the position of the particle in the box is $\Delta x = a$, where a is the width of the box.

From the uncertainty relation the uncertainty in the momentum is given by :

$$\Delta p_x \gtrsim \frac{h}{\Delta x} \gtrsim \frac{h}{a}$$

∴ the min. uncertainty in the momentum in + *ive* or – *ive* x-direction is $h/2a$, *i.e.*, the minimum possible momentum in either direction is $h/2a$.

Hence the ground state energy is

$$E_1 = \frac{p_x^2}{2m} = \frac{1}{2m}\left(\frac{h}{2a}\right)^2 = \frac{h^2}{8ma^2} = \frac{(2\pi)^2}{8ma^2}\left(\frac{h}{2\pi}\right)^2$$

$$= \frac{\pi^2 \hbar^2}{2ma^2}.$$

10. (*a*) A beam of electrons, each of energy E, is incident on a rectangular potential barrier of width a and height V_0, where $V_0 > E$. Obtain an expression for the transmission-coefficient through the barrier.

(*b*) Explain the phenomenon of α-decay of a radio-active nucleus.

11. A beam of particles each of mass m and energy E, moving in a region of zero potential energy, approaches a rectangular potential barrier of width a and height V_0, where $V_0 > E$.

If $\beta a >> 1$, where $\beta = \sqrt{\frac{2m(V_0 - E)}{\hbar^2}}$, prove that the transmission : coefficient is given by

$$T = \frac{16E}{V_0}\left(1 - \frac{E}{V_0}\right) e^{-2\beta a}$$

12. Find the reflection and transmission coefficients for a rectangular barrier of width a and height V_0 for the case where $E > V_0$. Show that the transmission coefficient is 1 for certain value of the energy, given by :

$$E = \frac{n^2 \pi^2 \hbar^2}{2ma^2} + V_0, \text{ where } n = 1, 2, 3, ...$$

13. Explain the problem of the leaking of a particle through a rectangular potential barrier of finite width and explain theory of α-particle decay. (Bangalore, 2005)

14. Show that the reflection coefficient R for a step barrier for the case $E > V_0$ is given by:

$$R = \left[\frac{1 - \sqrt{1 - V_0 / E}}{1 + \sqrt{1 - V_0 / E}}\right]^2$$

15. Explain why the quantum number n in the energy equation for a particle in one dimensional box cannot take zero value. (N.U., 2006)

CHAPTER 6

THE HYDROGEN ATOM

The hydrogen atom is a system of two particles, a proton and a single electron bound by electrostatic force of attraction. It, being the simplest atom, forms the basis for the theoretical treatment of more complex atomic systems. Bohr's theory of the hydrogen atom marked the beginning of the old quantum theory of atomic structure. Wave mechanics had its beginning when Schrödinger in 1926 gave the solution of the wave equation for the hydrogen atom. Subsequently there was extensive development of quantum mechanical theory of the hydrogen atom by Heisenberg, Max Born, and Jordan, before the treatment was finally given by Pauli.

The quantum mechanical treatment given in this chapter is due to Sommerfeld. It differs in some minor details from that of Schrödinger.

6.1. WAVE EQUATION FOR THE HYDROGEN ATOM

In the hydrogen atom the charge of the proton is $+e$ and that of the electron $-e$. Therefore, the electrostatic potential energy of the system in the absence of external fields is (in SI units) :

$$V = \frac{e(-e)}{4\pi\varepsilon_0 r} = -\frac{e^2}{4\pi\varepsilon_0 r} \quad \text{... (1)}$$

where r is the distance between the particles and ε_0 the permittivity of free space.

The proton is 1836 times heavier than the electron. So for convenience the proton can be considered to be stationary with the electron in motion around it. The time-independent Schrödinger's wave equation in three dimensions for the electron is :

$$\left[-\frac{\hbar^2}{2m}\nabla^2 + V\right]\psi = E\psi \quad \text{... (2)}$$

where m is the mass of the electron,

V is its potential energy,

E is its total energy,

$\psi(x, y, z)$ is the wave function for the electron, and

$\nabla^2 = \frac{\partial^2}{\partial x^2} + \frac{\partial^2}{\partial y^2} + \frac{\partial^2}{\partial z^2}$ is the Laplacian of $\psi(x, y, z)$ in the Cartesian coordinates x, y, z. We write Eq. (2) in a convenient form as :

$$\nabla^2\psi + \frac{2m}{\hbar^2}(E-V)\psi = 0 \quad \text{... (3)}$$

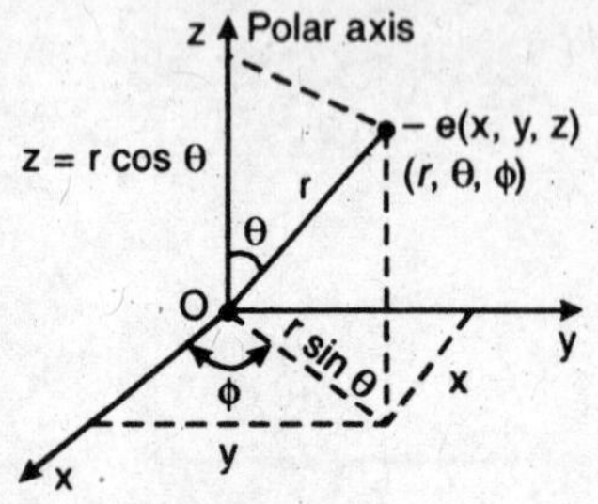

Fig. 6.1

The variables in this equation cannot be separated in the Cartesian coordinates. Therefore, the Cartesian coordinates of the electron relative to the proton are replaced by the spherical polar coordinates (r, θ, ϕ) and the Laplacian operator ∇^2 is transformed into these coordinates by using the equations: (See Fig. 6.1)

$$x = r\sin\theta\cos\phi$$

$$y = r\sin\theta\sin\phi$$

$$z = r\cos\theta$$

The Laplacian operator, in spherical polar coordinates, is :

$$\nabla^2 = \frac{1}{r^2}\frac{\partial}{\partial r}\left(r^2\frac{\partial}{\partial r}\right) + \frac{1}{r^2\sin\theta}\frac{\partial}{\partial\theta}\left(\sin\theta\frac{\partial}{\partial\theta}\right) + \frac{1}{r^2\sin^2\theta}\frac{\partial^2}{\partial\phi^2} \quad \text{... (4)}$$

Therefore, the Schrödinger equation in spherical polar coordinates becomes :

$$\frac{1}{r^2}\frac{\partial}{\partial r}\left(r^2\frac{\partial\psi}{\partial r}\right) + \frac{1}{r^2\sin\theta}\frac{\partial}{\partial\theta}\left(\sin\theta\frac{\partial\psi}{\partial\theta}\right) + \frac{1}{r^2\sin^2\theta}\frac{\partial^2\psi}{\partial\phi^2} + \frac{2m}{\hbar^2}\left[E + \frac{e^2}{4\pi\varepsilon_0 r}\right]\psi = 0 \quad \text{... (5)}$$

In this equation the wave-function ψ is a function of (r, θ, ϕ).

Separation of Variables

The equation in spherical polar coordinates can be easily separated into three equations, each involving a single independent variable. For this purpose, we assume the wave-function $\psi(r, \theta, \phi)$ to be a product of three functions,

$$\psi(r, \theta, \phi) = R(r)\,Q(\theta)\,F(\phi) \quad \text{... (6a)}$$

where $R(r)$ is a function of r alone,

$Q(\theta)$ is a function of θ alone and

$F(\phi)$ is a function of ϕ alone.

(**Note :** we use the symbols Q and F for the functions of θ and ϕ respectively and not the symbols Θ and Φ to avoid any confusion in writing).

The function $R(r)$ will show the variation of the wave function ψ along a *radius vector* from the nucleus, when θ and ϕ are constant. The function $Q(\theta)$ will show the variation of ψ with *zenith angle* θ along a circle on a sphere with nucleus as the centre, when r and ϕ are constant. The function $F(\phi)$ will show the variation of ψ with *azimuthal angle* ϕ along a circle with centre on OZ, where r and θ are constant.

In a simple form Eq. (6a) is written as :

$$\psi = RQF \quad \text{... (6b)}$$

Substituting this equation into Eq. (5), we get

$$\frac{QF}{r^2}\frac{d}{dr}\left(r^2\frac{dR}{dr}\right)+\frac{RF}{r^2\sin\theta}\frac{d}{d\theta}\left(\sin\theta\frac{dQ}{d\theta}\right)+\frac{RQ}{r^2\sin^2\theta}\frac{d^2F}{d\phi^2}$$

$$+\frac{2m}{\hbar^2}\left(E+\frac{e^2}{4\pi\varepsilon_0 r}\right)RQF=0 \quad \text{... (7)}$$

In this equation we have used ordinary derivatives instead of partial derivatives because each function depends on only one variable.

Now multiplying Eq. (7) by $\dfrac{r^2\sin^2\theta}{RQF}$, we get

$$\frac{\sin^2\theta}{R}\frac{d}{dr}\left(r^2\frac{dR}{dr}\right)+\frac{\sin\theta}{Q}\frac{d}{d\theta}\left(\sin\theta\frac{dQ}{d\theta}\right)+\frac{1}{F}\frac{d^2F}{d\phi^2}+\frac{2m}{\hbar^2}\left(E+\frac{e^2}{4\pi\varepsilon_0 r}\right)r^2\sin^2\theta=0$$

Transposing the third term to the right-hand side, we get

$$\frac{\sin^2\theta}{R}\frac{d}{dr}\left(r^2\frac{dR}{dr}\right)+\frac{\sin\theta}{Q}\frac{d}{d\theta}\left(\sin\theta\frac{dQ}{d\theta}\right)+\frac{2m}{\hbar^2}\left(E+\frac{e^2}{4\pi\varepsilon_0 r}\right)r^2\sin^2\theta=-\frac{1}{F}\frac{d^2F}{d\phi^2} \quad \text{... (8)}$$

Azimuthal Wave Equation, or the ϕ Equation

The left side of Eq. (8) is a function of r and θ and the right side is a function of ϕ only. Thus each side can be varied independently of the other. Therefore, the equation will be true only if both sides are equal to the same constant. This constant is denoted by m_l^2, where m_l is called the *orbital magnetic quantum number*.

Therefore, the right side of Eq. (8) becomes :

$$-\frac{1}{F}\frac{d^2F}{d\phi^2}=m_l^2$$

or

$$\frac{d^2F}{d\phi^2}+m_l^2F=0 \quad \text{... (9)}$$

This is the *first* of the *three* differential equations, and is called the *azimuthal wave equation*, or the ϕ equation. In the solution of Eq. (9) we will see that m_l must be a positive or negative integer or zero.

Polar and Radial Wave Equations

Equating the left side of Eq. (8) to m_l^2 and then dividing it by $\sin^2\theta$, we get :

$$\frac{1}{R}\frac{d}{dr}\left(r^2\frac{dR}{dr}\right)+\frac{1}{Q\sin\theta}\frac{d}{d\theta}\left(\sin\theta\frac{dQ}{d\theta}\right)+\frac{2mr^2}{\hbar^2}\left(E+\frac{e^2}{4\pi\varepsilon_0 r}\right)=\frac{m_l^2}{\sin^2\theta}$$

Transporing the second term on the left side to the right side, we get :

$$\frac{1}{R}\frac{d}{dr}\left(r^2\frac{dR}{dr}\right)+\frac{2mr^2}{\hbar^2}\left(E+\frac{e^2}{4\pi\varepsilon_0 r}\right)=\frac{m_l^2}{\sin^2\theta}-\frac{1}{Q\sin\theta}\frac{d}{d\theta}\left(\sin\theta\frac{dQ}{d\theta}\right) \quad \text{... (10)}$$

The left side of this equation is a function of r only, while the right side is a function of θ only, and hence both sides of the equation must be equal to the same constant. We denote this constant by β.

Equating both sides of the equation separately to the same constant β, we get the following equations :

$$\frac{m_l^2}{\sin^2\theta} - \frac{1}{Q\sin\theta}\frac{d}{d\theta}\left(\sin\theta\frac{dQ}{d\theta}\right) = \beta \quad \text{... (11)}$$

This equation is called the *polar wave equation or the* θ *equation.*

$$\frac{1}{R}\frac{d}{dr}\left(r^2\frac{dR}{dr}\right) + \frac{2mr^2}{\hbar^2}\left(E + \frac{e^2}{4\pi\varepsilon_0 r}\right) = \beta \quad \text{... (12)}$$

This equation is called the *radial wave equation.* Thus the Schrödinger wave equation (5) for the hydrogen atom has been separated into three equations (9), (11) and (12). Each of the equations depends on only one variable.

6.2. SOLUTION OF THE AZIMUTHAL WAVE EQUATION

The azimuthal wave equation :

$$\frac{d^2F}{d\phi^2} + m_l^2 F = 0 \quad \text{... (1)}$$

is a simple differential equation. The solution of this equation is :

$$F(\phi) = Ae^{i m_l \phi} \quad \text{... (2)}$$

where A is a constant and $i = \sqrt{-1}$. The wave function should have a single value for a given value of ϕ and should not change if ϕ is changed by 2π radians (because this brings us back to the same position). The condition for this requirement is

$$F(\phi + 2\pi) = F(\phi) \quad \text{... (3)}$$

Hence

$$Ae^{i m_l(\phi+2\pi)} = Ae^{i m_l \phi} \quad \text{... (4)}$$

Since the term $Ae^{i m_l \phi}$ is not zero, we divide Eq. (4) by this term and obtain :

$$e^{2\pi i m_l} = 1$$

By Euler's equation : $e^{i\theta} = \cos\theta + i\sin\theta$

we have $\cos 2\pi m_l + i \sin 2\pi m_l = 1$

Equating the real parts on the two sides of this equation, we get :

$$\cos 2\pi m_l = 1 \qquad \therefore \quad 2\pi\, m_l = 0,\ \pm 2\pi,\ \pm 4\pi,\ \pm 6\pi\ \ldots.$$

or

$$m_l = o,\ \pm 1,\ \pm 2,\ \pm 3, \quad \text{.... (5)}$$

The parameter m_l is called the *orbital magnetic quantum number* for the hydrogen atom.

Normalization of the Azimuthal Wave-Function: The normalization condition for the wave function $F(\phi)$ is :

$$\int_0^{2\pi} FF^*\, d\phi = 1 \quad \text{... (6)}$$

$$\therefore \quad \int_0^{2\pi}\left(Ae^{i m_l\phi}\right)\left(Ae^{i m_l\phi}\right)^* d\phi = 1$$

or
$$\int_0^{2\pi} AA^* e^{i m_l\phi} e^{-i m_l\phi} d\phi = 1$$

or
$$A^2 \int_0^{2\pi} d\phi = 1$$

or
$$A^2 (2\pi) = 1$$

Hence
$$A = \frac{1}{\sqrt{2\pi}} \quad \text{... (7)}$$

Substituting the value of the constant A in Eq. (2) : the solution of the azimuthal wave equation is,

$$F_{m_l}(\phi) = \frac{1}{\sqrt{2\pi}} e^{i m_l \phi} \quad \text{... (8)}$$

6.3. SOLUTION OF THE POLAR WAVE EQUATION

The polar wave equation, or the θ equation is (see Sec. 6.1)

$$\frac{m_l^2}{\sin^2\theta} - \frac{1}{Q\sin\theta}\frac{d}{d\theta}\left(\sin\theta\frac{dQ}{d\theta}\right) = \beta$$

Multiplying this equation by Q and rearranging the terms, we get :

$$\frac{1}{\sin\theta}\frac{d}{d\theta}\left(\sin\theta\frac{dQ}{d\theta}\right) + \left(\beta - \frac{m_l^2}{\sin^2\theta}\right)Q = 0 \quad \text{... (1)}$$

To solve this equation, we substitute

$$x = \cos\theta$$

$$\therefore \quad \sin\theta = \sqrt{1-x^2}$$

Then
$$\frac{dQ}{d\theta} = \frac{dQ}{dx}\frac{dx}{d\theta} = -\sin\theta\frac{dQ}{dx} \quad \text{... (2)}$$

$$\therefore \quad \frac{d}{d\theta} = -\sin\theta\frac{d}{dx} \quad \text{... (3)}$$

From Eq. (2),we get

$$\sin\theta\frac{dQ}{d\theta} = -\sin^2\theta\frac{dQ}{dx} = -\left(1-x^2\right)\frac{dQ}{dx}$$

And from Eq. (3), we have

$$\frac{1}{\sin\theta}\frac{d}{d\theta} = -\frac{d}{dx}$$

Substituting for these expressions in Eq. (1) :

$$-\frac{d}{dx}\left[-\left(1-x^2\right)\frac{dQ}{dx}\right] + \left(\beta - \frac{m_l^2}{1-x^2}\right)Q = 0$$

or
$$\frac{d}{dx}\left[\left(1-x^2\right)\frac{dQ}{dx}\right] + \left(\beta - \frac{m_l^2}{1-x^2}\right)Q = 0 \quad \text{... (4)}$$

This equation is known as *Legendre's equation.* The solutions of this equation satisfy the conditions of single-valuedness and continuity of the wave function Q if the constant β is of the form :

$$\beta = (k + m_l)(k + m_l + 1) \quad \text{... (5)}$$

where k and m_l are each zero or an integer. Therefore, we substitute $k + m_l = l$, so that

$$\beta = l(l+1) \quad \text{... (6)}$$

where $l = 0, 1, 2, 3, \ldots\ldots$

Thus l must be zero or a positive integer. The parameter l is called the *orbital angular momentum quantum number.* For a given value of l the absolute value $|m_l|$ of m_l must be equal to or less than l. That is $|m_l| \le l$,

i.e. $m_l = 0, \ \pm 1, \ \pm 2, \ \ldots\ldots \pm l$

The solutions of Eq. (4) are the associated. Legendre functions of degree l and order $|m_l|$.

The solutions are written as

$$Q_{lm_l}(\theta) = N_{lm_l} P_l^m(\cos\theta) \quad \text{... (7)}$$

where N_{lm_l} is the normalization constant given by

$$N_{lm_l} = \sqrt{\frac{(2l+1)(l - m_l)}{2(l + m_l)!}} \quad \text{... (8)}$$

The values of the Legendre functions for some values of l and $|m_l|$ are :

$P_0^0(\cos\theta) = 1$	$P_1^1(\cos\theta) = \sin\theta$
$P_1^0(\cos\theta) = \cos\theta$	$P_2^1(\cos\theta) = 3\sin\theta\cos\theta$
$P_2^0(\cos\theta) = \frac{1}{2}(3\cos^2\theta - 1)$	$P_3^1(\cos\theta) = \frac{3}{2}\sin\theta(5\cos^2\theta - 1)$
$P_3^0(\cos\theta) = \frac{1}{2}(5\cos^2\theta - 3\cos\theta)$	and so on.

6.4. RADIAL WAVE EQUATION

The radial wave equation is (see Sec.6.1) :

$$\frac{1}{R}\frac{d}{dr}\left(r^2\frac{dR}{dr}\right) + \frac{2m\ r^2}{\hbar^2}\left[E + \frac{e^2}{4\pi\varepsilon_0 r}\right] = \beta \quad \text{... (1)}$$

Multiplying this equation by R/r^2 and rearranging the terms, we get

$$\frac{1}{r^2}\frac{d}{dr}\left(r^2\frac{dR}{dr}\right) + \left[\frac{2m}{\hbar^2}\left(E + \frac{e^2}{4\pi\varepsilon_0 r}\right) - \frac{\beta}{r^2}\right]R = 0$$

Substituting $\beta = l(l+1)$, we get

$$\frac{1}{r^2}\frac{d}{dr}\left(r^2\frac{dR}{dr}\right)+\left[\frac{2m}{\hbar^2}\left(E+\frac{e^2}{4\pi\varepsilon_0 r}\right)-\frac{l(l+1)}{r^2}\right]R=0$$

Simplifying the first term, we obtain

$$\frac{d^2R}{dr^2}+\frac{2}{r}\frac{dR}{dr}+\left[\frac{2m}{\hbar^2}\left(E+\frac{e^2}{4\pi\varepsilon_0 r}\right)-\frac{l(l+1)}{r^2}\right]R=0 \quad \text{... (2)}$$

where l is the *orbital angular mometum quantum number,* and the other symbols have their usual meaning.

The solution of the radial wave equation for the wave function $R(r)$ is complicated. So it is not solved here in detail. Its solution for a special case, *i.e.* the ground state of the hydrogen atom will be given in Sec. 6.6. In the following paragraphs, we discuss a few points of its solution.

The radial wave equation is the only equation that contains a term involving the total energy E. The energy E can be positive or negative. When E is positive, the electron is unbound to the proton. This case occurs for large values of r. In this case the wave equation (2) becomes similar to that for a free particle, and so its solution gives finite wave function $R(r)$ for a positive value of E.

When E is negative, the electron is bound to the proton. In this case the solutions of the wave equation give finite wave functions only for total energies given by :

$$E_n = -\frac{me^4}{32\pi^2\varepsilon_0^2\hbar^2}\cdot\frac{1}{n^2} \quad \text{... (3)}$$

or

$$E_n = -\frac{m\,e^4}{8\varepsilon_0^2\,h^2}\cdot\frac{1}{n^2} \quad \text{... (4)}$$

where n can have the values given by

$$n = 1,\ 2,\ 3,\ \ldots$$

The parameter n is called the *total quantum number* or the *principal quantum number.*

The expression for E_n agrees with that obtained by the Bohr theory of hydrogen atom.

From the solution for the ground state of the hydrogen atom, for which the quantum numbers have values

$$m_l = 0,\quad l = 0,\quad n = 1,$$

the expression for the most probable distance of the electron from the proton has been obtained as

$$\frac{4\pi\,\varepsilon_0\hbar^2}{m\,e^2}$$

This expression agrees with that for the radius of the first Bohr orbit, and it is usually denoted by a_0.

Therefore, $$a_0 = \frac{4\pi\varepsilon_0\hbar^2}{m\,e^2} \quad \text{... (5)}$$

or $$a_o = \frac{\varepsilon_o h^2}{\pi m\ e^2} \qquad \text{... (6)}$$

Radial Wave-Function and Complete Wave-Function

The solution of the radial wave equation for the radial wave-function for a given value of the principal quantum number n and the orbital quantum number l, and the derivation of an expression for the normalization constant require complicated mathematical details. So we state only the expression for normalized radial wave-function $R_{nl}(r)$ for the hydrogen atom as :

$$R_{nl}(r) = -\left[\left(\frac{2}{na_0}\right)^3 \frac{(n-l-1)!}{2n\{(n+1)!\}^3}\right]^{1/2} .e^{-\rho/2}\rho^l .\ L_{n+1}^{2l+1}(\rho) \qquad \text{... (7)}$$

where $n = 1, 2, 3, ...$

$$\rho = \alpha r = \left(\frac{me^2}{2\pi\varepsilon_0 \hbar^2 n}\right) r = \left(\frac{2}{na_0}\right) r \qquad \text{... (8)}$$

The function $L_{n+1}^{2l+1}(\rho)$ are associated Laguerre functions, defined by

$$L_r^s = \frac{d^s}{d\rho^s} L_r(\rho)$$

where $L_r(\rho)$ are the Laguerre polynomials defined as

$$L_r(\rho) = e^\rho \frac{d^r}{d\rho^r}\left(\rho^r e^{-\rho}\right)$$

The complete wave-function for the hydrogen atom is written as :

$$\psi nlm(r, \theta, \phi) = R_{nl}(r) Q_{lm_l}(\theta) F_{m_l}(\phi) \qquad \text{... (9)}$$

where $n = 1, 2, 3, 4, ...$

$l = 0, 1, 2, 3, ...(n-1)$

$m_l = 0, \pm 1, \pm 2, \pm 3, ... \pm l,$

and $F_{m_l}(\phi), Q_{l_{m_l}}(\theta)$, and $R_{1n}(r)$ are given by Eq. (8) (Sec. 6.2), Eq.(7) (Sec. 6.3) and Eq. (7) (Sec.6.4).

6.5. QUANTUM NUMBERS: n, l, m_l

The special feature of the quantum mechanical theory of the hydrogen atom is the occurrence of the three quantum numbers:

(*i*) Total quantum number, or principal quantum number, n,

(*ii*) Orbital angular momentum quantum number, l, and

(*iii*) Orbital magnetic quantum number, m_l.

In the system of spherical polar coordinates, the variables which lead to the occurrence of the quantum numbers n, l, and m_l in the solutions of the three parts of Schrödinger's equation for the hydrogen atom are respectively, length of the radius vector r, zenith angle θ, and azimuthal angle ϕ. The solutions are finite and well-behaved only if the following conditions are satisfied by the quantum numbers:

(i) m_l must be 0 or a positive or negative integer $(0, \pm 1, \pm 2, \pm 3, \ldots\ldots)$.

(ii) l must be zero or a positive integer equal to or greater than the magnitude $|m_l|$ of m_l,

i.e. $\quad l \geq |m_l|$

or $\quad |m_l| \leq l$

This inequality can be expressed as a condition for m_l in the form :

$$m_l = 0, \ \pm 1, \ \pm 2, \ \pm 3, \ \ldots\ldots, \pm l.$$

(iii) n must be a positive integer equal to or greater than $(l+1)$, *i.e.*

$$n \geq l+1$$

or

$$l+1 \leq n$$

or

$$l \leq (n-1)$$

This inequality can be expressed as a condition for l in the form :

$$l = 0, \ 1, \ 2, \ 3, \ \ldots\ldots, (n-1)$$

A summary of the three quantum numbers $n, l,$ and m_l with their permissible values is as follows:

(1) Total quantum number : $n = 1, \ 2, \ 3, \ \ldots\ldots$

(2) Orbital angular momentum quantum number : $l = 0, 1, 2, 3, \ldots\ldots, n-1$.

(3) Orbital magnetic quantum nunmber : $m_l = 0, \ \pm 1, \ \pm 2, \ \pm 3, \ \ldots\ldots, \pm l$.

6.6. SOLUTION OF RADIAL WAVE EQUATION FOR THE GROUND STATE

The radial part of the time-independent Schrodinger's wave equation for the hydrogen atom is :

$$\frac{d^2R}{dr^2} + \frac{2}{r}\cdot\frac{dR}{dr} + \left[\frac{2m}{\hbar^2}\left(E + \frac{e^2}{4\pi\varepsilon_0 r}\right) - \frac{l(l+1)}{r^2}\right]R = 0 \quad \ldots. (1)$$

where l is the orbital angular momentum quantum number, and other symbols have their usual meaning.

For the ground state of the hydrogen atom the quantum numbers have their smallest possible values, *i.e.* $n=1$, $l=0$ and $m_l = 0$. Putting $l=0$ in Eq. (1), we get the equation for the ground state as :

$$\frac{d^2R}{dr^2} + \frac{2}{r}\frac{dR}{dr} + \frac{2m}{\hbar^2}\left(E + \frac{e^2}{4\pi\varepsilon_0 r}\right)R = 0 \quad \ldots (2)$$

The simplest solution of Eq. (2) is :

$$R(r) = Ae^{-\alpha r} \quad \ldots(3)$$

where α is a constant , and A is the normalization constant.

From Eq. (3) it is evident that:

(i) R is finite for all values of r. It has a large value only near the proton.

(ii) For each value or r, R has one value only.

(iii) R is continuous.

From Eq. (3), we obtain

$$\frac{dR}{dr} = -A\alpha e^{-\alpha r} = -\alpha A e^{-\alpha r} = -\alpha R$$

and
$$\frac{d^2R}{dr^2} = -\alpha\frac{dR}{dr} = -\alpha(-\alpha R) = \alpha^2 R$$

Substituting the expressions for these differential coefficients in Eq. (2), we get :

$$\therefore \quad \alpha^2 R - \frac{2\alpha R}{r} + \frac{2m}{\hbar^2}\left(E + \frac{e^2}{4\pi\varepsilon_0 r}\right)R = 0$$

Since *R (r)* is not zero, we divide both sides of this equation by *R (r)* and after rearrangement of the terms, we get :

$$\left(\alpha^2 + \frac{2mE}{\hbar^2}\right) = \frac{1}{r}\left(2\alpha - \frac{me^2}{2\pi\varepsilon_0\hbar^2}\right) \quad \text{... (4}$$

The left side of Eq. (4) is independent of *r*, and since the equation must be true for any value of *r*, both sides of this equation must be zero. Thus, equating the right side of Eq. (4) to zero,

$$2\alpha - \frac{me^2}{2\pi\varepsilon_0\hbar^2} = 0$$

or
$$\alpha = \frac{me^2}{4\pi\varepsilon_0\hbar^2} \quad \text{... (5)}$$

$$\therefore \quad \frac{1}{\alpha} = \frac{4\pi\varepsilon_0\hbar^2}{me^2}$$

The *reciprocal* of α is the radius a_o of the first Bohr orbit.

Thus
$$a_0 = \frac{4\pi\varepsilon_0\hbar^2}{me^2} = \frac{\varepsilon_0 h^2}{\pi m e^2} \quad \text{... (6)}$$

Similarly equating the left side of Eq. (4) to zero.

$$\alpha^2 + \frac{2mE}{\hbar^2} = 0$$

or
$$E = -\frac{\hbar^2\alpha^2}{2m} \quad \text{... (7)}$$

Substituting the value of α in this equation,

$$E = -\frac{\hbar^2}{2m}\left(\frac{me^2}{4\pi\varepsilon_0\hbar^2}\right)^2$$

$$= -\frac{me^4}{32\pi^2\varepsilon_0^2\hbar^2} \quad \text{... (8a)}$$

Substituting $\hbar = h/2\pi$, we get,

$$E = -\frac{me^4}{8\varepsilon_0^2 h^2} \quad \text{... (8b)}$$

The total energy E of the electron, as given by Eq. (8*a*) or (8*b*) is the same as that derived by the Bohr theory for $n = 1$. Therefore, this is lowest energy-level for the electron in the hydrogen atom and is called the ground state energy of the hydrogen atom.

Since the value of the constant $\alpha = \frac{1}{a_0}$, and that of the normalization constant :

$$A = 2\left(\frac{1}{a_0}\right)^{3/2}$$

the solution of the radial wave equation for the ground state is :

$$R_{1,0}(r) = 2\left(\frac{1}{a_0}\right)^{3/2} .e^{-r/a_0} \quad \text{... (9)}$$

Most Probable Position of the Electron in the Ground State

To obtain the probability of finding the electron between r and $(r+dr)$ from the nucleus, we describe two concentric spheres about the nucleus with radii r and $(r+dr)$. The volume of the shell between these spheres is $4\pi r^2 dr$.

The probability of finding the electron within this shell is given by :

$$P = |R(r)|^2 \times 4\pi r^2 \quad \text{... (10)}$$

$$= \left(Ae^{-\alpha r}\right)^2 \times 4\pi r^2 dr \qquad \because \quad R(r) = Ae^{-\alpha r}$$

$$= 4\pi A r^2 e^{-2\alpha r} dr \quad \text{... (11)}$$

Because of the factor r^2 the probability is small at small distances from the nucleus, and because of the factor $e^{-2\alpha r}$ it is also small of large distances. The most probable position of the electron will be where P is maximum as shown in Fig.6.2.

Suppose at $r = r_1$, P is maximum.

Differentiating Eq. (11) with respect to r,

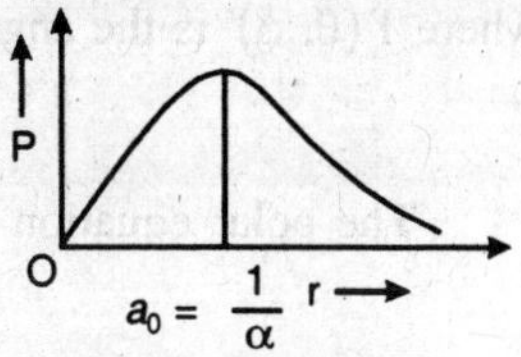

Fig. 6.2

$$\frac{dP}{dr} = 4\pi A\left[r^2 e^{-2\alpha r}(-2\alpha) + 2re^{-2\alpha r}\right]dr$$

$$= 8\pi A r e^{-2ar}[-r\alpha + 1]dr$$

At $r = r_1$, P is maximum,

$$\therefore \quad \left(\frac{dP}{dr}\right)_{r=r_1} = 0$$

Hence $\quad -r_1\alpha + 1 = 0$

or $$r_1 = \frac{1}{\alpha} = \frac{4\pi\varepsilon_0\hbar^2}{m\,e^2} = a_0$$

Thus the most probable position of the electron is at a distance equal to the radius of the first Bohr orbit. The wave function $R(r) = Ae^{-\alpha r}$ therefore, represents an *s*-state with smallest circular orbit.

Note: In our foregoing discussion the equations require a certain correction. We have considered the proton to be stationary. In reality both the orbital electron and the proton revolve around a common centre of mass. To make correction for the motion of the proton, we should replace the mass *m* of the electron by its reduced mass :

$$m' = \frac{m}{1 + m/M}$$

where *M* is the mass of the proton.

6.7. INTERPRETATION OF THE QUANTUM NUMBERS

We have seen that there are three quantum numbers *n, l,* and m_l in the quantum mechanical treatment of the hydrogen atom.

The quantum number *n* is associated with the total energy of the electron. So it is called the *principal quantum number* or the *total quantum number.*

Now we will show that the quantum numbers *l* and m_l are related to the angular momentum of the electron.

The operator for the square of the orbital angular momentum is [See Sec. 4.4, Eq. (19)]

$$\hat{L}^2 = -\hbar^2\left[\frac{1}{\sin\theta}\frac{\partial}{\partial\theta}\left(\sin\theta\frac{\partial}{\partial\theta}\right) + \frac{1}{\sin^2\theta}\frac{\partial^2}{\partial\phi^2}\right] \quad \text{... (1)}$$

It means that the operator, acting on the angular part of the wave-function, reproduces the same wave-function multiplied by the square of the orbital angular momentum.

$$\therefore \quad -\hbar^2\left[\frac{1}{\sin\theta}\frac{\partial}{\partial\theta}\left(\sin\theta\frac{\partial}{\partial\theta}\right) + \frac{1}{\sin^2\theta}\frac{\partial^2}{\partial\phi^2}\right]Y(\theta,\phi) = L^2 Y(\theta,\phi) \quad \text{.... (2)}$$

or $$\hat{L}^2 Y(\theta,\phi) = L^2 Y(\theta,\phi) \quad \text{... (3)}$$

where $Y(\theta, \phi)$ is the angular part of $\psi(r, \theta, \phi)$; and it is given by

$$Y(\theta,\phi) = Q(\theta)F(\phi) \quad \text{... (4)}$$

The polar equation and the azimuthal wave equation respectively are :

$$\frac{1}{\sin\theta}\frac{d}{d\theta}\left(\sin\theta\frac{dQ}{d\theta}\right) + \left[l(l+1) - \frac{m_l^2}{\sin^2\theta}\right]Q = 0 \quad \text{... (5)}$$

$$\frac{d^2F}{d\phi^2} + m_l^2 F = 0 \quad \text{... (6)}$$

From Eq. (6)

$$m_l^2 = -\frac{1}{F}\frac{d^2F}{d\phi^2} \quad \text{... (7)}$$

Subsituting this expression for m_l^2 in Eq. (5) :

$$\frac{1}{\sin\theta}\frac{d}{d\theta}\left(\sin\theta\frac{dQ}{d\theta}\right)+\left[l(l+1)+\frac{1}{\sin^2\theta.F}\frac{d^2F}{d\phi^2}\right]Q=0$$

Multiplying this equation by F

$$\frac{F}{\sin\theta}\frac{d}{d\theta}\left(\sin\theta\frac{dQ}{d\theta}\right)+\left[l(l+1)F+\frac{1}{\sin^2\theta}\frac{d^2F}{d\phi^2}\right]Q=0$$

or
$$\frac{1}{\sin\theta}\frac{\partial}{d\theta}\left(\sin\theta\frac{\partial\, QF}{\partial\,\theta}\right)+\frac{1}{\sin^2\theta}\frac{\partial^2 QF}{\partial\,\phi^2}=-l(l+1)QF$$

or
$$\left[\frac{1}{\sin\theta}\frac{\partial}{\partial\,\theta}\left(\sin\theta\frac{\partial}{\partial\,\theta}\right)+\frac{1}{\sin^2\theta}\frac{\partial^2}{\partial\,\phi^2}\right]Y(\theta,\phi)=-l(l+1)Y(\theta,\phi)$$

Multiplying this equation by $-\hbar^2$

$$-\hbar^2\left[\frac{1}{\sin\theta}\frac{\partial}{\partial\,\theta}\left(\sin\theta\frac{\partial}{\partial\,\theta}\right)+\frac{1}{\sin^2\theta}\frac{\partial^2}{\partial\,\phi^2}\right]Y(\theta,\phi)=l(l+1)\hbar^2Y(\theta,\phi) \quad \text{... (8)}$$

or
$$\hat{L}^2Y(\theta,\phi)=l(l+1)\hbar^2Y(\theta,\phi) \quad \text{... (9)}$$

This equation shows that $Y(\theta,\phi)$ is an eigen function of the operator $\hat{L}^2$ and the eigen value of the operator is $l(l+1)\hbar^2$.

Comparing Eqs.(3) and (9), we find the magnitude of the orbital angular momentum is given by :

$$L=\hbar\sqrt{l(l+1)} \quad \text{... (10)}$$

Thus the quantum number l determines the magnitude of the orbital angular momentum, and therefore, it is called the *orbital-angular momentum quantum number or orbital quantum number.*

The operator for the z-component of the orbital angular momentum is

$$\hat{L}_z=\frac{\hbar}{i}\frac{\partial}{\partial\,\phi}$$

$\therefore$
$$\frac{\hbar}{i}\frac{\partial}{\partial\,\phi}F(\phi)=L_zF(\phi)$$

or
$$\hat{L}_zF(\phi)=L_zF(\phi) \quad \text{... (11)}$$

where L_z is the z-component of the angular momentum. A solution of the azimuthal wave equation for the hydrogen atom is :

$$F(\phi)=Ae^{im_l\phi}$$

Differentiating this equation with respect to ϕ,

$$\frac{\partial F(\phi)}{\partial \phi} = Aim_l e^{im_l\phi} = im_l F(\phi)$$

Multiplying this equation by $\hbar / i$,

$$\frac{\hbar}{i}\frac{\partial F(\phi)}{\partial \phi} = \frac{\hbar}{i} im_l F(\phi) = \hbar m_l F(\phi)$$

$$\hat{L}_z F(\phi) = \hbar m_l F(\phi) \qquad \text{... (12)}$$

This equation shows that $F(\phi)$ is an eigen-function of the operator $\hat{L}_z$ and the eigen-value of the operator is $m_l\hbar$. Comparing Eqs. (11) and (12) the z-component of the angular momentum is given by,

$$L_z = m_l \hbar \qquad \text{... (13)}$$

Thus the quantum number m_l determines tne z-component of the angular momentum. When a magnetic field is applied along the z-axis, the degeneracy of the quantum state having the same value of n and l but different values of m_l can be removed. Therefore, this quantum number is called the *orbital magnetic quantum number.*

SOLVED EXAMPLES

Example 6.1. *Calculate the total energy of the electron in the first Bohr orbit, in electron volt. (Given: electron rest mass* $m = 9.11 \times 10^{-31}$ kg, *electron charge* $e = 1.6 \times 10^{-19}$ C, *Planck's constant* $h = 6.63 \times 10^{-34}$ Js, *permittivity of free space* $\varepsilon_0 = 8.85 \times 10^{-12}$ C^2/Nm^2 (F/m) *and* $1 \text{eV} = 1.6 \times 10^{-19}$ J

Solution

$$E_n = -\frac{me^4}{32\pi^2 \varepsilon_0^2 \hbar^2 n^2}$$

For the ground state $n = 1$, and since $\hbar = \dfrac{h}{2\pi}$

$$\therefore \quad E_1 = -\frac{me^4}{8\,\varepsilon_0^2 h^2}$$

$$= -\frac{9.11 \times 10^{-31} \times (1.6 \times 10^{-19})^4}{8 \times (8.85 \times 10^{-12})^2 \times (6.63 \times 10^{-34})^2}$$

$$= -\frac{59.7 \times 10^{-19}}{2.754} = \mathbf{-21.68 \times 10^{-19}\ J}$$

Now E_1 in eV is given by

$$E_1 = -\frac{21.68 \times 10^{-19}}{1.6 \times 10^{-19}} = -13.55 \text{ eV} = \mathbf{-13.6\ eV}$$

Example 6.2. *The solution of the radial part of Schrodinger's wave equation for the ground state of the hydrogen atom is*

$$R(r) = Ae^{-r/a_0}$$

where a_0 is the radius of the first Bohr orbit, and A is the normalization constant. Evaluate this constant.

Solution:

We have,

$$R(r) = Ae^{-r/a_0} \quad \text{... (1)}$$

The normalization condition for the total wave function $\psi(r,\theta,\psi)$ is

$$\iiint \psi(r,\theta,\phi)\psi^*(r,\theta,\psi)\,d\tau = 1 \quad \text{... (2)}$$

where $d\tau$ is the volume element in spherical polar coordinates :

$$d\tau = (r\sin\theta\, d\phi)(rd\theta)\,dr$$
$$= (r^2 dr)(\sin\theta\, d\theta)(d\phi) \quad \text{... (3)}$$

The total wave function is the product of the three functions $R(r)$, $Q(\theta)$,$F(\phi)$.

$$\therefore \quad \psi(r,\theta,\phi) = RQF \quad \text{... (4)}$$

Hence the normalization condition (Eq.2) becomes

$$\iiint (RR^*)(QQ^*)(FF^*)(r^2 dr)(\sin\theta\, d\theta)(d\phi) = 1$$

$$\int_0^\infty RR^* r^2 dr \int_0^\pi QQ^* \sin\theta\, d\theta \int_0^{2\pi} FF^* d\phi = 1 \quad \text{...(5)}$$

Hence for the radial wave function the normalization condition is :

$$\int_0^\infty RR^* r^2 dr = 1$$

$$\int_0^\infty \left(Ae^{-r/a_0}\right)\left(Ae^{-r/a_0}\right)^* r^2 dr = 0$$

$$A^2 \int_0^\infty r^2\, e^{-2r/a_0} dr = 1 \quad \text{... (6)}$$

The integral can be evaluated by the process of integration by parts. It is found that

$$\int_0^\infty r^2 e^{-2r/a_0} dr = \frac{a_0^3}{4} \quad \text{... (7)}$$

Substituting this value in Eq. 6, we get

$$A^2\left(\frac{a_0^3}{4}\right)=1$$

$$\therefore \qquad A=2\left(\frac{1}{a_0}\right)^{3/2} \qquad \text{... (8)}$$

This is the value of the normalization constant. Now the wave function for the ground state is expressed as :

$$R(r)=2\left(\frac{1}{a_0}\right)^{3/2}.e^{-r/a_0} \qquad \text{... (9)}$$

Example 6.3. *The wave function* $\psi(r,\theta,\phi)$ *of the hydrogen atom for 1s state is*

$$\psi(1s)=\left(\frac{1}{\pi a_0^3}\right)^{1/2} e^{-r/a_0}$$

Show that the wave function is normalized, and find the average distance of the electron from the nucleus, in 1s orbital, given that

$$\int_0^\infty x^n e^{-ax}dx=\frac{\Gamma(n+1)}{a^{n+1}}$$

Solution.

(*i*) The normalization condition for the complete wave function in 1s state is :

$$\iiint \psi(1s)\psi^*(1s)\,d\tau=1$$

or

$$\iiint |\psi(1s)|^2\,d\tau=1 \qquad \text{... (1)}$$

where $d\tau$ is the volume element given by,

$$d\tau=(r\sin\theta\,d\phi)(rd\theta)dr=(r^2dr)(\sin\theta\,d\theta)(d\phi)$$

Now we evaluate the integral on left side of Eq. (1)

$$\iiint |\psi(1s)|^2 d\tau=\iiint \frac{1}{\pi a_0^3}e^{-2r/a_0}(r^2dr)(\sin\theta\,d\theta)(d\phi)$$

$$=\frac{1}{\pi a_0^3}\int_0^\infty r^2e^{-2r/a_0}dr\int_0^\pi \sin\theta\,d\theta\int_0^{2\pi}d\phi \qquad \text{... (2)}$$

The values of the integrals are

$$\int_0^\infty r^2e^{-2r/a_0}dr=\frac{\Gamma(2+1)}{(2/a_0)^3}=2\times\frac{a_0^3}{8}=\frac{a_0^3}{4}$$

$$\int_0^{\pi} \sin\theta\, d\theta = 2\int_0^{\pi/2} \sin\theta\, d\theta = 2 \quad \text{and} \quad \int_0^{2\pi} d\phi = 2\pi$$

Substituting these values in Eq. (2),

$$\iiint |\psi_1|^2\, d\tau = \frac{1}{\pi a_0^3} \times \frac{a_0^3}{4} \times 2 \times 2\pi = 1$$

Hence the wave function is normalized.

(*ii*) **Expectation value of *r* in 1s state**

$$< r > = \iiint \psi^*(1s) r \psi(1s) d\tau$$

$$= \iiint \left(\frac{1}{\pi a_0^3}\right)^{1/2} e^{-r/a_0} r \left(\frac{1}{\pi a_0^3}\right)^{1/2} e^{-r/a_0} (r^2 dr)(\sin\theta\, d\theta)(d\phi)$$

$$= \frac{1}{\pi a_0^3} \int_0^{\infty} r^3 e^{-2r/a_0} dr \int_0^{\pi} \sin\theta\, d\theta \int_0^{2\pi} d\phi \qquad ...(3)$$

The values of the integrals are :

$$\int_0^{\infty} r^3 e^{-2r/a_0} dr = \frac{\Gamma(3+1)}{(2/a_0)^4} = \frac{3\times 2\times 1}{1} \times \frac{a_0^4}{16} = \frac{3a_0^4}{8}$$

$$\int_0^{\pi} \sin\theta\;\, d\theta = 2, \quad \text{and} \quad \int_0^{2\pi} d\phi = 2\pi \cdot$$

Hence from Eq. (3), we have

$$< r > = \frac{1}{\pi a_0^3} \times \frac{3a_0^4}{8} \times 2 \times 2\pi = \frac{3}{2} a_0 .$$

Example 6.4. *The normalized wave function of the hydrogen atom for 1s state is*

$$\psi(1s) = \left(\frac{1}{\pi a_0^3}\right)^{1/2} e^{-r/a_0}$$

where $a_0 = \dfrac{4\pi\varepsilon_0 \hbar^2}{m e^2}$ *is the Bohr radius. Find the expectation value of the potential energy of the electron in 1s state, given that*

$$\int_0^{\infty} x^n e^{-ax} dx = \frac{\Gamma(n+1)}{a^{n+1}}$$

Solution. The potential energy of the electron at distance r from nucleus is given by :

$$V = -\frac{e^2}{4\pi\varepsilon_0 r} \quad \text{(in SI units)}$$

The expectation value of the potential energy is given by :

$$\langle V \rangle = \iiint \psi^*(1s) V \psi(1s)\, d\tau$$

$$= \iiint \left(\frac{1}{\pi a_0^3}\right)^{1/2} e^{-r/a_0} \left(-\frac{e^2}{4\pi\varepsilon_0 r}\right)\left(\frac{1}{\pi a_0^3}\right)^{1/2} e^{-r/a_0} \left(r^2 dr\right)(\sin\theta\, d\theta)(d\phi)$$

$$= -\left(\frac{e^2}{4\pi\varepsilon_0}\right)\frac{1}{\pi a_0^3}\int_0^\infty r e^{-2r/a_0} dr \int_0^\pi \sin\theta\, d\theta \int_0^{2\pi} d\phi$$

The values of the integrals are

$$\int_0^\infty r e^{-2r/a_0} dr = \frac{\Gamma(1+1)}{(2/a_0)^2}$$

$$= \frac{1}{1} \times \frac{a_0^2}{4} = \frac{a_0^2}{4}$$

$$\int_0^\pi \sin\theta\, d\theta = 2. \quad \text{and} \quad \int_0^{2\pi} d\phi = 2\pi.$$

Hence

$$\langle V \rangle = -\left(\frac{e^2}{4\pi\varepsilon_0}\right)\frac{1}{\pi a_0^3} \times \frac{a_0^2}{4} \times 2 \times 2\pi$$

$$= -\frac{e^2}{4\pi\varepsilon_0 a_0} = -\frac{e^2}{4\pi\varepsilon_0} \times \frac{m e^2}{4\pi\varepsilon_0 \hbar^2}$$

$$= -\frac{m e^4}{(4\pi\,\varepsilon_0)^2\, \hbar^2}$$

QUESTIONS AND PROBLEMS

1. (*a*) Write the time-independent Schrödinger wave equation for the hydrogen atom in spherical polar coordinates and separate it into three differential equations for the three parts of the total wave-function.

   (*b*) Solve the azimuthal wave equation and show that the magnetic quantum number m_l must be zero or a positive or negative integer. (Bangalore, 2005)

2. (*a*) State the radial part of the time-independent Schrödinger wave equation for the hydrogen atom with interpretation of the wave-function. (Mysore, 2004)

(*b*) Apply this equation to find the energy of the atom in the ground state.

$$\left(\textbf{Ans. } E_1 = -\frac{m e^4}{32\pi^2\varepsilon_0^2\hbar^2}\right)$$

3. Write down the radial part of the time-independent Schrödinger wave equation for the hydrogen atom and solve the equation to obtain the eigen values of the energy of atom.

$$\left(\textbf{Ans. } E_n = -\frac{m e^2}{32\pi^2\varepsilon_0^2\hbar^2}\frac{1}{n^2}\right)$$

4. State Schödinger's equation for hydrogen atom in spherical polar coordinates. Explain the significance of various quantum numbers defining a state of the system. What is the order degeneracy of a certain energy state? (Gorakhpur, 2004)

5. (*a*) Explain how the problem of the hydrogen atom can be solved quantum-mechanically. Solve the radial part of the Schrödinger equation for the hydrogen atom and obtain the eigen-values of the energy. Explain the degeneracy in the spectrum.

6. The complete wave function of the hydrogen atom for $2p$ state is

$$\psi_{210} = \frac{1}{4}\left(\frac{1}{2\pi a_0^3}\right)^{1/2}\frac{r}{a_0}e^{-r/2a_0}\cos\theta$$

Prove that the wave function is normalized. Given that

$$\int_0^\infty x^n e^{-ax}\,dx = \frac{\Gamma(n+1)}{a^{n+1}}.$$

7. Find the expectation value of the distance of the electron from the nucleus in the hydrogen atom in $2p$ state. (**Ans.** $5a_0$)

8. Write the significance of quantum numbers n and l. (N.U., 2006)

CHAPTER 7

ELECTRON SPIN

The quantum theory of the hydrogen atom explains satisfactorily certain properties of the hydrogen atom without the use of the postulates introduced by Bohr. But it cannot explain the fine structure of spectral lines and anomalous Zeeman effect. For explanation of these phenomena and other atomic phenomena the hypothesis of electron spin and the exclusion principle were introduced. In this chapter we shall study the elcctron spin and the exclusion principle.

7.1. ORBITAL MAGNETIC DIPOLE MOMENT AND ORBITAL ANGULAR MOMENTUM OF AN ELECTRON.

Let an electron of mass m be rotating with speed v in a circular orbit of radius r round the nucleus of an atom. An electron circulating round the nucleus is a small current loop. So it has an *orbital magnetic dipole moment* of magnitude μ_1 given by

$$\mu_l = IA \qquad \text{... (1)}$$

where I is the conventional current in the direction opposite to that of v, and A is the area of the loop. The current is equivalent to the rate at which the electronic charge passes any given point on the orbit.

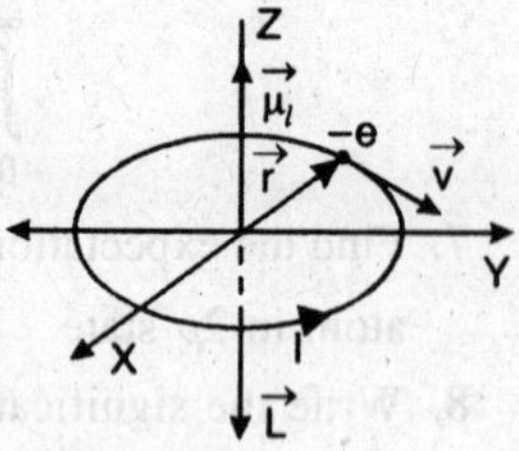

Fig 7.1

$$\therefore \qquad I = -\frac{e}{T} = -\frac{e}{2\pi r / v} = -\frac{ev}{2\pi r}$$

where T is the time of one revolution of the electron round the nucleus, and $-e$ is the electronic charge.

Hence from Eq. (1), we have

$$\mu_l = -\frac{ev}{2\pi r}(\pi r^2) = -\frac{evr}{2} \qquad \text{... (2)}$$

The minus sign has been inserted in the expression for the current, because the electronic charge is $-e$. In vector form Eq. (2) is written as

$$\vec{\mu}_l = -\frac{e\,\vec{r} \times \vec{v}}{2} \qquad \text{... (3)}$$

This equation shows that the direction of $\vec{\mu}_l$ is opposite to that of the vector product $\vec{r} \times \vec{v}$.

In Fig.7.1 the direction of $\vec{\mu}_l$ is perpendicular to the plane of the orbit and pointing upwards along the positive direction of the z-axis

Orbital Angular Momentum:

The orbital angular momentum $\vec{L}$ of the electron is given by the vector product

$$\vec{L} = m\,\vec{r} \times \vec{v} \qquad \text{... (4)}$$

In Fig.7.1 the direction of $\vec{L}$ is perpendicular to the plane of the orbit and pointing downwards, *i.e.* along the negative direction of the z- axis.

Relation between $\vec{\mu}_l$ and $\vec{L}$:

Dividing Eq. (3) by (4) , we obtain

$$\frac{\vec{\mu}_l}{\vec{L}} = -\frac{e}{2m}$$

$$\therefore \qquad \vec{\mu}_l = -\frac{e}{2m}\vec{L} \qquad \text{... (5)}$$

The minus sign shows that $\vec{\mu}_l$ and $\vec{L}$ are in opposite directions.

The magnitude L of *the orbital angular momentum* $\vec{L}$ of an electron in an atom is quantized, *i.e.* it can have only certain values. These values are given by (See Sec. 6.7)

$$L = \sqrt{l(l+1)}\,\hbar \qquad \text{....(6)}$$

where l is the *orbital angular momentum quantum number*, and $\hbar = h/2\pi$.

The permissible values of l are

$$l = 0, 1, 2, \ldots\ldots (n-1).$$

Now from Eq. (5), the magnitude of $\vec{\mu}_l$ is given by

$$\mu_l = \frac{e}{2m}L \qquad \text{...(7)}$$

or,

$$\mu_l = \frac{e}{2m}\sqrt{l(l+1)}\,\hbar \qquad \text{...(8)}$$

This equation gives the expression for the *magnitude of the orbital magnetic dipole moment* $\vec{\mu}_l$, and shows that the magnitude μ_l must also be quantized.

Bohr Magneton:

According to Bohr's theory of the hydrogen atom, the angular momentum L of the electron takes on only those values which are integral multiples of $\hbar$, i.e.

$$L = n\hbar$$

Substituting the value of L for the ground state $(n = 1)$ in Eq. (7) we get

$$\mu_1 = \frac{e}{2m}\hbar = \frac{eh}{4\pi m}$$

The magnetic moment given by this equation when the electron is in the first Bohr orbit is called the *Bohr magneton* and it is denoted by μ_B.

Thus $$\mu_B = \frac{eh}{4\pi m} \quad \text{.... (9)}$$

Now Eq.(8) can be expressed in terms of the Bohr magneton:

$$\mu_1 = \frac{e}{2m}\sqrt{l(l+1)}\frac{h}{2\pi} = \sqrt{l(l+1)}\frac{eh}{4\pi m} \quad \text{... 10(a)}$$

$$= \sqrt{l(l+1)}\,\mu_B$$

or $$\vec{\mu_l} = \vec{l}_{\mu B} \quad \text{... 10(b)}$$

where the vector $\vec{l}$ has the magnitude $\sqrt{l(l+1)}$.

To provide a reference direction for measurement of the components of $\vec{\mu_l}$ and $\vec{L}$ in that direction, we assume that a uniform magnetic field having its direction parallel to a z-axis is applied to the atom. Then the z-components of μ_1 and $\vec{L}$ along that direction can be measured. In terms of the z-components $\mu_{l,z}$ and L_z, Eq. (5) is written as :

$$\mu_{l,z} = -\frac{e}{2m}L_z \quad \text{... (11)}$$

The component L_z of the *orbital angular momentum* $\vec{L}$ is quantized, it can have only the values given by

$$L_z = m_1\frac{h}{2\pi} = m_1\hbar \quad \text{... (12)}$$

The parameter m_l is the *orbital magnetic quantum number*. The permissible values of m_l are:

$$m_l = 0, \pm 1, \pm 2, \quad ... \pm l$$

Substituting the value of L_z in Eq. (11), we get :

$$\mu_{l,z} = -\frac{e}{2m}\left(m_l\frac{h}{2\pi}\right) = -m_l\frac{eh}{4\pi m}$$

$$= -m_l\mu_B \quad \text{... (13)}$$

Gyromagnetic ratio of the orbital electron:

It is defined as the ratio of the orbital magnetic dipole moment $\vec{\mu}_l$ to the orbital angular momentum $\vec{L}$ of the electron. Thus from Eq. (5) the ratio is given by :

$$\frac{\vec{\mu}_l}{\vec{L}} = -\frac{e}{2m} \quad \text{... (14)}$$

7.2. SPIN ANGULAR MOMENTUM AND SPIN MAGNETIC DIPOLE MOMENT OF AN ELECTRON

In 1925 Goudsmit and Uhlenbeck introduced the hypothesis that an electron in an atom can be regarded as a charged sphere rotating or spinning about an axis through its centre of mass. Due to the spinning motion it has an *intrinsic spin angular momentum* $\vec{S}$, and an *intrinsic spin magnetic dipole moment* $\vec{\mu}_s$.

Because the electron is negatively charged the vectors $\vec{\mu}_s$ and $\vec{S}$ are in opposite directions, and therefore they are related by :

$$\vec{\mu}_s = -\frac{e}{m}\vec{S} \quad \text{... (1)}$$

The magnitude S of the spin angular momentum $\vec{S}$ of any electron is quantized and it is given by

$$S = \sqrt{s(s+1)}\,\hbar \quad \text{... (2)}$$

The parameter s is called the *spin angular momentum quantum number*. It has the single value 1/2, *i.e.* $s = \frac{1}{2}$.

Therefore, the value of S is given by

$$S = \sqrt{\frac{1}{2}\left(\frac{1}{2}+1\right)}\,\hbar = \frac{\sqrt{3}}{2}\,\hbar = 0.866\,\hbar \quad \text{... (3)}$$

From Eq. (1) the magnitude μ_s of the *spin magnetic dipole moment* is given by :

$$\mu_s = \frac{e}{m}S = \frac{e}{m}\sqrt{s(s+1)}\,\hbar \quad \text{...(4)}$$

This equation shows that μ_s is also quantized.

Since $s = \frac{1}{2}$,

$$\mu_s = \frac{e}{m}\frac{\sqrt{3}}{2}\hbar = \frac{\sqrt{3}}{2}\frac{e\hbar}{m} \quad \text{... (5)}$$

This equation gives the magnitude of the spin magnet dipole moment.

For providing a reference direction for measurement, we assume that a uniform magnetic field having its direction parallel to a z-axis is applied to the atom. Then the z-components of $\vec{\mu}_s$ and $\vec{S}$ can be measured. Now in terms of the z-components $\mu_{s,z}$ and S_z, Eq. (1) is written as

$$\mu_{s,z} = -\frac{e}{m} S_z \qquad \text{... (6)}$$

The component S_z of the *spin angular momentum* is quantized, it can have only the values given by :

$$S_z = m_s \frac{h}{2\pi} = m_s \hbar \qquad \text{... (7)}$$

The parameter m_s is called the *spin magnetic quantum number*. m_s has only two permissible values:

$$m_s = +\frac{1}{2} \text{ and } -\frac{1}{2}.$$

When $m_s = +\frac{1}{2}$, the electron is said to be spin up, and when $m_s = -\frac{1}{2}$ the electron is said to be *spin down*.

Since $m_s = \pm\frac{1}{2}$, the possible components of the spin angular momentum $\vec{S}$ along the z-axis are given by

$$S_z = \pm\frac{1}{2}\hbar \qquad \text{... (8)}$$

Now substituting the value of S_z in Eq. (6) we get the z-component of the spin magnetic dipole moment:

$$\mu_{s,z} = -\frac{e}{m}(m_s\hbar) = -m_s \frac{e\hbar}{m} \qquad \text{... (9)}$$

This equation shows that the component $\mu_{s,z}$ is also quantized.

Since $m_s = \pm\frac{1}{2}$, the possible components of the *spin magnetic dipole moment* along the z-axis are given by :

$$\mu_{s,z} = \pm\frac{e\hbar}{2m} = \pm\frac{eh}{4\pi m} = \pm\mu_B \qquad \text{...(10)}$$

Gyromagnetic ratio of the electron spin:

It is defined as the ratio of the spin magnetic dipole moment $\vec{\mu}_s$ to the spin angular momentum $\vec{S}$ of the electron.

Thus from Eq. (1) it is given by

$$\frac{\vec{\mu}_s}{\vec{S}} = -\frac{e}{m} \qquad \text{... (11)}$$

7.3. SPIN-ORBIT COUPLING

Let an electron of mass m be rotating in a circular orbit of radius r round a proton of a one-electron atom. Viewed from the frame of reference of the electron the proton with its positive charge e is moving in a circular orbit of radius r round the electron. Therefore the proton produces a magnetic field of flux density $\vec{B}$ at the position of the electron. Thus the electron finds itself in the magnetic field due to its own orbital motion.

This magnetic field acts on the electron's *spin magnetic dipole moment* $\vec{\mu}_s$. The potential energy V_m of a magnetic dipole of moment $\vec{\mu}_s$ in the magnetic field is given by :

$$V_m = -\mu_s B \cos\theta \qquad \text{... (1)}$$

where θ is the angle between the direction of $\vec{\mu}_s$ and that of $\vec{B}$ which is along the z-axis (Fig.7.2).

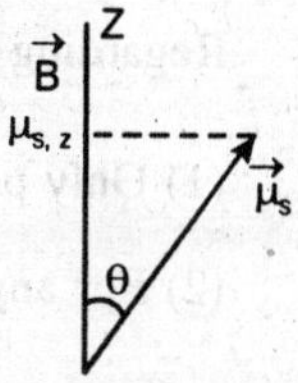

Fig 7.2

In Eq. (7), $\mu_s \cos\theta$ is the component of the vector $\vec{\mu}_s$ in the direction of $\vec{B}$. This component is $\mu_{s,z}$ which has two quantized values : $\pm\frac{e\hbar}{2m}$ (See Sec. 7.2, Eq. 10) ... (2)

$$\therefore \qquad \mu_s \cos\theta = \mu_{s,z} = \pm\frac{e\hbar}{2m} \qquad \text{... (3)}$$

Substituting for $\mu_s \cos\theta$ in Eq. (1) we obtain

$$V_m = \pm\frac{e\hbar}{2m} B \qquad \text{... (4)}$$

This expression gives the change of energy of an electron due to the spin-orbit coupling.

If the energy of an electron in a given atomic quantum state in the absence of spin-orbit coupling is E then depending on the orientation of the spin angular momentum vector $\vec{S}$, the total energy of the electron in the presence of the coupling will be

$$E + \frac{e\hbar}{2m} B, \qquad \text{or} \qquad E - \frac{e\hbar}{2m} B$$

Therefore every quantum state (except s-state) will split into two separate substates. Consequently every spectral line will split into two component lines.

7.4 QUANTUM NUMBERS *j* AND m_j

Quantum Number *j*:

Each electron in an atom has the *orbital angular momentum* $\vec{L}$ *and spin angular momentum* $\vec{S}$. The resultant angular momentum is called the *total angular momentum*. It is denoted by the vector $\vec{J}$ and is given by the vector sum of the vectors $\vec{L}$ and $\vec{S}$:

$$\vec{J} = \vec{L} + \vec{S} \quad \text{... (1)}$$

The magnitude J of the total angular momentum is quantized, *i.e.* it can have only certain values given by :

$$J = \sqrt{j(j+1)}\,\hbar \quad \text{... (2)}$$

where the parameter j is called the *total angular momentum quantum number*. Its permissible values are given by

$$j = l \pm s \quad \text{... (3)}$$

where l is the orbital angular momentum quantum number having possible values:

$$l = 0, 1, 2 \ \dots (n-1).$$

and s is the spin *angular momentum quantum number* having the single value :

$$s = \frac{1}{2}.$$

$$\therefore \qquad j = l \pm \frac{1}{2} \quad \text{... (4)}$$

Regarding the permissible values of j, the following points are to be noted:

(1) Only positive values of j are permissible, so that for $l = 0$, j has only one value $j = \frac{1}{2}$.

(2) For any given value of l except for $l=0$, j can have only the following two values :

$$j = l + \frac{1}{2}, \text{ and } j = l - \frac{1}{2},$$

so that an allowed value of j is always an odd multiple of $\frac{1}{2}$.

Use of the Quantum Number j:

Relative orientations of the vectors $\vec{J}$, $\vec{L}$ **and** $\vec{S}$

From the knowledge of the total angular momentum quantum number j, the orbital angular momentum quantum number l and the spin angular momentum quantum number s, we can determine the relative orientations of the vectors $\vec{J}, \vec{L}$, and $\vec{S}$. In the case of one-electron atom there are only two relative orientations of the vectors:

(*i*) for $j = l + s$, in this case $J > L$, and

(*ii*) for $j = l - s$, in this case $J < L$.

We now draw vector diagrams for the two cases: (*i*) $j = l + s$, and (*ii*) $j = l - s$.

(*i*) When $l=1$, then $j = 1 + \frac{1}{2} = \frac{3}{2}$, because $s = \frac{1}{2}$.

Therefore, the magnitudes of the vectors

$\vec{J}, \vec{L}$ and $\vec{S}$ are respectively given by

$$J=\sqrt{j(j+1)}\,\hbar=\sqrt{\frac{3}{2}\left(\frac{3}{2}+1\right)}\,\hbar=\frac{\sqrt{15}}{2}\,\hbar=1.936\ \hbar$$

$$L=\sqrt{l(l+1)}\,\hbar=\sqrt{1(1+1)}\,\hbar=\sqrt{2}\,\hbar=1.414\ \hbar$$

$$S=\sqrt{s(s+1)}\,\hbar=\sqrt{\frac{1}{2}\left(\frac{1}{2}+1\right)}\,\hbar=\frac{\sqrt{3}}{2}\,\hbar=0.866\ \hbar$$

(*ii*) When $l=1$, then $j=1-\frac{1}{2}=\frac{1}{2}$, because $s=\frac{1}{2}$.

Therefore, the magnitudes of the vectors are :

$$J=\sqrt{j(j+1)}\,\hbar=\sqrt{\frac{1}{2}\left(\frac{3}{2}\right)}\,\hbar=\frac{\sqrt{3}}{2}\,\hbar=0.866\ \hbar$$

$$L=\sqrt{l(l+1)}\,\hbar=\sqrt{1(1+1)}\,\hbar=\sqrt{2}\,\hbar=1.414\ \hbar$$

$$S=\sqrt{s(s+1)}\,\hbar=\sqrt{\frac{1}{2}\left(\frac{1}{2}+1\right)}\,\hbar=\frac{\sqrt{3}}{2}\,\hbar=0.866\ \hbar$$

The relative orientations of the vectors for the two cases are shown in Fig. 7.3. In each figure the lengths of the sides of the triangle are proportional to the magnitudes of the corresponding vectors.

For $j=l+s=\frac{3}{2}$ For $j=l-s=\frac{1}{2}$

Fig. 7.3

Quantum Number m_j:

The z-component J_z of the total angular momentum $\vec{J}$ is quantized; it can have only the values given by :

$$J_z=m_j\frac{h}{2\pi}=m_j\hbar \qquad \text{... (5)}$$

The parameter m_j is called the *total magnetic quantum number*.

The permissible values of m_j range from $+j$ through O to $-j$ in integral steps, *i.e.*

$$m_j=j,\quad j-1,\quad j-2,\,..........,\,-j \qquad \text{... (6)}$$

Thus an allowed value of m_j is an odd multiple of $\frac{1}{2}$.

Example: For $j = \frac{5}{2}$, the allowed values of m_j are : $m_j = \frac{5}{2}, \frac{3}{2}, \frac{1}{2}, -\frac{1}{2}, -\frac{3}{2}, -\frac{5}{2}$.

Thus for a given value of j there are $(2j+1)$ values of m_j.

Precession of $\vec{L}$ and $\vec{S}$ about $\vec{J}$:

Angular momenta $\vec{L}$ and $\vec{S}$ interact magnetically. Consequently they exert torques on each other. In the absence of an external magnetic field, the total angular momentum is conserved. Therefore the internal torques produce the precession of $\vec{L}$ and $\vec{S}$ around the direction of their resultant J (Fig. 7.4*a*).

Precession of $\vec{J}$ about $\vec{B}$ and precession of $\vec{L}$ and $\vec{S}$ about $\vec{J}$:

If an external magnetic field of flux density $\vec{B}$ is applied to the atom, then $\vec{J}$ precesses about the direction of $\vec{B}$, and $\vec{L}$ and $\vec{S}$ continue to precess about $\vec{J}$ (Fig. 7.4 *b*).

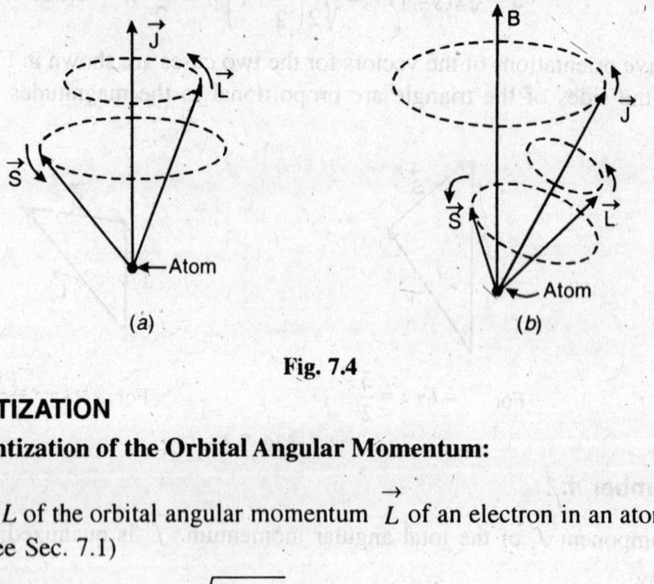

Fig. 7.4

7.5. SPACE QUANTIZATION

(*a*) Space Quantization of the Orbital Angular Momentum:

The magnitude L of the orbital angular momentum $\vec{L}$ of an electron in an atom is quantized and it is given by (See Sec. 7.1)

$$L = \sqrt{l(l+1)}\,\hbar \qquad \text{... (1)}$$

where l is the *orbital angular momentum quantum number* having the permissible values given by

$$l = 0, 1, 2, \ldots, n-1$$

where n is the principal quantum number. For providing a reference direction for measurement, we assume that a uniform magnetic field of flux density $\vec{B}$ and having its direction parallel to a z-axis is applied to the atom.

Then the component L_z of the vector $\vec{L}$ along the z-axis is also quantized and it is given by :

$$L_z = m_l \hbar \qquad \text{... (2)}$$

where m_l is the orbital magnetic quantum number.

The permissible values of m_l for a given value of l are given by :

$$m_l = l, l-1, l-2, ..., o, ..., -l$$

That is for a given value of l, the number of possible values of m_l is $(2l+1)$. The angle θ between the direction of the vector $\vec{L}$ and the z-axis is given by (Fig. 7.5)

$$\cos\theta = \frac{L_z}{L} = \frac{m_l \hbar}{\sqrt{l(l+1)}\hbar} = \frac{m_l}{\sqrt{l(l+1)}} \quad ... (3)$$

This equation shows that the direction of *the orbital angular momentum vector* $\vec{L}$ *is also quantized* with respect to the direction of an external magnetic field, and for a given value of l, there are $(2l+1)$ possible orientations of the vector $\vec{L}$ with respect to the direction of the external magnetic field. This fact is called the *space quantization of the orbital angular* momentum of the electron.

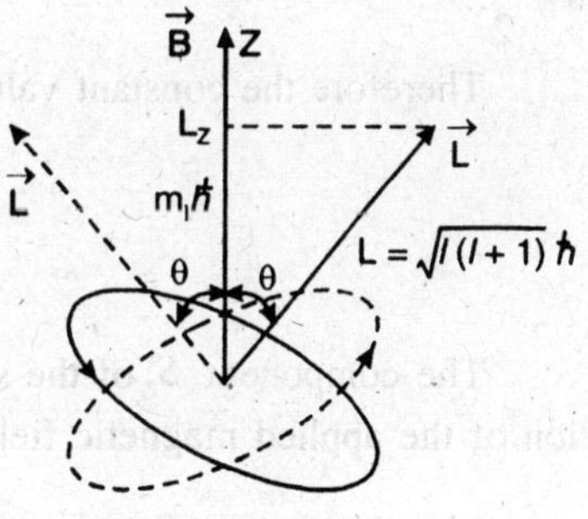

Fig. 7.5

Example:

(*i*) For $l = 0$

$m_l = 0$

$\therefore$ $L_z = 0$

(*ii*) For $l = 1$

$m_l = 1, \ 0, \ -1$

$\therefore$ $L_z = \hbar, 0, -\hbar$

(*iii*) For $l = 2$

$m_l = 2, \ 1, \ 0, \ -1, \ -2$

$\therefore$ $L_z = 2\hbar, \ \hbar, \ 0, \ -\hbar, \ 2\hbar$

It should be noted that m_l is always less than $\sqrt{l(l+1)}$.

$\therefore$ $$m_l\hbar < \sqrt{l(l+1)}\hbar$$

i.e. $$L_z < L$$

$\therefore$ the vector $\vec{L}$ can never be exactly parallel or antiparallel to the magnetic field.

The space quantization of the orbital angular momentum of an electron for $l = 2$ is shown in Fig. 7.6.

The torque due to the magnetic field acting on the magnetic dipole gives rise to precession of the angular momentum vector $\vec{L}$ about the direction of the magnetic field $\vec{B}$, as shown in Fig.7.5. In this motion the same angle of inclination θ with the direction of $\vec{B}$ is maintained.

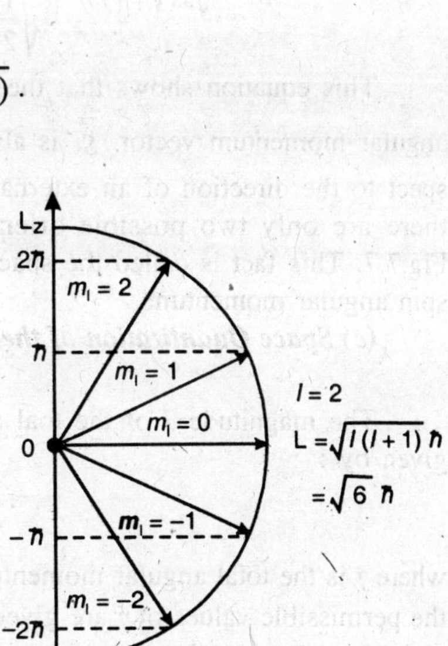

Fig 7.6

(b) Space Quantization of the Spin Angular Momenum

The magnitude S of the spin angular momentum $\vec{S}$ of an electron is quantized and it is given by (See Sec. 7.2) :

$$S = \sqrt{s(s+1)}\,\hbar \quad \text{... (1)}$$

where s is the spin angular momentum quantum number. It has only one permissible value: $s = \frac{1}{2}$.

Therefore the constant value of the magnitude S is :

$$S = \sqrt{\frac{1}{2}\left(\frac{1}{2}+1\right)}\,\hbar = \frac{\sqrt{3}}{2}\hbar \quad \text{... (2)}$$

The component S_z of the spin angular momentum $\vec{S}$ along the z-axis *i.e.* along the direction of the applied magnetic field is also quantized, and it is given by

$$S_z = m_s\hbar \quad \text{... (3)}$$

where m_s is the spin magnetic quantum number. m_s has only two permissible values, $m_s = +\frac{1}{2}$, and $m_s = -\frac{1}{2}$.

The angle θ between the direction of the vector $\vec{S}$ and the z-axis is given by :

$$\cos\theta = \frac{S_z}{S} = \frac{m_s\hbar}{\sqrt{s(s+1)}\,\hbar} = \frac{\pm\frac{1}{2}\hbar}{\sqrt{\frac{1}{2}\left(\frac{1}{2}+1\right)}\,\hbar} = \frac{\pm\frac{1}{2}\hbar}{\frac{\sqrt{3}}{2}\hbar} = \pm\frac{1}{\sqrt{3}}$$

This equation shows that the direction of the spin angular momentum vector $\vec{S}$ is also quantized with respect to the direction of an external magnetic field, and there are only two possible orientations as shown in Fig.7.7. This fact is called the space quantization of the spin angular momentum.

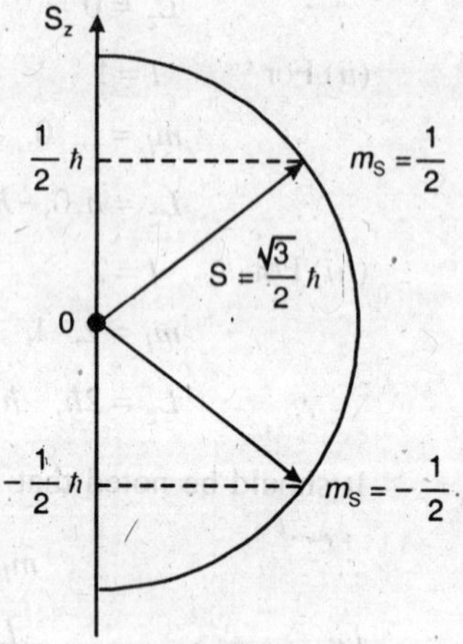

Fig 7.7

(c) Space Quantization of the Total Angular Momentum

The magnitude J of the toal angular momentum $\vec{J}$ of an electron is quantized and it is given by :

$$J = \sqrt{j(j+1)}\,\hbar \quad \text{... (1)}$$

where j is the total angular momentum quantum number. For a given value of l except for $l = 0$, the permissible values of j are given by :

$$j = l + \frac{1}{2}, \quad j = l - \frac{1}{2}.$$

The component J_z of the vector $\vec{J}$ along the z-axis is also quantized and it is given by :

$$J_z = m_j \hbar \quad \text{... (2)}$$

where m_j is the total magnetic quantum number.

For a given value of j, the possible values of m_j are given by :

$$m_j = j,\ j-1,\ j-2,\ ...,\ -j.$$

Thus for a given value of j, the number of possible values of m_j is $2j+1$.

Now the angle θ between the direction of the vector $\vec{J}$ and the z-axis is given by (Fig. 7.8) :

$$\cos\theta = \frac{J_z}{J} = \frac{m_j \hbar}{\sqrt{j(j+1)}\,\hbar} = \frac{m_j}{\sqrt{j(j+1)}} \quad \text{... (3)}$$

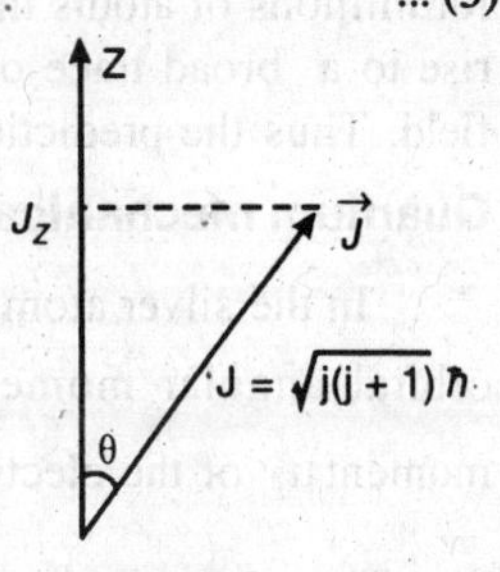

Fig. 7.8

This equation shows that the direction of the total angular momentum vector is also quantized with respect to the direction of an external magnetic field, and for a given value of j, there are $(2j+1)$ possible orientations of the $\vec{J}$ with respect to the direction of the external magnetic field.

This fact is called the space quantization of the total angular momentum $\vec{J}$.

7.6. STERN AND GERLACH EXPERIMENT

Space quantization of spin angular momentum of an electron was first demonstrated by O. Stern and W. Gerlach in an experiment performed by them in 1921.

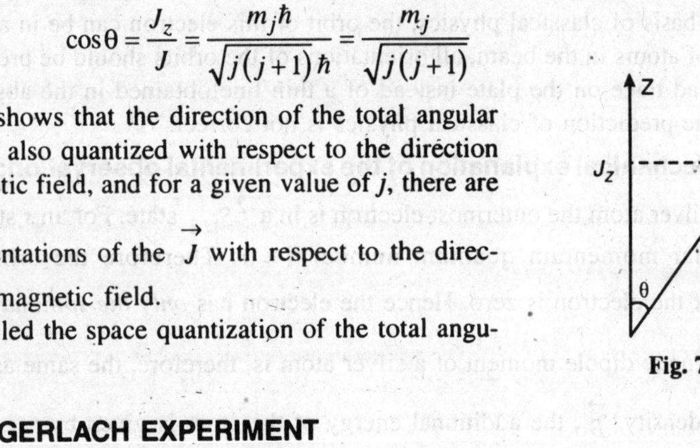

Fig. 7.9

Apparatus:

The experimental arrangement is shown in Fig. 7.9(a). *O* is a small electric oven having a slit-shaped opening. S_1 and S_2 are slits for obtaining a narrow beam of silver atoms. *N* and *S* are the poles of a strong electromagnet. One pole is in the form of a knife-edge and the other in the form of a channel parallel to the knife-edge (Fig.7.9(*b*)), so that the magnetic field between the poles is inhomogeneous, *i.e.* has a large space rate of variation. *P* is a glass detector plate. The entire apparatus is enclosed in a highly evacuated glass chamber.

Method :

Silver is vaporized in the oven. A narrow beam of silver atoms is allowed to pass through the inhomogeneous magnetic field and is recorded on the plate *P*.

When the magnetic field is off, a thin straight line trace is obtained on *P* (Fig. 7.9(c)). When the magnetic field is turned on, the trace is divided into two lines (Fig. 7.9 (c)) except at the ends where the effect of the inhomogeneous magnetic field is not large.

Explanation:

Silver (Ag) has the atomic number $Z = 47$. The outermost electron is in the 5s state and all inner shells and subshells are closed. Therefore, this 5s electron alone is responsible for the magnetic moment of the atom.

On the basis of classical physics, the orbit of this electron can be in any plane in space. So for millions of atoms in the beam, all orientations of the orbits should be present. This would give rise to a broad trace on the plate instead of a thin line obtained in the absence of the magnetic field. Thus the prediction of classical physics is not correct.

Quantum mechanical explanation of the experimental observation:

In the silver atom the outermost electron is in a ${}^2S_{1/2}$ state. For an *s* state of an electron, the orbital angular momentum quantum number $l = 0$. Therefore the orbital magnetic dipole moment $\vec{\mu}_l$ of the electron is zero. Hence the electron has *only the spin magnetic dipole moment* $\vec{\mu}_s$. The magnetic dipole moment of a silver atom is, therefore, the same as $\vec{\mu}_s$. In the magnetic field of flux density $\vec{B}$, the additional energy of the atom is given by :

$$E = -\mu_s B \cos\theta \qquad \text{... (1)}$$

where θ is the angle between the direction of $\vec{\mu}_s$ and the direction of $\vec{B}$.

$\mu_s \cos\theta$ is the component of $\vec{\mu}_s$ in the direction of $\vec{B}$. This component is $\mu_{S,Z}$ which has two quantized values $\pm\dfrac{e\hbar}{2m}$.

$$\therefore \qquad E = -\pm\frac{e\hbar}{2m}B = \pm\mu_B B \qquad \text{... (2)}$$

where μ_B is the Bohr magneton $e\hbar/2m$. In a uniform field each atomic magnetic dipole experiences a torque, which tends to orient it parallel to the field. In the inhomogeneous field the atomic dipole also experiences a force which tends to accelerate it.

Suppose the silver atom enters the magnetic field with a velocity v along the *y*-axis (the axes are shown in Fig. 7.9). The magnetic force F_z acting on the atom along the z-axis is determined by differentiating Eq.(2) with respect to *z*. This gives

$$F_z = \frac{dE}{dz} = \pm\mu_B\frac{dB}{dz} \qquad \text{... (3)}$$

The acceleration a of the atom is given by :

$$a = \frac{F_z}{m} = \pm \frac{\mu_B}{m}\frac{dB}{dz} \quad \text{... (4)}$$

The time t taken by the atom to travel through the field with velocity v is given by :

$$t = \frac{L}{v}$$

where L is the length of the path through the field.

The displacement d of the atom in the z-direction on emerging from the field is given by

$$d = \frac{1}{2}at^2 = \frac{1}{2}\left(\pm\frac{\mu_B}{m}\cdot\frac{dB}{dz}\right)\left(\frac{L}{v}\right)^2$$

$$= \pm\frac{1}{2}\cdot\frac{\mu_B}{m}\cdot\frac{dB}{dz}\cdot\frac{L^2}{v^2} \quad \text{... (5)}$$

Assuming that the distribution of speeds among the atoms in the source is given by Maxwell-Boltzmann speed distribution law, the most probable speed of a silver atom is given by :

$$v_p = \sqrt{\frac{2kT}{m}} \quad \text{... (6)}$$

where k is Boltzmann's constant, T is the absolute temperature of the source, and m is the mass of a silver atom. Assuming that $v = v_p$, from Eq. (5) we get

$$d = \pm\frac{1}{2}\cdot\frac{\mu_B}{m}\cdot\frac{dB}{dz}\cdot\frac{L^2 m}{2kT}$$

$$= \pm\frac{1}{4}\cdot\frac{\mu_B}{kT}\cdot L^2\cdot\frac{dB}{dz} \quad \text{... (7)}$$

This expression gives the theoretical value of d. It is found that the theoretical value is in agreement with the measured experimental value.

Conclusion: Thus the postulate of space quantization and of the existence of electron spin is verified.

7.7 PAULI'S EXCLUSION PRINCIPLE

Quantum Numbers:

In order to specify the quantum state of an electron in an atom the appropriate set of the following quantum numbers must be assigned to each electron in the atom:

(1) Principal quantum number n,

(2) Orbital angular momentum quantum number l,

(3) Orbital magnetic quantum number m_l,

(4) Spin magnetic quantum number m_s.

The permissible values which these quantum numbers can take on are as follows:

$$n = 1, 2, 3, ...$$

$$l = 0, 1, 2, ...(n-1)$$

$$m_l = 0, \pm 1, \pm 2, ... \pm l$$

$$m_s = +\frac{1}{2} \text{ or } -\frac{1}{2}.$$

The following conditions must be satisfied by the quantum numbers:

$$l \le (n-1) \quad \text{and} \quad -l \le m_l \le l$$

It is seen that for any value of l, there are $2l+1$ different values of m_l.

Statement of the Principle: For assignment of all the electrons in an atom to appropriate quantum states W. Pauli in 1925 enunciated the fundamental principle known as *Pauli's exclusion principle* which is stated as follows:

No two electrons in any one atom can be in the same quantum state.

Since quantum state of each electron is specified by four quantum numbers: *n, l, m_l and m_s*, the principle is usually stated as follows:

No *two electrons in any one atom can have the same set of four quantum numbers, n, l, m_l and m_s*.

Explanation: According to the principle, each electron in an atom must have a different set of the four quantum numbers. If the four quantum numbers of two electrons are identical, the one of the two electrons will be excluded from the electronic configuration of an atom. Therefore the principle is called the exclusion principle.

Application:

The principle can be applied to find the number of electrons in a given shell and subshell of an atom. The electrons in an atom, having the same value of n are said to be in the same electron shell. Corresponding to n = 1, ,2 3, ... the shells are called *K, L, M,* ......, respectively. The maximum number of electrons in a shell of given quantum number n is $2n^2$. A shell is divided into subshells corresponding to different values of the quantum number l. For $l = 0$, 1, 2, 3, ..., the subshells are called *s, p, d, f,* ..... subshells. The maximum number of electrons in a subshell of given value of l and different values of m_l and m_s is $2(2l+1)$.

We consider distribution of electrons in K and L shells :

(1) *K shell:* (*i*) $n = 1$

∴ the max. no. of electrons in K shell $= 2n^2 = 2$

(*ii*) $l \le (n-1)$ ∴ $l = 1-1 = 0$

hence $m_l = 0$

Corresponding to $l = 0$, there is one subshell designated as 1s.

No. of Is electrons $= 2(2l+1) = 2(2\times 0+1) = 2.$

For one electron $m_s = +\frac{1}{2}$ and for the other $m_s = -\frac{1}{2}$.

Thus the two sets of the quantum numbers specifying the quantum states of two 1s electrons are:

n	l	m_l	m_s
1	0	0	$+\frac{1}{2}$
1	0	0	$-\frac{1}{2}$

(2) **L shell:** (*i*) $n=2$

$\therefore$ the max. no. of electrons in L shell= $2n^2 = 2\times 2^2 = 8$

(*ii*) $l \leq (n-1)$ $\therefore$ $l=0$ and 1

hence $m_l = -1, 0, +1$

Corresponding to $l=0$ and $l=1$, the subshells are designated as 2s and 2p respectively.

No. of 2s electrons $= 2(2l+1) = 2(2\times 0+1) = 2$

No. of 2p electrons $= 2(2l+1) = 2(2\times 1+1) = 6$

Thus the eight sets of quantum numbers specifying the quantum states of two 2s electrons and six 2p electrons are :

n	l	m_l	m_s
2	0	0	$-\frac{1}{2}$
2	0	0	$+\frac{1}{2}$
2	1	-1	$-\frac{1}{2}$
2	1	-1	$+\frac{1}{2}$
2	1	0	$-\frac{1}{2}$
2	1	0	$+\frac{1}{2}$
2	1	+1	$-\frac{1}{2}$
2	1	+1	$+\frac{1}{2}$

Maximum possible number of electrons in a shell of principal quantum number *n*: A subshell is specified by the principal quantum number *n*, and the orbital angular momentum quantum number *l* where

$$l = 0, 1, 2, \ldots\ldots, (n-1).$$

For any value of *l* the possible values of the orbital magnetic quantum number m_l are

$$m_l = 0, \pm 1, \pm 2, \ldots\ldots, \pm l.$$

Thus there are $(2l+1)$ different values of m_l for any value of *l*.

There are two possible values of the spin magnetic quantum number m_s $\left(+\frac{1}{2} \textit{ and } -\frac{1}{2}\right)$ for any value of m_l.

$\therefore$ the maximum number of electrons which each subshell contain $= 2(2l+1)$

Thus there are $(2l+1)$ different values of m_l for any value of l.

There are two possible values of the spin magnetic quantum number $m_s\left(+\frac{1}{2} and -\frac{1}{2}\right)$ for any value of m_l.

∴ the maximum number of electrons which each subshell contain $= 2(2l+1)$

∴ the maximum number of electrons in a shell of principal quantum number n is given by

$$\sum_{l=0}^{l=n-1} 2(2l+1) = 2[1+3+5+......+\{2(n-1)+1\}]$$

$$= 2[1+3+5+.........+2n-1]$$

$$= 2\times\frac{n}{2}[\textit{first term} + \textit{last term}]$$

$$= n[1+2n-1] = 2n^2$$

SOLVED EXAMPLES

Example 7.1 *What is the Bohr Magneton? Calculate its value given that*

$e = 1.6\times10^{-19}$ C, $h = 6.626\times10^{-34}$ Js, $m = 9.11\times10^{-31}$ kg.

Solution

The Bohr Magneton is given by

$$\mu_B = \frac{eh}{4\pi m} = \frac{1.6\times10^{-19}\times6.626\times10^{-34}}{4\times3.14\times9.11\times10^{-31}}$$

$$= \frac{1.6\times6.626\times10^{-22}}{4\times3.14\times9.11} = \frac{10.602\times10^{-22}}{114.42}$$

$$= 0.092659\times10^{-22} = 9.27\times10^{-24}\ \text{Am}^2$$

or $\quad \boldsymbol{\mu_B = 9.27\times10^{-24}}$ **J/Wb/m²**

Note: $1\,\text{Wb/m}^2 = 1\frac{\text{N}}{\text{Cm/s}} = 1\,\text{N/Am}$

The unit Wb/m^2 is called the tesla (T) so that 1 Wb/m^2 = 1T

Example 7.2. *A beam of electrons enters a uniform magnetic field of flux densit 1.5 Wb/m². Find the energy difference between electrons whose spins are parallel and antiparallel to the field. (the Bohr magneton* $\mu_B = 9.27\times10^{-24}$ J/T *).*

Solution. In the magnetic field the additional energy of an electron having its spin parallel to the field is given by

$$E_1 = +\frac{eh}{2m}B = +\mu_B B$$

and the additional energy of an electron having its spin antiparallel to the field is given by :

$$E_2 = -\mu_B B$$

∴ the energy difference is

$$E_1 - E_2 = 2\mu_B B$$

$$= 2 \times 9.27 \times 10^{-24} \times 1.5 \text{ J}$$

$$= 27.81 \text{ J}$$

$$= \frac{27.81 \times 10^{-24}}{1.6 \times 10^{-19}} = \mathbf{1.738 \times 10^{-4} eV}$$

Example 7.3. *In the stern-Gerlach experiment a beam of silver atoms passes through a magnetic field of gradient 1.5T / mm which is along the z-axis. The length of the path in the field is 3.5 cm. The speed of atoms is 750 m/s. Find the displacement of the atoms in the positive z-direction when they emerge from the field. The mass m of a silver atom is* 1.8×10^{-25} kg, *and the Bohr magneton is* 9.27×10^{-24} J/T.

Solution:

$$d = +\frac{\mu_B}{2m} \cdot \frac{dB}{dz}\left(\frac{L}{v}\right)^2 = \frac{\mu_B}{2m} \cdot \frac{dB}{dz} \cdot \frac{L^2}{v^2}$$

$$= \frac{9.27 \times 10^{-24}}{2 \times 1.8 \times 10^{-25}} \times 1.5 \times 10^3 \times \frac{(3.5 \times 10^{-2})^2}{(7.5 \times 10^2)^2}$$

$$= \frac{9.27 \times 1.5 \times 3.5^2}{2 \times 1.8 \times 7.5^2} \times 10^{-4}$$

$$= \frac{170.33}{202.5} \times 10^{-4} = 8.41 \times 10^{-5} \text{ m}$$

$$= \mathbf{0.0841 \text{ mm}}$$

QUESTIONS AND PROBLEMS

1. Obtain classically the relation between the orbital magnetic dipole moment $\vec{\mu}_L$ and the orbital angular momentum of an electron. $\left[\textbf{Ans. } \vec{\mu}_L = -\frac{e}{2m}\vec{L}\right]$
2. Show that the component L_z in a given direction z of the orbital angular momentum $\vec{L}$ can never be equal to the magnitude of $\vec{L}$.
3. An electron is in a quantum state for which the magnitude of the orbital angular momentum $\vec{L}$ is $2\sqrt{3}\,\hbar$. Find the number of projections of the electron's orbital magnetic dipole moment on a z-axis. **[Ans. 7]**
4. Explain spin-orbit coupling. (Baroda, 2005)
5. Explain space quantization of electron spin. (Gujarat, 2006)
6. Describe the Stern-Gerlach experiment for verification of space quantization.
7. State and explain Pauli's exclusion principle. 2006)
8. **Discuss the result of Stern - Gerlach experiment.** (N.U., 2006)
9. Define the Bohr Magneton and give its expression. (N.U., 2006)

APPENDIX 1

Relation between Relativistic Energy E and Relativistic Momentum p for a particle

The total relativistic energy E of a particle of rest mass m_0 moving with velocity v is given by :

$$E = mc^2 \quad \text{... (1)}$$

or

$$E = \frac{m_o c^2}{\sqrt{1 - v^2/c^2}}$$

Squaring both the sides of this equation :

$$E^2\left(1 - \frac{v^2}{c^2}\right) = m_0{}^2 c^4 \quad \text{.... (2)}$$

The relativistic momentum p of the particle is

$$p = mv = \frac{Ev}{c^2}$$

Squaring both the sides of this equation:

$$p^2 = \frac{E^2 v^2}{c^4}$$

$$\therefore \quad p^2 c^2 = \frac{E^2 v^2}{c^2}$$

or

$$\frac{E^2 v^2}{c^2} = p^2 c^2 \quad \text{... (3)}$$

Now adding Eqs. (2) and (3), we get

$$E^2 = p^2 c^2 + m_0{}^2 c^4$$

$$E = \left(p^2 c^2 + m_0{}^2 c^4\right)^{1/2} \quad \text{... (4)}$$

APPENDIX 2

Some Physical Constants and Units

Quantity	*Symbol*	*Value*
Angstrom Unit	Å	10^{-10} m
Avogadro's number	N	6.023×10^{23} mole^{-1}
Bohr radius	a_0	5.2918×10^{-11} m
Bohr magneton	$\frac{e\hbar}{2m}$	9.27×10^{-24} J/T
Boltzmann's constant	k	1.3806×10^{-23} J/K
Compton wavelength of electron	$\lambda_0 = \frac{h}{m_0 c}$	0.02426 Å
Electron Charge	e	1.6022×10^{-19} C
Electron rest mass	m_0	9.1096×10^{-31} kg
Electron volt	eV	1.6022×10^{-19} J
Electron rest energy	m_0c^2	5.1×10^{5} eV
Ideal gas constant	R	8.3142 J / mol K
Neutron rest mass	m_n	1.6749×10^{-27} kg
Permeability of free space	μ_0	$4\pi\times10^{-7}$ Wb/Am (H/m)
Permittivity of free space	ε_0	8.8542×10^{-12} C^2/Nm^2 (F/m)
Planck's constant	h	6.6256×10^{-34} Js
	$\hbar = \frac{h}{2\pi}$	1.0546×10^{-34} Js
Proton rest mass	m_p	1.6726×10^{-27} kg
Speed of light in free space	c	2.9979×10^{8} m/s
Stefan's constant	σ	5.6697×10^{-8} W/m^{2}K^4

APPENDIX 3

Probability Current Density

The product of the wave function $\psi(x,y,z,t)$ for a particle in motion, and its complex conjugate $\psi^*(x,y,z,t)$ has been interpreted as the probability density $P(x,y,z)$ in three dimensions (see Section 4.3), *i.e.* the probability per unit volume for finding this particle at position (x,y,z) at time t. It follows that if $dx|dy|dz$ is the volume element surrounding the point at (x,y,z), the probability that the particle will be found within this volume element at the time t is $P(x,y,z)\,dx|dy|dz = \psi(x,y,z,t)\,\psi^*(x,y,z,t)\,dxdydz$. The overall probability over whole of the space is always unity, *i.e.*,

$$\int_{-\infty}^{\infty} P(x,y,z)\,dxdydz = 1$$

On the basis of the preceding interpretation the probability may be regarded as flowing from one region of space to another like a fluid. Therefore although the probability in a region changes with time, its total value over whole of the space is conserved. It is, therefore, possible to deduce for probability an equation of continuity expressing the law of conservation of probability. For this purpose we now define the probability current and probability current density.

Probability Current : The probability current through any area in the region is defined as the probability flowing normally through the area per unit time.

It is a scalar quantity and as probability is a dimensionless quantity, SI unit is per second, *i.e.*, 1/s.

Probability Current Density : The probability current density at a point in the region is defined as the probability flowing per unit area per unit time in the direction normal to the unit area surrounding the point.

It is a vector quantity denoted by the symbol $\vec{S}$. Its SI unit is per square metre per second, i.e., $1/m^2s$.

Equation of Continuity for Probability

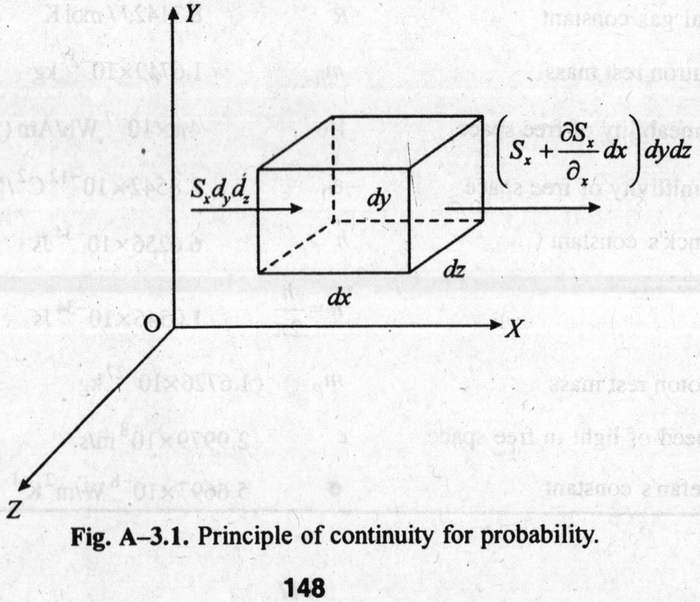

Fig. A–3.1. Principle of continuity for probability.

We consider the flow of probability through the volume element (Fig. A–3.1) whose sides have the lengths *dx, dy, dz* parallel to the rectangular coordinate axes *OX, OY, OZ* respectively. The volume element may have different probability currents through its different faces.

Let S_x be the probability current density at the left face of the volume element.

Then the probability current flowing into the volume element through the left face $= S_x dydz$

That flowing out of the right face $= \left(S_x + \frac{\partial S_x}{\partial x}dx\right)dydz$

Therefore the increase in the probability per unit time due to the flow in the positive *X*-direction

$$= S_x dydz - \left(S_x + \frac{\partial S_x}{\partial x}dx\right)dydz$$

$$= -\frac{\partial S_x}{\partial x}dxdydz$$

The total increase in the probability in the volume element due to the flow in and out of all faces of the volume *dxdydz* will be

$$= -\left[\frac{\partial S_x}{\partial x} + \frac{\partial S_y}{\partial y} + \frac{\partial S_z}{\partial z}\right]dxdydz$$

∴ the increase in the probability per unit time per unit volume

$$= -\left[\frac{\partial S_x}{\partial x} + \frac{\partial S_y}{\partial y} + \frac{\partial S_z}{\partial z}\right]$$

$$= -\text{div}\,\vec{S}$$

where $\vec{S}$ is the probability current density vector. But the increase in the probability per unit volume [*i.e.*, probability density $P(x,y,z)$] per unit time

$$= \frac{\partial P(x,y,z)}{\partial t}$$

Since the increase in the probability per unit time per unit volume is equal to the increase in the probability density per unit time, we have

$$-\text{div}\,\vec{S} = \frac{\partial P(x,y,z)}{\partial t}$$

or $$\frac{\partial P}{\partial t} = -\text{div}\,\vec{S} \qquad ...(1)$$

Eq. (1) is called the equation of continuity for probability. The equation expresses the law of conservation for probability, which may be stated as follows. The rate of the increase of the probability with time of finding the particle within a small volume element is equal to the rate of the flow of the probability with time into this volume element through the bounding surface of the volume element.

Probability Current Density for One Dimensional Motion

For one dimensional motion of the particle the equation of continuity from the general equation is obtained as follows :

$$\frac{\partial P}{\partial t} = -\text{div}\,\vec{S}$$

$$= -\left[\vec{i}\frac{\partial}{\partial x}+\vec{j}\frac{\partial}{\partial y}+\vec{k}\frac{\partial}{\partial z}\right].\left[\vec{i}\,S_x+\vec{j}\,S_y+\vec{k}\,S_z\right]$$

where $\vec{i}, \vec{j}, \vec{k}$ are unit vectors in the positive directions of the axes OX, OY, OZ respectively.

Taking the scalar product on the right hand side of the equation, we get

$$\frac{\partial P}{\partial t} = -\left[\frac{\partial S_x}{\partial x}+\frac{\partial S_y}{\partial y}+\frac{\partial S_z}{\partial z}\right] \quad \text{....(2)}$$

∴ for the motion in the positive x–direction this equation is transformed to

$$\frac{\partial P}{\partial t} = -\frac{\partial S_x}{\partial x} \quad \text{...(3)}$$

From Eq. (3), we have $\qquad dS_x = -\frac{\partial P}{\partial t}dx$

Integrating this equation, we get $\qquad S_x = -\frac{\partial}{\partial t}\int P dx$

But the probability density $\qquad P = \psi(x,t)\,\psi^*(x,t)$

where $\psi(x,t)$ is the wave function for the particle at the position x and at the time t, and $\psi^*(x,t)$ is its complex conjugate.

Hence, we have $\qquad S_x = -\frac{\partial}{\partial t}\int \psi(x,t)\psi^*(x,t)dx$

or $\qquad S_x = -\frac{\partial}{\partial t}\int \psi\psi^*\, dx \quad \text{...(4)}$

For convenience we have dropped the variables x and t from $\psi(x,t)$ and $\psi^*(x, t)$

Now the Schrodinger equations for $\psi(x,t)$ and $\psi^*(x,t)$ are

$$i\hbar\frac{\partial \psi}{\partial t} = -\frac{\hbar^2}{2m}\frac{\partial^2\psi}{\partial x^2}+V\psi \quad \text{...(5)}$$

$$-i\hbar\frac{\partial \psi^*}{\partial t} = -\frac{\hbar^2}{2m}\frac{\partial^2\psi^*}{\partial x^2}+V\psi^* \quad \text{...(6)}$$

Multiplying Eq. (5) by ψ^* and Eq. (6) by ψ, we get

$$i\hbar\psi^*\frac{\partial \psi}{\partial t} = -\frac{\hbar^2}{2m}\psi^*\frac{\partial^2\psi}{\partial x^2}+\psi^* V\psi \quad \text{...(7)}$$

$$-i\hbar\psi^*\frac{\partial \psi^*}{\partial t} = -\frac{\hbar^2}{2m}\psi\frac{\partial^2\psi^*}{\partial x^2}+\psi V\psi^* \quad \text{...(8)}$$

Subtracting Eq. (8) from Eq. (7), we get

$$i\hbar\left(\psi^*\frac{\partial \psi}{\partial t}+\psi\frac{\partial \psi^*}{\partial t}\right) = -\frac{\hbar^2}{2m}\left[\psi^*\frac{\partial^2\psi}{\partial x^2}-\psi\frac{\partial^2\psi^*}{\partial x^2}\right]$$

or $\qquad i\hbar\frac{\partial}{\partial t}(\psi\psi^*) = -\frac{\hbar^2}{2m}\frac{\partial}{\partial x}\left[\psi^*\frac{\partial \psi}{\partial x}-\psi\frac{\partial \psi^*}{\partial x}\right]$

or $$\frac{\partial}{\partial t}(\psi\psi^*) = \frac{i\hbar}{2m}\frac{\partial}{\partial x}\left[\psi^*\frac{\partial\psi}{\partial x} - \psi\frac{\partial\psi^*}{\partial x}\right] \quad ...(9)$$

Substituting this equation into Eq. (4), we get

$$S_x = -\frac{i\hbar}{2m}\int\frac{\partial}{\partial x}\left[\psi^*\frac{\partial\psi}{\partial x} - \psi\frac{\partial\psi^*}{dx}\right]dx$$

$$= -\frac{i\hbar}{2m}\left[\psi^*\frac{\partial\psi}{\partial x} - \psi\frac{\partial\psi^*}{\partial x}\right] \quad ...(10)$$

This is the required expression for the probability current density S_x in the positive x-direction.

To show that the probability current density for a free particle is equal to the product of its probability density and its speed.

For a free particle moving in the positive x-direction the momentum p_x at position x is given by

$$\frac{\hbar}{i}\frac{\partial\psi}{\partial x} = p_x\psi$$

$$\therefore \quad \frac{\partial\psi}{\partial x} = \frac{i}{\hbar}p_x\psi \quad ...(11)$$

and $$\frac{i}{i}\frac{\partial\psi^*}{\partial x} = p_x\psi^*$$

$$\therefore \quad \frac{\partial\psi^*}{\partial x} = -\frac{i}{\hbar}p_x\psi^* \quad ...(12)$$

Substituting Eqs. (11) and (12) in Eq. (10), we get

$$S_x = -\frac{i\hbar}{2m}\left[\psi^*\frac{i}{\hbar}p_x\psi + \psi\frac{i}{\hbar}p_x\psi^*\right]$$

Simplifying the right hand side, we get

$$= \frac{1}{m}(\psi\psi^* p_x) = (\psi\psi^*)\frac{p_x}{m}$$

or $$S_x = (\psi\psi^*)\frac{mv_x}{m} = (\psi\psi^*)v_x \quad ...(13a)$$

This equation shows that the probability current density S_x in the positive x-direction is equal to the product of the probability density $\psi\psi^*$ and the speed of the particle in the same direction,

Since $p_x = \hbar k$, we also have

$$S_x = (\psi\psi^*)\frac{p_x}{m} = (\psi\psi^*)\frac{\hbar k}{m} \quad ...(13b)$$

Index